The Specter of Communism in Hawaii

T. Michael Holmes

University of Hawaii Press
HONOLULU

Printed in the United States of America

94 95 96 97 98 99 5 4 3 2 1

Library of Congress Cataloging-in-Publication Data
Holmes, T. Michael, 1934–
The specter of Communism in Hawaii / T. Michael Holmes.
p. cm.
Includes bibliographical references and index.
ISBN 0-8248-1550-5 (alk. paper)
1. Anti-communist movements—Hawaii—History—20th century.
2. Communism—Hawaii—History—20th century. 3. Labor movement—Hawaii—History—20th century. 4. Hawaii—Politics and government—1900–1959. I. Title.
HX91.H3H65 1994
320.5'32'09969—dc20 93-45841
CIP

University of Hawaii Press books are printed on acid-free paper and meet the guidelines for permanence and durability of the Council on Library Resources

Designed by Paula Newcomb

For my sons, Tom and Dan

Contents

Preface

This is not a history of communism in Hawaii, although much of that history will be revealed in these pages. This work is about the struggle against the perceived or purported threat of communism in Hawaii, Hawaii's version of the McCarthy era. It begins with the labor movement in Hawaii in the 1930s, moves into the political arena at the end of World War II, and concludes in 1954, the year of the "Democratic Revolution" in Hawaii, with the anti-Communist movement substantially spent.

The project was begun more than twenty years ago, in 1972. Coming to the University of Hawaii as a doctoral candidate in 1969, I knew little Hawaiian history. My major field was American foreign policy, with a special interest in the domestic political manifestations of the cold war. Having grown up in southern California, I was acutely aware of the political career of Richard M. Nixon. The year I entered college, in 1952, Nixon's role in the Alger Hiss case secured him the vice-presidency. At the time, the phenomenon known as McCarthyism had galvanized the American public. As a young college student who worshiped Walter Lippmann and George Kennan, I was disturbed by the rhetorical excesses of the more virulent forms of anticommunism.

I came to the University of Hawaii to study with Walter Johnson, editor of the papers of Adlai Stevenson. Professor Johnson came to Hawaii after a distinguished career in the history department at the University of Chicago. He came to love Hawaii and transferred many of his social interests to the Islands. It was Walter Johnson who introduced me to Hawaii's experience during the McCarthy era. Together, we formulated the outline for my doctoral dissertation.

The study of anticommunism in Hawaii proved to be a fascinating and fruitful subject for a doctoral dissertation. There is an interesting symmetry to the topic, as the governmental attack against the perceived threat of communism in Hawaii included executive, legislative, and judicial actions. Another factor that made the project rewarding was that many of the principal actors in the events discussed were still alive and willing to talk.

Publication plans with the University of Hawaii Press were delayed when I left Hawaii for Switzerland in 1976. Fifteen years later, spurred by the disintegration of the Soviet Union, I came back to the University of Hawaii Press with the idea of reviving the project. The Press was enthusiastic. The result is what you see here.

The time lag has proven beneficial for the book. Part One, principally based on secondary sources, draws from some valuable work that was not available in the mid-1970s, particularly Sanford Zalburg's biography of Jack Hall, *A Spark Is Struck* (1979), and Edward D. Beechert's labor history *Working in Hawaii* (1985). It also reconfirms the timeless value of Lawrence H. Fuchs' landmark work *Hawaii Pono* (1961) and the sensitive perceptions of Gavan Daws' *Shoal of Time* (1968).

Part Two of this work, "The Specter Emerges," focuses on a single year. That year begins on Armistice Day in 1947 and concludes with the general election of 1948. It includes Governor Ingram M. Stainback's Armistice Day declaration of war against communism; the appearance of a volatile pamphlet, *The Truth about Communism in Hawaii*, by an avowed former communist named Ichiro Izuka; the suspension, hearing, and dismissal of school teachers John and Aiko Reinecke; a revolt in the ranks of the International Longshoremen's and Warehousemen's Union (ILWU) led by Amos Ignacio; and a political season conducted in the shadow of the specter of communism. This single year established a foundation for the anticommunist agenda that was followed for the next six years in the territory of Hawaii.

Part Three, "The Specter Grows," documents the next five years of the crusade against communism in the territory of Hawaii, including the 1949 longshore strike; the visit of the House Committee on Un-American Activities in 1950; and Hawaii's Smith Act trial in 1952 and 1953. This trial of the so-called Hawaii Seven, which included Jack Hall, regional director of the ILWU, lasted twenty-two months from arrest to conviction and marked the last major thrust of militant anticommunism in Hawaii.

Parts Two and Three reflect a substantial amount of original research, from sources including the transcript of the hearing of John and Aiko Reinecke by the territorial commissioners of public instruction (1947), which ran to more than 4,000 pages; the transcript of testimony given before the House Committee on Un-American Activities (1950), over 500 pages; and the transcript of Hawaii's Smith Act trial (1952–1953), over 16,000 pages.

Parts Two and Three also draw on interviews and letters between the author and twenty-two individuals who were participants in the events documented here. This dimension of the work has been enhanced by the addition of sixteen relevant interviews from the John A. Burns Oral History Project, conducted between 1975 and 1984 by Stuart Gerry Brown, Paul Hooper, and Dan Boylan. I am particularly indebted to Dan Boylan, who generously assisted me in obtaining the maximum value from this treasury of primary source material. Oral history, of course, must be used with discretion; memory tends to be very selective. Whatever its limitations, however, oral history brings the writer into more intimate contact with his subjects than any other medium.

I made heavy use of the newspapers of the time, notably the *Honolulu Advertiser*, the *Honolulu Star-Bulletin*, and the *Honolulu Record*. Neighbor island papers were consulted at appropriate times, specifically the *Hilo Tribune-Herald*, the *Maui News*, and Kauai's *Garden Island*. Labor publications such as the *Voice of Labor*, the *Kauai Herald*, the *Herald*, the *ILWU Dispatcher*, and the *ILWU Reporter* were also useful. The newspaper of the Hawaii Residents' Association, *IMUA Spotlight*, was of considerable interest. There has been a debate among historians over whether newspaper copy can be considered primary source material. My opinion is affirmative. Newspapers not only provided me a substantial amount of factual information but gave me a feeling for the times about which I have written that could not have been duplicated by any other source. In those early days of television, newspapers were still the primary shapers of public opinion.

It would be impossible to acknowledge all of the people who have contributed to this work. To the archivists and librarians at the Hawaii State Archives and the Hawaiian Collection of the Sinclair and, later, Hamilton libraries at the University of Hawaii, my deepest thanks. It was with real sadness that I learned, when I returned to the University of Hawaii in 1991, of the untimely death of David Kittleson. His assistance, back in 1972 and 1973, was invaluable. Another archivist I would like to acknowledge is Gene Vrana of the ILWU library in San Francisco. In the 1970s I did not have the luxury of visiting San Francisco, but for one week in March 1992 I made up for that earlier omission. Mr. Vrana took an extraordinary interest in what I was doing and proved to be exceptionally helpful. He commented one day that his father had been involved in the first Smith Act case. The name Vrana did not register with me, but I recognized his full name, Eugene Dennis Vrana. His father, Eugene Dennis, had been general secretary of the Communist Party of the United States of America (CPUSA) and one of the defendants in the famous Foley Square case.

One cannot share the lives of those who have made our recent history without becoming deeply moved by some of them. I must acknowledge the rare privilege of coming to know John and Aiko Reinecke. Their gentle dignity, candor, and quiet good humor amazed me in the face of all they had endured in the name of anticommunism. On 1 July 1978, three days after he and Aiko had received a check for $250,000 from the State of Hawaii, John Reinecke wrote me a letter. The check was the result of the Reineckes' legislative "rehabilitation." John wanted to thank me for my role in making it possible for them to recover some of their lost pay and retirement benefits. In the fall of 1976, the *Hawaii Bar Journal* had devoted an entire issue to a piece I had written about the Reineckes titled "The Reinecke Case, a Study in Administrative Injustice." A copy was distributed to each member of the state legislature. My role in support of the Reineckes remains the greatest satisfaction of my professional life.

Walter Johnson would have been happy to see this work completed. Unfortunately, he died in 1985. A brilliant teacher and a dear friend, I wish I could thank him again for his unerring guidance and for the many wonderful hours we spent together at his home in Punaluu—probing history, politics, international relations, and the deeper mysteries of tennis.

I would like to thank Iris Wiley, executive editor at the University of Hawaii Press, for her encouragement in the late 1970s and again in 1991. I must also thank her for assigning this project to my current editors, Pam Kelley and Cheri Dunn, who have helped make the production of this work a real joy.

My special thanks go to my brother, Dick Holmes, for his thoughtful reading of this manuscript. And to my mother, without whom my return to writing would have been impossible, no words can begin to express my appreciation.

Finally, some of what you encounter here may seem terribly wrong or even silly from today's perspective. Although some of the anticommunist agenda was driven by hidden and unworthy motivations, most of it seems to have been driven by a deeply felt fear of an alien threat to the American way of life. I have sought to place the anticommunist movement in Hawaii in its proper context, but I have not backed away from expressing my opinions. The reader is entitled to know, to differ with, or to agree with the views of the author. I alone am responsible for any errors of fact or interpretation.

Acronyms

ACLU	American Civil Liberties Union
AFL	American Federation of Labor
CIO	Congress of Industrial Organizations
CPUSA	Communist Party of the United States of America
DNC	Democratic National Committee
FBI	Federal Bureau of Investigation
FLSA	Fair Labor Standards Act
HACU	Hawaiian Association of Civic Unity
HCLC	Hawaii Civil Liberties Committee
HSPA	Hawaiian Sugar Planters' Association
HUAC	House Un-American Activities Committee
IBU	Inland Boatmen's Union
ILA	International Longshoremen's Association
ILWU	International Longshoremen's and Warehousemen's Union
IWW	Industrial Workers of the World
KKK	Ku Klux Klan
NAACP	National Association for the Advancement of Colored People
NLRB	National Labor Relations Board
PAC	political action committee
ROTC	Reserve Officers' Training Corps
SUP	Sailors' Union of the Pacific
UCAPAWA	United Cannery Agricultural Packing and Allied Workers of America
UHW	Union of Hawaiian Workers

PART ONE

SETTING THE STAGE

Chapter 1

The Mainland

Most Americans think about anticommunism as a cold war phenomenon. In fact, anticommunism in the United States preceded the cold war; indeed, it even preceded the existence of the Soviet Union. It was initially linked to the nativist tradition of the nineteenth century, a tradition that was built upon a morbid fear of foreigners. Between 1880 and 1915 more than twenty million immigrants came to the United States, mostly from Europe. During that thirty-five years the population of the United States doubled, growing from fifty million to one hundred million. In 1915 immigrants represented fully 25 percent of the nation's population. With them they brought foreign ideas, including those of Karl Marx, Frederick Engels, and Vladimir Ilyich Ulyanov, better known as Lenin—ideas that pitted class against class.

It is no wonder that these ideas were of interest to the working class, for foreigners were disproportionately represented among the poor and the working. Many foreign workers gravitated toward the Industrial Workers of the World (IWW), a radical labor union that was founded in 1905. The "Wobblies," as they were known, focused on the exploitation of the working class and opposed U.S. entry into World War I. The IWW saw the war as a squabble among imperialists.

Opposition to entering the war would seem to have put the IWW on the side of Woodrow Wilson, who ran for reelection as president of the United States in 1916 under the banner "He kept us out of war." Walter Lippmann, then a young writer for the *New Republic,* knew better. In a letter to Herbert Croly in September 1916, Lippmann wrote, "What we're electing is a war President—not the man who kept us out of war."[1] On 6 April 1917, scarcely one month after Wilson's second inaugural, the United States entered World War I "to make the world safe for democracy." One of the events that made it easier for Wilson to enter the war was the March 1917 overthrow of the tsar of Russia (Nicholas II) and his replacement with the "democratic" Kerensky government.

Those who now opposed U.S. participation in the war, especially foreign radicals, were quickly isolated. The Immigration Act of 1917 called for the deportation of foreigners who were critical of the U.S.

government. George Creel's Committee on Public Education made it clear that "all opponents of the war effort were sinister agents of an enemy conspiracy."[2] The Sedition Act of 1918 went so far as to make "disloyal opinion and demeaning references to the flag or form of government" punishable by a prison term of up to twenty years. "Big Bill" Haywood of the IWW; Eugene Debs, the five-time presidential candidate of the Socialist party between the years 1900 and 1920; and Victor Berger, a member of the national executive committee of the Socialist party, were all sent to prison. Judge Kenesaw Mountain Landis, better known for his later service as major league baseball's first commissioner, said that he would have preferred to see Berger "lined up against a wall and shot."[3] Berger's conviction was later overturned by the Supreme Court.

With the Bolshevik Revolution in November 1917, anticommunism began to take on its cold war flavor. The Allied intervention during the Russian civil war also created a legacy of mistrust between the United States and the Soviet Union. On 7 November 1919, the second anniversary of the Bolshevik Revolution, Attorney General A. Mitchell Palmer launched raids against suspected radicals in twelve cities throughout the United States. Expanded raids began on 2 January 1920. Palmer wanted very much to become the Democratic party's presidential nominee in 1920. "My information," he said in justification of his actions, "showed that Communism in this country was an organization of thousands of aliens . . . direct allies of Trotsky, aliens of the same misshapen cast of mind and indecencies of character."[4] Palmer soon had plans to deport 3,500 "red aliens," the overwhelming majority of whom were American citizens. In the spring of 1920, Palmer was blocked by Secretary of Labor Louis F. Post, who canceled 2,202 deportation orders.[5]

Palmer, in a desperate effort to rebuild his credibility, predicted a massive onslaught of radical protests, assassinations, and bombings for May Day 1920. When they failed to materialize, Palmer was discredited in the eyes of much of the American public. His public career was finished when highly respected members of the legal community such as Roscoe Pound, Zachariah Chaffee, Jr., and Felix Frankfurter publicly denounced his tactics.

American prosperity in the 1920s coupled with a rather inauspicious start for the Soviet economy diminished interest in any perceived communist threat for the remainder of the decade. The issue resurfaced with the advent of the Great Depression. In 1930 great excitement was created in New York over some bogus documents that connected the Soviet Amtorg Trading Company with the dissemination of communist propaganda in the United States. Arch-conservative representative Hamilton Fish of New York led the fight to create a special committee of the United States House of Representatives. He sponsored a resolution to investigate "all entities, groups or individuals who are alleged to advise, teach or advocate the overthrow by force or violence of the Government of the United States, or attempt to undermine our republican form of government by inciting riots, sabotage or revolutionary disorders." Fish assured his colleagues, "It is not the purpose of this resolution to interfere with any group except the Communists in the United States, and we propose to deport all alien Communists." To add support, Fish pointed out that the jobs of those deported could be given to "honest, loyal Americans who are unemployed." The House voted the special committee into existence, 210 in favor, 18 opposed.[6]

A succession of special committees came and went before the creation of the House Committee on Un-American Activities (commonly known as the House Un-American Activities Committee, or HUAC) in 1938. HUAC was different from its predecesors in that it was a permanent committee of the House of Representatives. HUAC was created as a result of an unlikely joint effort of Samuel Dickstein, from New York City's Lower East Side, and Martin Dies, from east Texas. Dickstein was a Russian immigrant, the son of a rabbi. He saw HUAC as an instrument that could be used to fight Nazism in the United States. Dies' father had also represented east Texas in the House of Representatives, making his reputation as an enemy of Bolsheviks and the League of Nations. The son had inherited the father's tendencies, and he saw HUAC as a vehicle to fight the scourge of communism in the United States. After the bill creating HUAC passed, by a vote of 191 to 41, Dies was named chairman of the committee. When committee members were named, Dickstein, to his dismay, was not included.

During the 1930s many thoughtful Americans came to question the ability of the U.S. economy to survive. Noted critic Edmund Wilson, who experienced his own brief flirtation with the Communist party, put it this way in 1930—long before the most severe period of the Great Depression:

> There are today in the United States, according to the census director, something like nine million men out of work; our cities are scenes of privation and misery on a scale which sickens the imagination; our agricultural life is bankrupt; our industry, in shifting to the South, has reverted almost to the horrible conditions, before the Factory Acts, of the England of a hundred years ago, and the fight of the unions there for recognition is all to begin again; so many banks are failing that the newspapers do not dare to print the truth about them. And when we look to South America or to the European countries west of Russia, we see only the same economic chaos, the same lack of capacity or will to deal with it, and the same resultant suffering. May we not well fear that what has broken down, in the course of one catastrophic year, is not simply the machinery of representative government, but the capitalist system itself.[7]

As World War II approached, the Communist Party of the United States of America (CPUSA) found itself on a political roller coaster. Connected with the foreign policy of the Soviet Union since its creation in 1919, the CPUSA was heard as a forceful voice against Nazi Germany in the mid-1930s. With the signing of the Nazi-Soviet nonaggression pact of 1939, the Party lost many adherents who had signed up during the period of disillusionment of the Great Depression or the times of enthusiasm associated with communist support for the Republican cause during the Spanish civil war (1936–1939).

After the Nazi attack of the Soviet Union in June of 1941, the picture changed. By the end of that fateful year, the United States was allied with the Soviet Union against Hitler's forces. Under the leadership of Earl Browder, the CPUSA became the Communist Political Association, a kind of educational society, and steered clear of politics. Browder contended that the friendly relations between the United States and the Soviet Union would survive the victory. William Z. Foster, who succeeded to the leadership of the CPUSA when it was reorganized and repoliticized in the summer of 1945, did not share Browder's optimism.

Contrary to popular opinion, the CPUSA was never an illegal organization in the United States. It could be found listed in the telephone directories of most major cities; it regularly published a variety of political propaganda that was widely available; some of the party's adherents ran for public office bearing the Communist party label; it even held public rallies in such open places as New York City's Madison Square Garden.

Bills were proposed, from time to time, that would have outlawed the party, but none was successful. The Mundt-Nixon bill of 1948 probably came as close to outlawing the Communist party as any piece of legislation during the cold war. It is not clear, however, that this was the intention of the bill. Some members of Congress supported the legislation because it outlawed the Communist party, while others supported it because it did not. Richard Nixon, in his floor management of the bill, emphasized that he didn't want to outlaw the Communist party but merely wanted to control it. Roger Morris, in his biography of Nixon, saw it this way: "Clearly an assault on civil liberties, Mundt-Nixon's requirements of registration by what it defined *a priori* as a conspiracy amounted to banishment of a political party and idea, and harbored in its veiled language chaotic confusion."[8]

Thomas E. Dewey, the Republican candidate for president in 1948, was less subtle, calling the bill "nothing but the method of Hitler and Stalin . . . an attempt to beat down ideas with a club . . . a surrender of everything we believe in." Mundt-Nixon passed in the House on 18 May 1948, by a vote of 319 to 58, but it was "summarily scuttled," without coming to a vote, in the Senate.[9]

Some elements of Mundt-Nixon found their way into the Internal

Security Act of 1950, although Senator Pat McCarran, a Republican from Nevada, was careful to point out that the purpose of the bill was not to outlaw the Communist party. Yet thousands of people in the United States lost jobs, suffered deportation, or even went to jail for their alleged activities as members of this "legal" entity. No sector of the population was more subject to virulent anticommunism in the United States during the years immediately after World War II than organized labor. And no labor leader was hounded with such determination as was Harry Bridges, the Australian-born president of the International Longshoremen's and Warehousemen's Union (ILWU). In 1939 and again in 1941 Bridges was subjected to highly publicized deportation hearings because of his alleged membership in the Communist party. Failing in its first attempt, the federal government was successful in a second hearing that featured a procession of disreputable and perjured witnesses. In 1945 Bridges' deportation was overturned by the U.S. Supreme Court. Justice Frank Murphy, commenting on the government's unrelenting quest to deport Bridges, proclaimed:

> The record in this case will stand forever as a monument to man's intolerance of man. Seldom, if ever in the history of this nation, has there been such a concentrated and relentless crusade to deport an individual because he dared to exercise the freedom that belongs to him as a human being and that is guaranteed to him by the Constitution. . . . When the immutable freedoms guaranteed by the Bill of Rights have been so openly and concededly ignored, the full wrath of constitutional condemnation descends upon the action taken by the government.[10]

When Bridges finally became a citizen, shortly after the Supreme Court decision in 1945, Judge Thomas C. Foley of San Francisco declared: "You will make a fine citizen. Any man who has fought so long and so hard for citizenship as you have will certainly value and appreciate it."[11]

But that was not the end of the U.S. government's efforts to get rid of Harry Bridges. In 1950 Bridges and his two witnesses, Henry Schmidt and Bob Robertson, were convicted of having perjured themselves at his 1945 naturalization hearing. Three years later, that conviction was overturned by the Supreme Court. The government countered by filing a civil suit to have Bridges "denaturalized." The case came to trial before Judge Irving Goodman in 1955, without a jury. Judge Goodman concluded that "the government has failed to prove the allegations of its complaint as to respondent's alleged membership in the Communist Party by clear and convincing evidence."[12] The decision did not address the question of whether Bridges' citizenship could have been revoked in a civil proceeding had the government been able to prove that he had been a member of the Communist party.

The anticommunist thrust of the federal government was to affect

Harry Bridges at the organizational level as well as the personal. In 1947 Congress passed the Taft-Hartley Act, over the veto of President Harry S Truman. This act, which was considered by organized labor to be a significant step backward after the New Deal gains of the 1930s, contained a requirement that all union leaders sign annual affidavits declaring that they were not members of the Communist party. Although Truman opposed portions of Taft-Hartley dealing with the operation of labor unions in the United States, he was determined to lead the fight against communism. To this end, on 12 March 1947 Truman signed Executive Order 9835 to ensure that no communists were present in the U.S. government. In the next five years the Loyalty Review Board, established to review the loyalty of government employees, supervised the investigation of four million government employees, brought charges against over nine thousand individuals, and dismissed 379 as security risks. No spies were ever uncovered by the Loyalty Review Board.[13]

Executive Order 9835 did not directly affect Harry Bridges, but it did encourage the Congress of Industrial Organizations (CIO) to take a close look at itself. Beginning in 1947, the CIO sought to rid itself of the red taint frequently attributed to it. On 13 April 1947 Irving Potash, a vice-president of the Fur and Leather Workers Union and a member of the Communist party national committee, warned his CIO brothers, "Not one of you will buy peace for yourselves by joining a witch hunt."[14] Potash's warning did not deter the CIO.

Bridges was at the center of the storm when the CIO expelled the ILWU on 29 August 1950. In a *New Yorker* interview in 1962, Arthur Goldberg, general counsel for the CIO at the time of the communist purges, made a telling point. Describing the "careful, judicial" conduct of the CIO lawyers in the ILWU case, Goldberg explained their procedures: "For instance, we established in detail and beyond doubt that Harry Bridges steadily followed the Communist line."[15] This quotation bears close scrutiny, for it captures the essence of much of the anticommunism of the cold war period. Goldberg was stating the obvious when he pointed out that many of the views of Harry Bridges were similar to those held by the Communist party. Bridges was quick to admit these shared views. But he also called attention to significant points of divergence with the views and actions of the Communist party. His point was that sharing a particular view with a communist doesn't make you one. In the eyes of many in the United States, including the leadership of the CIO, Harry Bridges was dead wrong on this point.

Monsignor Charles Owen Rice, in company with Philip Murray of the CIO, led the assault on the communist elements in labor in 1947. Rice, one of the nation's most militant crusaders against communism, wrote thirty years later:

> The American trade union movement would be healthier today if Phil Murray had not purged the CIO and if a strong, broad-based Communist minority had been able to survive in the trade unions. . . . I think I wasted a lot of time on a crusade that did more harm than good. Far better had I concentrated exclusively on building strong, honest unions, exposing crooks, organizing the unorganized and confronting the might of unchecked monopoly and aggrandizement.[16]

Unions were not the only institution having difficulty with the communist issue. In the August 1947 annual report of the American Civil Liberties Union (ACLU), it was observed: "The climate of opinion in which freedom of public debate and minority dissent functioned with few restraints during the war years and after has undergone a sharply unfavorable change."[17] This same ACLU, an organization that traditionally had opposed the concept of "guilt by association," had, in 1940, expelled Elizabeth Gurley Brown, an avowed communist, from its board of directors by a vote of 10 to 9. After World War II, the ACLU's concern about communism within its ranks grew. In 1953 the board of directors modified the membership application to read that "only those whose devotion to civil liberties is not qualified by adherence to Communist, Fascist, KKK, or other totalitarian doctrine" were welcome to join. This reference to communism was found to be offensive to a majority of the membership by a vote of 21,271 to 18,995. In spite of this expression of the ACLU members' opinion, the board of directors voted 14 to 4 to retain the language on the basis of powers that had earlier been extended to them by the membership.[18]

There can be little doubt that Truman's loyalty program had unintended consequences both inside and outside of government. Clifford R. Durr, a member of the Federal Communications Commission during the Truman administration, recalled: "In a talk with President Truman at the White House in June 1948, he frankly told me that he had signed the Order to take the ball away from J. Parnell Thomas." Thomas, a Republican representative from New Jersey, was chairman of HUAC during the Eightieth Congress. Durr went on to say that Truman had indicated that if things got out of control, "he would modify the Order and even repeal it, if necessary."[19] The government's loyalty program was considerably broadened before Truman left office, with the passage of the McCarran Act. To Truman's credit, it was passed over his veto.

In 1948 the Justice Department discovered another means to apply pressure to the Communist party, the Smith Act. Properly known as the Alien Registration Act of 1940, the Smith Act grew out of congressional efforts to have Harry Bridges deported. During debate on the bill, Representative Howard Smith was asked, "Will this bill, as presently proposed, give Congress authority to handle the Bridges case?" The Virginia Democrat responded, "That is exactly what it was designed to do."[20] In the final minutes before the vote on the bill, a conspiracy provision was added to Smith Act, making it illegal to teach or advocate the overthrow of the United States government by force or violence. It was the only part of the Smith Act that did not deal with immigration matters. Smith, however, was clear about the importance of the newly added conspiracy section. He called it "the very heart of the legislation," remarking, "We have laws against aliens who advocate the overthrow of this government by force, but do you know that there is nothing in the world to prevent a treasonable American citizen from doing so?"[21]

Passed by the House, the Smith Act languished in the Senate for almost a year. While the Smith Act was waiting for Senate action, Representative A. Leonard Allen, a Louisiana Democrat, introduced a bill calling for the deportation of Harry Bridges. In 1939 Bridges had successfully fought the government's first effort to deport him. The Allen bill was passed by the House of Representatives by a vote of 330 to 42 on 14 June 1940. Five days later, Attorney General Robert H. Jackson sent a strongly worded memorandum to the Senate Committee on Immigration, pointing out the bill's obvious constitutional deficiencies—it was clearly a bill of attainder—and called for its rejection by the Senate.

By the spring of 1940, events in Europe, particularly the Nazi-Soviet nonaggression pact, had aroused the American people to threats of subversion. Senator Tom Conally, a Texas Democrat, expressed eagerness to secure legislation because, "It will have a very fine effect on the public mind, and assure the public that Congress is doing something about the so-called 'fifth column' and in correcting subversive activities."[22] The Senate ducked the Allen bill and passed the Smith Act, which was signed into law by President Franklin D. Roosevelt on 28 June 1940.

Prior to 1948 the Smith Act had been used only once, against a friendless group of Trotskyites in Minneapolis during World War II. In a remarkable bit of irony, the *Daily Worker,* with its distinctly Stalinist point of view, praised the U.S. government for its decisive action in the case: "The American people can find no objection to the destruction of the Fifth Column in this country. On the contrary, they must insist on it."[23]

The Communist party was less appreciative when, on 20 July 1948, twelve of the top leaders of the CPUSA were indicted in New York for "teaching and advocating the overthrow of the United States government by force and violence" in violation of the Smith Act. The trial of eleven of the twelve (William Z. Foster was dropped owing to ill health) party leaders began on 17 January 1949. On 14 October 1949 all eleven were found guilty. Their conviction was upheld by the U.S. Court of Appeals and, on 4 June 1951, by the U.S. Supreme Court in *Dennis v. United States* (341 U.S. 494). In his majority decision, Chief Justice Fred M. Vinson accepted a reinterpretation of the "clear and present danger" doctrine that had first been enunciated by Justice Oliver Wendell Holmes, Jr., in *Schenck v. United States* (249 U.S. 47) in 1919. Vinson said that it was sufficient that the conspirators were willing to overthrow the government if and when possible. Further, he held that the probability of success in an attempt to overthrow the government was too hard a measure and, therefore, not a proper one. "An attempt to overthrow the Government by force, even though doomed from the outset, is sufficient evil for Congress to prevent."[24] Justices Hugo Black and William O. Douglas dissented. In his dissent, Justice Black wrote: "Public opinion being what it now is, few will protest the conviction of the Communist petitioners. There is hope, however, that in calmer times, when the present passions and fears subside, this or some later court will restore the First Amendment liberties to the high, preferred place where they belong in a free society." Once the *Dennis* decision had affirmed the government's position with regard to the Smith Act, the door was open to go after the so-called second string communists. Before the Justice Department was finished, there had been additional Smith Act trials in New York, Los Angeles, Baltimore, Pittsburgh, Seattle, Detroit, Saint Louis, Philadelphia, and, as we shall see, Honolulu.[25]

While the first Smith Act defendants were awaiting their trial in New York, the 1948 presidential election was in progress. That election pitted two of Franklin D. Roosevelt's former vice-presidents against each other for the Democratic party's nomination. Realizing early on that Truman, who had acceded to the presidency when Roosevelt died in 1945, controlled the party's nomination processes, Henry Wallace, Roosevelt's vice-president from 1941 to 1945, formed the Independent Progressive party. Wallace's refusal to repudiate Communist party support undoubtedly cost him many votes and helped to establish Harry Truman's anticommunist credentials in the eyes of many American voters. Ironically, this split in the Democratic party arguably aided Truman in his stunning upset victory over Governor Thomas E. Dewey of New York, the Republican standard-bearer. Wallace lamented: "If the Communists would have a ticket of their own, the New Party would lose 100,000 votes, but gain four million." Joseph R. Starobin, in his work *American Communism in Crisis, 1943–1957*, pointed out: "Verbally, Wallace defended the right of the Communists to be acknowledged as a political force under the protection of the Constitution. He viewed them as wrong in their perception of the world, but defended their right to be wrong."[26]

In that same year, 1948, a young man was making his reputation in the House of Representatives using anticommunism as his key weapon. Richard M. Nixon entered the House in 1947 by defeating a popular five-term Democratic incumbent, Jerry Voorhis. Nixon biographer Stephen E. Ambrose wrote: "Nixon's campaign came to center on a charge that Voorhis was a Communist sympathizer who had Communist support. This was absolutely untrue, as Nixon knew perfectly well. . . . In point of fact, Voorhis . . . had become anathema to the Communist Party, because [he] had denounced Russian aggression in Eastern Europe."[27] Nixon created confusion in the Voorhis camp with his allegations that Voorhis had been endorsed by the National Citizens' Political Action Committee (he had not been) and by a meaningless comparison of Voorhis' voting record with that of Vito Marcantonio, American Labor party congressman from New York. Nixon saved his best for last. The weekend before the election, on 2–3 November 1946, the Nixon campaign unleashed a "boiler room" calling blitz. The callers would say to registered voters within the district, "This is a friend of yours, but I can't tell you my name. I just wanted you to know that Jerry Voorhis is a communist" and hang up. The callers were paid nine dollars a day and "sworn to secrecy."[28] Another Nixon biographer, Fawn M. Brodie, relates an encounter between Nixon and a Voorhis aide, Stanley Long. When Long accused him of having lied about Voorhis' communist connections, Nixon was alleged to have said: "Of course I knew Jerry Voorhis wasn't a Communist. . . . The important thing is to win. You're just being naive."[29]

After entering the House of Representatives, Nixon had the good political fortune to become a member of the House Committee on Un-American Activities. It was as a member of HUAC that Nixon was able to introduce the Mundt-Nixon bill and have his historic rendezvous with Alger Hiss. Alger Hiss, as an official in the State Department, had played important roles in the Dumbarton Oaks Conference (1944), the Yalta Conference (1945), and the United Nations Conference on International Organization in San Francisco (1945), where the United Nations Charter was adopted. In 1947 he became president of the Carnegie Endowment for International Peace. Then, in 1948, Hiss was identified in a HUAC hearing by Whittaker Chambers, a brilliant but tormented former communist, as having been a fellow member of the Communist party from 1934 to 1938. Hiss, a graduate of Johns Hopkins and Harvard Law School, was a protégé of Felix Frankfurter and a law clerk for Justice Oliver Wendell Holmes, Jr. The accusation stunned the nation's foreign policy establishment. Hiss denied ever having been a member of the Communist party and, initially, denied even knowing Chambers. He later admitted having known Chambers under the assumed name George Crosley. Nixon tenaciously pursued the case when others on HUAC wanted to drop it as a "hot potato" because Hiss had impeccable credentials in the political establishment. In January 1950 Alger Hiss was finally convicted of perjury for having lied to the committee about his past activities. Hiss was sentenced to a five-year prison term. He served forty-four months in the federal penitentiary at Lewisburg, Pennsylvania.

Looking back at Nixon's role in the Hiss case, Walter Goodman, a historian generally critical of HUAC, gave the future president high marks:

> Nixon's career was famously expedited by the Hiss case . . . but the qualities he showed on the Committee would have carried him forward in any event. He was smart, energetic, and a very fast learner of what he needed to know. He could be dogged yet agile; he had a nice instinct for when to bet high and when to cut his losses. The Committee had helped to make him, but he, more than any other member, had been responsible for giving the Committee its great year. As that year drew to a close, no one could doubt that Richard Nixon's future was exceedingly bright. As for the Committee itself, however, it would not again attain the resplendency of 1948.[30]

The question of Alger Hiss' guilt or innocence has long been debated in American political circles. Harry Truman was quoted by Henry Nicholson, his favorite Secret Service agent, as having said: "Dean Acheson tells me Alger Hiss is innocent. After reading the evidence in the papers, I think the s.o.b. is guilty, and I hope they hang him."[31] The nation, including many who wanted to believe in Hiss' innocence, appeared to agree that Hiss, at the very least, had lied to HUAC.[32]

One month after the Hiss conviction in January 1950, the nation saw the first arrests of members of the alleged spy ring led by the German-born nuclear physicist Klaus Fuchs. During the spring and summer, the names of his coconspirators in the so-called implosion conspiracy grabbed the attention of the American public as they were arrested: Harry Gold, David Greenglass, Arthur Dean Slack, Julius Rosenberg, Morton Sobel. The nation could only wonder about the role these alleged spies had played in the Soviet Union's first successful nuclear detonation in Siberia in September of 1949.[33]

Communist North Korea invaded South Korea on 25 June 1950. By the middle of September the United Nations forces in Korea were in danger of being driven into the sea. Small wonder that Congress was in a mood to pass the McCarran Act over President Truman's veto. On 22 September the Internal Security Act of 1950 passed the House by a vote of 286 to 48.[34] On 23 September it passed the Senate, 57 to 10.[35] The act provided for the registration of all communists and communist front organizations with the Justice Department. It required that all communist and communist front propaganda be labeled as such. It stipulated that all members of the Communist party and communist front organizations be barred from jobs in the U.S. government and the defense industries. The act also gave the attorney general the right to deny passports to members of the Communist party and communist front organizations. There were extensive provisions for dealing with aliens. Noncitizens could be deported and naturalized citizens could be denaturalized if they were found to be in violation of those provisions of the law. At the time the McCarran Act passed, J. Edgar Hoover, director of the Federal Bureau of Investigation (FBI), estimated it would affect about 550,000 communists and fellow travelers, about 10 percent of whom were actually Communist party members.[36]

In his veto message Truman had complained that the McCarran Act would aid potential enemies by requiring a complete public list of vital defense plants, laboratories, and other installations. The Justice Department and the FBI would have to waste immense amounts of time and energy in attempting to carry out the law's unworkable registration provisions. The act would deprive the country of the great contributions of many aliens in intelligence matters. It would antagonize friendly governments. It would put the government of the United States into the thought control business. And it would give government officials vast powers to harrass all of our citizens in the exercise of their right of free speech.[37]

On 13 October 1950 Attorney General J. Howard McGrath was quoted as saying: "We cannot fight communism by placing totalitarian power in any hand. And I think the bill placed such power in the hands of the Attorney General. I don't want it any more than I want it in any other hands."[38] On 23 October 1950 the "reluctant" Justice Department began a roundup of alien communists. Eighty-six were arrested in the first group, including David Hyun, a former Hawaii resident of Korean origin then living in Los Angeles. Under the law, the attorney general had the power to hold these individuals for up to six months, pending deportation. On 1 January 1951 the *Honolulu Star-Bulletin* announced that there were 64,000 aliens to be registered under the Internal Security Act of 1950, just in the territory of Hawaii.[39]

Richard Nixon was elected to the U.S. Senate in 1951 with popular support created by the conviction of Alger Hiss. In a vicious campaign, Nixon dubbed his opponent, Helen Gahagan Douglas, the "Pink Lady." The Nixon campaign circulated a "pink sheet" showing that Mrs. Douglas had voted with the infamous left-winger Vito Marcantonio on 354 occasions while she was a member of the House of Representatives. Over half a million copies were distributed to the California voters. As Fawn Brodie points out:

> Nixon, himself, had voted with Marcantonio 112 times. Of the 354 votes, most were non-controversial and minor; only 76 were key "roll-call" votes. Of these, Douglas had voted with Marcantonio 66 times, 53 times with a majority of the Democratic party. Of the 13 in which she did not vote with the party, 11 dealt with housing, rent, and price controls. Two dealt with internal security, the Mundt-Nixon bill, which she opposed and the McCarran internal security bill, where she voted to sustain Truman's veto. On all foreign policy issues she had voted with the bi-partisan "contain-

> ment of Russia" majority, save the Greek-Turkish aid bill. On ten crucial roll-call votes she had voted against Marcantonio.[40]

The entire campaign was a disaster for Mrs. Douglas. Wherever she turned, she was on the defensive. Nixon won by over 680,000 votes.

By 1952 Nixon was ready for bigger things. Nixon's anticommunist credentials were among the reasons for his selection as Dwight D. Eisenhower's running mate in the presidential election of 1952. Eisenhower was attempting to outflank Senator Joseph McCarthy, the Republican "loose cannon" of the anticommunist movement.

Senator Joseph R. McCarthy, Republican of Wisconsin, was an American phenomenon. He entered the field of anticommunism in 1950 and virtually dominated it for the better part of five years. A shameless, pathological liar, McCarthy had been elected to the U.S. Senate in the Republican year 1946. His principal competition during the Republican primary came from Robert M. LaFollette, Jr. In the wake of the dissolution of the Progressive party of Wisconsin, base of the LaFollette dynasty for decades, the son of "Fighting Bob" LaFollette expected his Progressive constituency to follow him into the Republican fold. They did not, leaving the door open for young Joe McCarthy, "Tail Gunner Joe," as he fraudulently called himself. McCarthy asked Wisconsin Republicans why they should vote for LaFollette, who remained on his "Virginia plantation" instead of coming home to Wisconsin to defend his record. LaFollette clearly underestimated McCarthy's appeal and paid for it by losing the Republican primary by 5,400 votes out of 410,000 votes cast.[41]

McCarthy's first three years in the Senate were undistinguished, to say the least. He was known as the "Pepsi Cola Kid" for his efforts to have sugar controls lifted so that the soft drink industry could get back to business as usual. McCarthy was well paid for his efforts by the soft drink lobby. He also found pay dirt in the housing industry, doing favors on Capitol Hill for Lustron Corporation.

In January of 1950, with his reelection campaign two and one-half years away, McCarthy had dinner with a small group of supporters at the Colony Restaurant in Washington, D.C. One of those present on that fateful occasion was Father Edmund A. Walsh, dean of the Georgetown School of Foreign Service. History "credits" Father Walsh with having turned McCarthy in the direction of anticommunism.

McCarthy's first anticommunist speech came one month later. On 9 February 1950 McCarthy addressed the Republican women of Wheeling, West Virginia. Here was his theme:

> Today we are engaged in a final, all-out battle between Communistic atheism and Christianity. The modern champions of Communism have selected this as the time. . . . The war is on. . . .

> Six years ago . . . there were within the Soviet orbit 180,000,000 people. Lined up on the antitotalitarian side there were . . . roughly 1,625,000,000 people. Today, only six years later, there are 800,000,000 people under the absolute domination of Soviet Russia. . . . On our side, the figure has shrunk to around 500,000,000. . . . In less than six years the odds have changed from nine to one in our favor to eight to five against us. This indicates the tempo of Communism's victories and American defeats in the Cold War. As one of our outstanding historical figures once said, "When a great democracy is destroyed, it will not be because of enemies from without, but rather because of enemies within."

McCarthy continued, his tone revealing the antielite bias characterizing much of the anticommunist rhetoric of the day:

> The reason why we find ourselves in a position of impotency is not because our only powerful potential enemy has sent men to invade our shores, but rather because of the traitorous actions of those who have been treated so well by this Nation. It has not been the less fortunate or members of minority groups who have been selling this Nation out, but rather those who have had all the benefits that the wealthiest nation on earth has to offer—the finest homes, the finest college education, the finest jobs in Government we can give.
>
> This is glaringly true in the State Department. There the young men who were born with silver spoons in their mouths are the ones who have been the worst.[42]

McCarthy went on to say that he had the names of 205 known communists who worked at the State Department. This number was to change frequently in the next few weeks: At Salt Lake City and Reno, the number he used was 57; in a speech before the Senate on 20 February it was 81; before the Tydings Committee he used the number 10; in executive sessions he used the number 116; and so it went. McCarthy's 20 February speech before the Senate was a six-hour circus in which the senator, who had entered with the bulging briefcase that was to become his trademark, began throwing cases at his colleagues. Hour after hour, he referred to cases by number. Some were identified only as individuals who worked for the United Nations or the Voice of America. Case 14 was "primarily a morals case." Case 41 was significant because he was so staunchly anticommunist that Secretary of State Dean Acheson had fired him! Case 3 was the same as case 4. Case 9 was the same as case 77. On and on it went. As Richard Rovere, a noted journalist who covered McCarthy during the entire period of his ascendancy, said in his work *Senator Joe McCarthy:*

> It was a flabbergasting performance, lasting from late afternoon almost until midnight. Senators drifted in and out of the chamber as McCarthy, growing hoarser, redder, and less coherent, shuffled about the idiotic "dossiers" that were spread untidily over two desks and that were plainly as

> foreign to him as they were to the other Senators. Scott Lucas interrupted sixty-one times, mainly in a futile effort to make McCarthy straighten out his mixed-up numbers. . . . "I may say," [McCarthy protested,] "if the Senator [Lucas] is going to make a farce of this, I will not yield to him. I shall not answer any more silly questions of the Senator. This is too important, too serious a matter for that."[43]

Militant anticommunists who had preceded McCarthy were shocked by his recklessness. This was especially true of Richard Nixon, who had paved the way for McCarthy with the Hiss case. During the 1952 presidential election, whenever the issue of McCarthyism came up, Nixon cautiously deflected it by saying that there would be no McCarthyism if Truman had been more honest about subversive influences in his government. "The way to get rid of so-called McCarthyism," Nixon urged, "is to elect a new administration that will deal with the problem honestly."[44] President Truman was more blunt in condemnation of McCarthyism. When asked by a reporter whether he thought Senator McCarthy would be able to turn up any real communists in the State Department, Truman replied: "I think the greatest asset the Kremlin has is Senator McCarthy."[45]

One of the great Republican elder statesmen of the time, Henry Stimson, commented on Senator McCarthy's attacks against Dean Acheson in a 27 March 1950 letter to the *New York Times:*

> No matter what else may occur, the present charges have already spattered mud upon individuals of the highest integrity, and in the present state of the world the denial cannot always overtake the accusation. . . . The real motive of the accuser in this case is to cast discredit upon the Secretary of State of the United States. This man is not trying to get rid of known Communists in the State Department; he is hoping against hope that he will find some.[46]

Senator John Bricker, a conservative Republican from Ohio, was Thomas E. Dewey's running mate in the presidential election of 1944. Bricker reflected a substantial strain of contemporary Republican sentiment in his reputed remark to McCarthy in the Senate cloakroom: "Joe, you're a dirty son of a bitch, but there are times when you've got to have a son of a bitch around, and this is one of them."[47] The Democrats, for the most part, were simply ducking for cover.

By the end of March 1950 McCarthy was ready to let his battle against the State Department "stand or fall" on the basis of one case: the case of Owen Lattimore. Ironically, Lattimore, then director of the Walter Hines Page School of International Relations at Johns Hopkins University, had never been an employee of the State Department. He had, indeed, been a consultant for the State Department as he was then for the United Nations. Had the State Department followed the Far

East policy outlined by Lattimore in his trenchant 1949 work *The Situation in Asia*, the United States might well have avoided the disasters experienced in both Korea and Vietnam. Lattimore, a World War II aide to Chiang Kai-shek, had come to the realization that Chiang's regime was corrupt beyond redemption. Chiang Kai-shek, not the United States government, had lost China to the communists. This insight, which seems so obvious today, earned Lattimore the enmity of a powerful group loosely known as the China Lobby.

Writing in May 1950, Lattimore named the China Lobby as the source for McCarthy's charges against him. One of the "pressure organizations" supporting the China Lobby was the Constitutional Educational League of Joseph Kamp. "I later learned," Lattimore wrote, "that Kamp's pamphlet *America Betrayed*, which was distributed to members of Congress and editors all over the country just a week before McCarthy began his campaign, contained all the same charges against the same people in almost the same words."[48] Whatever the source of the charges, Lattimore would have his day before the Senate. When McCarthy's accusations began to receive national attention, the Senate appointed a subcommittee to investigate communist infiltration into government. The chairman of the subcommittee was Millard E. Tydings of Maryland, an old guard conservative southern Democrat. McCarthy was called before the Tydings Committee to prove his charges against Lattimore.

The hearing began on 6 April 1950 before a standing-room-only audience in the caucus room of the Senate office building. Lattimore opened with a systematic review of the charges and a stirring denunciation of McCarthy, charging that the senator had violated the responsibility of his high office:

> He [has] violated it by impairing the effectiveness of the United States Government in its relations with its friends and allies, and by making the Government of the United States an object of suspicion in the eyes of the anti-Communist world, and undoubtedly the laughing stock of Communist governments.
>
> He has violated it by instituting a reign of terror among officials and employees of the United States Government, no one of whom can be sure of safety from attack by the machine-gun of irresponsible publicity in Joseph McCarthy's hands.
>
> He has without authorization used secret documents obtained from government files. He has vilified citizens of the United States and accused them of high crime, without giving them an opportunity to defend themselves.
>
> He has refused to submit alleged documentary evidence to a duly constituted committee of the Senate.
>
> He has invited disrespect to himself and his high office by refusing to live up to his word. Twice on the floor of the Senate he stated that any

> charges he made under the cloak of immunity he would repeat in another place so that their falseness could be tested in a court of the United States. He said that if he should fail to do this he would resign. He has been called to repeat his charges so that they could be tested in a court of action. He has failed to do so. And he has not resigned.[49]

After the applause had died down, Senator Tydings told Lattimore: "I owe it to you and to the country to tell you that four members of the subcommittee [three Democrats and Senator Lodge] recently had a complete summary of your loyalty file read to us in the presence of Mr. J. Edgar Hoover, head of the Federal Bureau of Investigation. At the conclusion of the reading, it was the unanimous opinion of the subcommittee and of all others in the room [which included Attorney General J. Howard McGrath] that there is nothing in the files to show that you have ever been a Communist or have ever been connected with espionage."[50]

The centerpiece of McCarthy's case against Lattimore turned out to be a professional former communist by the name of Louis Budenz, whom we shall meet again in Hawaii. Budenz' testimony was rambling, unsubstantiated, and at times incoherent. When Lattimore's attorneys, Abe Fortas and Paul Porter, questioned Budenz, they asked why, when he had been interrogated by the FBI for more than three thousand hours between 1946 and 1950, he had never brought forward the name of Owen Lattimore as a security risk. They asked why, in 1947, when a State Department security officer specifically asked him about Lattimore, he had said that he knew of nothing that would indicate that Owen Lattimore was a communist. They asked why, in a 1949 draft of an article for *Colliers*, there had been no mention of Lattimore. Subcommittee counsel Edward P. Morgan asked why there were no charges against Lattimore in his most recent book. Budenz finally had an answer; he volunteered that "in another book which I am writing Mr. Lattimore is very prominent."[51]

A shred of dignity was salvaged for the Republican party on 1 June 1950 when Senator Margaret Chase Smith, a Republican from Maine, presented a "Declaration of Conscience," a statement in which she was joined by six Republican colleagues. "I speak as a Republican. I speak as a woman. I speak as a United States Senator. I speak as an American," Senator Smith intoned. "The United States Senate has long enjoyed worldwide respect as the greatest deliberative body in the world. But recently that deliberative character has too often been debased to the level of a forum of hate and character assassination sheltered by the shield of congressional immunity." In her conclusion Senator Smith said that she did not wish to see the Republicans "ride to political victory on the Four Horsemen of Calumny—Fear, Ignorance, Bigotry and Smear."

She added: "While it might be a fleeting victory for the Republican Party, it would be a more lasting defeat for the American people."[52]

One might have thought that McCarthy would slink away into the night after so poor a showing in the Lattimore case, but he did not. He continued to be a major force in American politics for another four years. Not until the Army-McCarthy hearings of 1954 was he finally brought down, censured by his colleagues in the United States Senate. McCarthy died three years later, at the age of forty-eight, a pathetic, alcoholic shell of his former self. He left behind a legacy of fear and hate.

The years from 1947 to 1953 will be the central focus of this work as we turn to Hawaii. Those years on the mainland of the United States are well sumarized in a brief paragraph from David H. Bennett's *The Party of Fear:*

> If communists or fellow travelers had dominated a few important unions after V-J day, they had been expelled from the CIO by 1947. If communists had played a key role in organizing Henry Wallace's Progressive Party presidential candidacy in 1948, these efforts resulted only in a crushing defeat. By 1953, membership had plummeted from fifty-four thousand to twenty-four thousand . . . and a significant percentage of this tiny group of card carrying communists were double agents, representatives of intelligence services.[53]

It can be argued, on the one hand, that it was precisely because of the strong anticommunist movement that the subversive elements in the United States were stopped in their tracks. On the other hand, it can be argued that communist influences were never the threat the anticommunists portrayed them to be.

Although McCarthy was not a major force in Hawaii, where local politics were emphasized over national more than on the mainland, many aspects of anticommunism on the mainland were repeated in Hawaii. Both on the mainland and in Hawaii all three branches of government were active in promoting anticommunism. Truman's Executive Order 9835 was a trigger for the Reinecke case in 1947; the House Committee on Un-American Activities held hearings in Hawaii in 1950; the "Hawaii Seven" were arrested, tried, and convicted of having violated the Smith Act in an ordeal that lasted from 1951 to 1953; organized labor in Hawaii, notably Harry Bridges' ILWU, experienced many of the same forms of harassment that were visited upon their mainland brothers and sisters; and the Democratic party in Hawaii had to overcome persistent charges of communist infiltration as did their colleagues from the mainland. Anticommunism in Hawaii had its own unique themes and variations, but it was the same song as on the mainland—just a different verse.

Chapter 2

The Territory of Hawaii

During the 1920s and 1930s there were some parallels between the territory of Hawaii and the mainland on the question of communism, but there were major differences. The differences were related, primarily, to Hawaii's geographic location and its plantation economy. Although there is no evidence of an organized radical movement in the 1920s, the *Honolulu Star-Bulletin* characterized a tragic incident at Hanapepe, Kauai, during the 1924 sugar strike in the most lurid terms. The "Hanapepe Massacre" saw sixteen strikers and four police officers die in a brief flurry of gunfire and knife attacks. The *Star-Bulletin* reacted as follows:

> On one side, we have a great majority of liberty-loving Americans. On the other side we have, first the labor "leaders" and their deluded, ignorant followers; second, their alien backers; third, the fringe of hangers-on—the professional agitators, the "Reds," the IWW's—who are egging on the Filipino leaders and preaching class warfare and the destruction of the American institutions . . . a heterogeneous group of "Reds," "Pinks," and "Yellows"—"wobblies" and communists and crack-brained demagogues —who have aligned themselves with the strikers and are doing their Bolshevik best to turn Hawaii into anarchy.[1]

Lawrence Fuchs, in his work *Hawaii Pono*, pointed out that "by crying 'subversion' or 'Communism' at every major effort at unionization during the forty years after annexation, oligarchy spokesmen had numbed the minds of Hawaii's workingmen." Fuchs went on to say:

> Before [Jack] Hall's arrival in Hawaii, the [Communist] party had made little headway in the Islands. In 1922, a small Marxist-oriented Japanese newspaper appeared on Kauai, and seven years later there emerged a small Marxist study group on Maui. But as late as 1936, according to a 1951 report of the Commission on Subversive Activities in the Territory, there were no more than sixty Communist party members on Hawaii's waterfront, most of whom were nonresident seamen.[2]

George Wright was president of the Honolulu Central Labor Council when he tried to organize Hawaii's workers into the United Workers of

Hawaii in 1922. Wright's campaign included a "Manifesto to the Workers of Hawaii." He sought racial cooperation and industrial unionism, concepts that were to be the backbone of the ILWU. But, as Hawaii labor historian Edward D. Beechert pointed out: "The manifesto immediately conjured up visions of the One Big Union campaign and the Industrial Workers of the World (IWW). Wright consistently denied any connection with the IWW or radicalism, despite the similarity of goals."[3]

The system of plantation labor in Hawaii, from its beginnings at Koloa Plantation on the island of Kauai in 1835 through World War II, was, at best, paternalistic; at its worst it was harshly punitive. From the first introduction of Chinese workers in 1852, to the massive importation of Japanese laborers during the 1880s and 1890s, to the injection of more than a hundred thousand Filipino laborers from 1910 to 1932, the sugar planters pitted one racial or ethnic group against another in their efforts to find and maintain a docile, compliant work force. Racial antipathies against Asians led to sporadic efforts to import European workers: Norwegians, Portuguese, Spanish, Germans, and Russians were introduced to Hawaiian plantation life. Relatively few remained for long in Hawaii; fewer still remained on the plantations. The territorial board of immigration reported that between 1905 and 1916 104,406 plantation workers were brought to Hawaii. Of that number, 44,989 had left Hawaii for the West Coast, 38,462 had returned to their countries of origin, and 20,955 remained in Hawaii.[4]

Of those who remained, large numbers fled the harsh isolation of plantation life to work in the cities, particularly Honolulu. The Hawaiian Sugar Planters' Association (HSPA), alarmed by the mobility of the work force, made grudging improvements in plantation living and working conditions, while continuing their search for more pliant workers. Richard Cooke, president of the HSPA in 1930, defended their approach in the face of critics who were arguing for a more adequately paid indigenous work force:

> We do know that if the policy of employing native born had been originally adopted, there would not have been any sugar or pineapple plantations, and extremely little in the way of other industrial development. From a strictly ethical standpoint, I can see little difference between the importation of foreign laborers and the importation of jute bags from India.[5]

The HSPA placed great pressure on the territorial Department of Public Instruction during the 1920s, believing that education was undermining their work force. At the HSPA's forty-ninth annual meeting in 1929, a compliant superintendent of public instruction told the assemblage, while describing his department's plans for vocational education as a means of keeping children of plantation workers satisfied with plantation life, "We are simply working for you, the same as any other person here or on the plantation is working for you." Cooke, wanting to be sure that nobody forgot the main point, reminded the audience, "As has been emphasized over and over again, the primary function of our plantations is not to produce sugar, but to pay dividends."[6]

The HSPA was really the voice of the "Big Five," the powerful factoring organizations that had come to control Hawaii's shipping and agriculture as increasing capital requirements drove the competition into their arms. The Big Five firms were Alexander & Baldwin, American Factors (H. Hackfeld before World War I), C. Brewer, Castle & Cooke, and Theo H. Davies. They not only controlled shipping and agriculture, they also had a lock on banking, insurance, utilities, ground transportation, wholesale merchandising, and retailing. Within the Big Five there was a maze of interlocking boards of directors that allowed a relatively small group of men at the top to manipulate Hawaii's economic life. These men tended to take a paternalistic view of their workers; they were vigorously antiunion. They had used the precept "divide and rule" to prevent the development of strong unions. During the late 1920s their strategy appeared to be working. After bruising strikes in 1920 and 1924, labor was under control and profits were large.

With the Great Depression came a sharp drop in the markets for sugar and pineapple, with a resulting oversupply of labor. Beechert points out, "When agricultural employment declined, the sugar industry undertook to return some 7,000 workers in 1932 to the Philippines at industry expense, thus avoiding further lay-offs which could contribute to the already heavy relief burden." Ironically, one of the long-cherished goals of Hawaii's politicians came to pass during this period. "Citizen employment" in the sugar industry, which had been only 15.9 percent of the work force in 1930, rose to 31.4 percent in 1936. Small wonder, when roughly 25 percent of the work force in Honolulu was without a job.[7]

The Great Depression also brought the New Deal. Section 7(a) of the National Industrial Recovery Act did much to encourage union membership in the United States. In addition, the exclusivity of the American Federation of Labor (AFL) and its craft orientation was being overtaken by the industrial organization approach of labor leaders such as John L. Lewis, head of the United Mine Workers and founder of the CIO. The National Labor Relations Act of 1935, more commonly known as the Wagner Act, gave further impetus to industrial unions. If Hawaii's plantation workers were to be unionized, the industrial model was the only one that made sense.

Since the late nineteenth century, Hawaii had been in constant contact with the West Coast labor movement through maritime workers, particularly the International Longshoremen's Association (ILA) and the Sailors' Union of the Pacific (SUP). The first major effort of the ILA to organize in Hawaii came during the 1901 waterfront strike against McCabe, Hamilton, & Renny and was defeated with the use of Japanese "scabs" recruited from the plantations. The ILA languished during the next decade, amidst demands from the national union that Asian workers be excluded. In 1912 the national union bent on the issue, with the proviso that Asian members not be allowed to transfer their membership to mainland locals. The final ILA strike in Hawaii came in 1916, ending with a compromise on wages but a refusal to recognize the union or allow a union shop. In Hawaii, as on the West Coast, a company union was established, giving employers complete control of the waterfront. The successor to the ILA, the ILWU, would eventually organize Hawaii's waterfront and plantation workers, but it was to be a vastly different union from its predecessor.

Although the success of any large organization is the product of the efforts of many, the man most closely associated with the ILWU's success in Hawaii is Jack Hall. Hall graduated from high school near Los Angeles in 1931, at the age of sixteen. The nation was sinking deeper and deeper into the Great Depression, and opportunities for a young high school graduate looked grim. Hall hitchhiked to San Francisco and, after a long wait, shipped out as an able bodied seaman aboard the *President Hoover.* He first saw Hawaii in 1932, an event he recalled for the *ILWU Reporter* in 1950: "It was daybreak. Rain clouds stood over the valleys. A light cool breeze fanned those of us who stood at the rail as the ship nosed her way into the channel. I was expectant—but a little tense and excited. I had the feeling that Hawaii was different—and it was."[8] In 1935 Hall made Honolulu his home port. But before that he was to go through a formative experience in California.

Hall's ship at the time, the *President Garfield,* was docked in Los Angeles while the Big Strike of 1934 was going on in San Francisco. The nineteen-year-old sailor caught a bus to the Bay Area and immersed himself in strike activities. He came away with his SUP union card, dated 16 September 1934, and a feeling that union work would be an important part of his future.

Hall returned to Hawaii in 1935 with a mission. Revels Cayton, business agent for the Marine Cooks and Stewards' Union in San Francisco, had seen potential in the lanky young sailor. "If Hall got $20 a week, he was living," said Cayton. "We needed a guy to meet the ships in Honolulu and talk to the guys." Cayton, then a member of the Communist party, recalled forty years later: "You could tell he could carry out that kind of job. Those were the days when labor was beginning to flex its muscles and we were looking for leaders."[9] Hall also got work from a feisty Hawaiian-German named Maxie Weisbarth, the local business agent for the SUP, and from the newly founded labor weekly *Voice of Labor.*

During Hall's career with the ILWU, there was much speculation about his alleged membership in the Communist party. Clearly, he was a member. Hall's own diary chronicled the fact: "Left on a trip around the world westward. *President Wilson*, December 13 [1935]. Arrived S.F. [San Francisco] March 25, 1936. Officially joined the CP [Communist party] early in 1936, presumably after March 25."[10] Jack Hall later told his half brother, John, that he had joined the Communist party to get all the help he could in his work as a labor organizer. In 1950 Jack Hall signed a Taft-Hartley affidavit stating that he was "not now" a member of the Communist party. There is no reason to believe that Hall perjured himself in the signing of such an affidavit. Hall was, above all, a pragmatic labor leader. When he thought it served his purposes to belong to the Communist party, he did so. When it was no longer in his interest, he got out. Jack Kimoto, onetime head of the Communist party in Hawaii, said that Hall should be remembered as a labor leader, not a Communist party leader.[11]

Although many communists had passed through Hawaii over the years, there does not seem to have been an actual party organization until 1937. A colorful seaman named Bill Bailey was sent to set one up. Bailey, a tall, handsome Irishman, came with a reputation. In 1935 the German passenger ship *Bremen* was docked in New York Harbor. On the rigging of the bow of the ship was a Nazi flag, illuminated at night by a large spotlight. In front of a crowd in the thousands that was there to protest the presence of the Nazi ship and behind the backs of a vigilant crew, Bailey snuck aboard, climbed the rigging, and cut down the hated flag. It was a performance much appreciated by the protesters but not the crew. Bailey took quite a beating at the hands of the Germans before being turned over to the harbor police, who were themselves none too gentle with the young radical.[12] Bailey was remembered in 1978 by Louis Goldblatt, secretary-treasurer of the ILWU for thirty-five years and Harry Bridges' point man in Hawaii: "Some of the old-timers," Goldblatt said, "still talk about Big Bill. . . . The guys still remember his speech calling for a Soviet America."[13]

Bailey was sent to Hawaii by William Schneiderman, head of the Communist party in California, after the west coast maritime strike of 1936–1937, to do some "political work."[14] He arrived as a yeoman aboard the *Lurline*, got a small room that he decorated with a hand-painted hammer and sickle on some red bunting, and started his search along the waterfront for radical workers who might form the nucleus of a Communist party organization in Hawaii. At his first membership meeting, Bailey is reported to have pointed to his flag and said: "That's my Bible. We've got to go out and visit people and talk and talk and begin to organize the workers." Then he signed up his guests as members of the Communist party, giving each of them a card that identified them as members of the "Travelers Club" for an initiation fee of ten cents.[15] In a 1992 interview, Bailey recalled that there were ten to twelve people in that first group.[16]

Shortly thereafter, Bailey was introduced to Jack Hall by Maxie Weisbarth as "another commie you ought to meet." Bailey gave Jack Hall some on-the-job training in labor organizing when the two of them went to Maui from 8 to 19 April 1937 to help Antonio Fagel organize Filipino sugar workers. Fagel was a disciple of the exiled Filipino labor leader Pablo Manlapit and headed up the Vibora Luviminda. Beechert describes that organization as follows:

> The Vibora Luviminda was an intensely Filipino organization, closely resembling the political-religious reform movements in the Philippines. The name was fashioned from the nickname of the patriot who had resisted the American occupation of the Philippines, General Artemio Y Rocorte, often known as Vibora (serpent) for his ability to strike American troops without warning, and the contraction of the three major island groups of the Philippines—Luzon, Visayas, and Mindanao—hence Vibora Luviminda. The appeal of Vibora Luviminda was explicitly nationalistic; it related more to the colonial status of the homeland than to the condition of the Filipino worker in Hawaii.[17]

While Bailey and Hall were helping Fagel to prepare for the labor action ahead, they tried to convince him that organizing along ethnic lines was counterproductive; he should consider all workers, regardless of race or ethnic background. Fagel replied that he would think about other ethnic groups after he had organized the Filipinos.

On 20 April 1937, the day after Bailey and Hall returned to Honolulu, the strike on Maui began. While Bailey returned to Maui, Hall was sent by Ed Berman to Kauai to assist the Port Allen longshoremen. Berman was editor of *Voice of Labor* and had recently been appointed unpaid director of the CIO for the territory of Hawaii. At this point in his life, Berman envisioned himself playing the role in Hawaiian labor history that Jack Hall would eventually occupy.

Bailey reported to Berman from Maui that he had seen some cylindrical tubes on the roof of a plantation mill. He determined, erroneously as it turned out, that there were machine guns on the roof. Berman printed a story in *Voice of Labor,* with Bailey's byline, under the headline "Maui Workers Faced with Machine Guns." When Bailey returned to Honolulu in mid-May, a waterfront policeman who had befriended him warned him that plans were under way at the police department to have Bailey arrested for violating the territory's Criminal Syndicalist

Act, a nasty piece of legislation left over from the red-baiting days of 1919 to 1923.[18] With the *Lurline* sailing on 20 May, Bailey had two choices: be on the *Lurline* or go to jail. Jack Kawano, a young longshore leader who had been among those Bailey brought into the Communist party during his stay in Hawaii, advised him to go. "We haven't got a lawyer," Kawano said. "You left your mark here. Get the hell out. You're not running out on us."[19]

Bailey left Hawaii, continuing a storied life that included service in the Spanish civil war as part of the Abraham Lincoln Battalion.[20] Bailey's successor as Communist party organizer in Hawaii arrived from California in 1938. Jack Kimoto had been born on Ewa Plantation and had spent three years of his childhood in Japan and seven years of his adult life in California. The Party needed a dedicated communist who understood the Asian population in Hawaii and Hawaii's plantation economy. Kimoto was their man.

While a flurry of loosely coordinated labor activity was taking place in Hawaii during the latter half of the 1930s, Harry Bridges was becoming the undisputed leader of the ILA on the West Coast. Then, on 11 August 1937, Bridges led the ILA's Pacific coast units out of the AFL and into the CIO. This exodus was the culmination of Bridges' long fight with Joe Ryan, the national president of the ILA. The fight began when Bridges defied Ryan's efforts to end the Big Strike of 1934 on terms congenial to West Coast shipping interests and ended with the creation of the ILWU. In the territory of Hawaii, both the Hilo and Honolulu longshoremen's associations had been granted ILA charters in November 1936. In October 1937 the Honolulu Longshoremen's Association became ILWU Local 1-37; the Hilo unit became ILWU Local 1-36.

Union prospects in the territory of Hawaii did not look good to National Labor Relations Board hearing officer George Pratt, who made the following observation in his 1937 NLRB report: "The mores of the Territory provide no place for a union for any of its employed inhabitants, and consequently, activity in looking toward such union organization and moves made toward it which are commonplace on the mainland become endowed with portentous and revolutionary significance when seen through island eyes."[21] Lawrence Judd, president of the Industrial Association of Hawaii, was not impressed by Pratt or the NLRB. Judd was quoted by the *Honolulu Star-Bulletin* on 22 April 1937 as saying, "I pay about as much attention to the NLRB as I do to the Desha Bathing Suit Law," a disdainful reference to a 1921 territorial ordinance requiring bathing suits to be covered in public.[22] The next year, 1938, was to bear out Pratt's concerns.

The year 1938 was marked by labor violence. In February the Inter-Island Steam Navigation Company was hit by a four-day strike by the

Inland Boatmen's Union. The sole purpose of the strike was to gain recognition of the IBU by Inter-Island. It was successful, largely owing to the announcement that an NLRB inspector would be arriving on 14 March. In connection with this short-lived action, Jack Hall was arrested, severely beaten, and held incommunicado for fourteen hours by the Honolulu police. John A. Burns, a policeman who would later become governor of the state of Hawaii, recalled the incident:

> I remember having seen him and heard what happened from the rest of the boys. Evidently he had shot his mouth off at this lineup [at the pier] where the cops were keeping the guys from going back to the boat. . . . Hall said something about it and so he was picked out as a trouble maker and they had bounced him off to the police station and booked him and took him up in the elevator and he got a few bouncing around [*sic*] in the elevator, which was not extremely unusual.[23]

On 26 May the IBU was once again on strike against Inter-Island. This time they were joined by the ILWU and the Metal Trades Council. The strike ended two and one-half months later with few substantive gains. But much had taken place to raise the territory's emotional temperature. On 28 June Louis E. Welch, business manager for the *Voice of Labor*, was arrested for assaulting two cab drivers he claimed were in the process of driving strike breakers to the docks. He pleaded "no contest" and was sentenced to nine months in jail. On 7 July a bomb threat was reported to have been made against the Inter-Island ship *Waialeale*. This later turned out to be a setup perpetrated by the AFL-affiliated Honolulu Waterfront Workers' Association. Charles B. Wilson, Jr., president of the union, was convicted of possession of dynamite for illegal purposes and sentenced to five years in prison. He served six months. Ed Berman, who was coordinating the strike, said that Wilson's Waterfront Workers' Association was actually a company union "disguised as an 'AFL' union to fight the CIO and democratic unionism."[24]

The *Waialeale* was again the center of attention on 22 July, when it docked at Hilo, manned by a nonunion crew. When longshoremen working at adjacent piers gathered to taunt the crew, Police Lieutenant Charles Warren lobbed a tear gas grenade into the midst of the protesters, ending the unplanned demonstration. Fearing violence, Inter-Island announced the cancellation of further sailings. Under pressure from local business and with assurances of public safety from Sheriff Henry K. Martin, Inter-Island announced on 28 July that sailings would be resumed. This announcement set the stage for what was, perhaps, the most important symbolic event in Hawaii's labor history, the "Hilo Massacre." Although no lives were lost, the name stuck.

When the *Waialeale* docked at Hilo on 1 August 1938, the ship was greeted by about 250 protesters, who had been carefully searched for weapons by the leaders of the protest and instructed not to engage in any violence. The police had painted two yellow lines on the pavement and ordered the assemblage to stay behind the lines. When they crossed the first line, tear gas grenades were used to disperse the crowd. Lieutenant Warren, who had been the prime instigator of the events of 22 July, was once again at the center of the action. Armed with a riot gun and a bayonet, he slapped one of the seated protesters across the face with his bayonet. When the injured man turned, Warren stabbed him in the shoulder. Warren then struck the next man in the line with the butt of his riot gun. At this point, sensing that the crowd was ready to explode, Warren fired a round of buckshot into the ground. The blast ricocheted into the closest protesters. With that, other policemen opened fire. Twenty-two shots were fired in all, sending fifty-one protesters—including two women—to Hilo Hospital for treatment. The most seriously injured was Bert Nakano, who became something of a martyr as multiple gunshot wounds in his foot and ankle left him with a permanent limp. Longshore leader Harry Kamoku reported to Ed Berman: "They shot us down like sheep."[25]

The Inter-Island strike ended two weeks later, on 15 August 1938, with the two strike leaders, Ed Berman and Jack Kawano, deeply divided. Berman wanted the strike to end; Kawano wanted it to continue. John E. Reinecke, a school teacher and radical labor supporter, summarized the results of the Inter-Island strike for the Hawaii Educational Association's Social-Economic Committee:

> So far as attainment of expressed objectives was concerned, the strike was a total failure for the drydock workers and the longshoremen. The Inter-Island succeeded completely in preventing the establishment of a union shop in any form and the wage increase which it conceded to seamen fell far short of West Coast scales which the IBU set as a standard. The ILWU gained nothing except some minor improvements in work conditions.[26]

Reinecke did cite the one lasting benefit of the strike for the cause of organized labor in Hawaii when he pointed out: "From the point of view of union organization, few events could have been more opportune than the Hilo shooting. A movement draws inspiration from its martyrs."[27]

Jack Hall, who was on Kauai and in Honolulu during the strike, saw two other benefits of the Inter-Island strike, which he expressed in the *Voice of Labor* on 18 August 1938:

> When the strike began, many people expected the Hawaiians in the Union to hold out for about four days. "The Hawaiians," they said, "are too easy going. All they want is a little fish and poi and their liquor." This slander has been disproved by the strike. The Hawaiians demonstrated to the

> world that they share the determination and stamina of workers everywhere.
>
> Particularly is this true of members of the ILWU. This small but disciplined band of workers demonstrated a militance and persistence which will stand as a model for all Hawaiian workers. And in Jack Kawano, their leader, they have produced as careful an organizer and as keen a negotiator as can be found anywhere.[28]

Hall would not always hold Kawano in such high regard, but there is no doubt about Kawano's importance during the early years of the ILWU in Hawaii.

Charges of communist domination of Hawaii's labor movement were frequent during the Inter-Island strike. They were not without foundation. As Fuchs pointed out:

> The leaders of the important strike against the Inter-Island Steamship Company—[Jack] Hall, Jack Kawano, and Ed Berman . . . were alleged to have frequented Communist meetings. Other key figures included Dr. John Reinecke . . . Jack D. Kimoto . . . and Robert McElrath, former seaman and delegate to the national convention of the Communist party held in New York City in 1940.[29]

In the summer of 1939 Jack Hall and Ichiro Izuka, leader of the Port Allen (Kauai) longshoremen, were invited to attend the California Labor School in San Francisco. They were aboard ship on 1 September 1939, the day Nazi Germany invaded Poland. The school was frequently referred to as an arm of the Communist party. Technically, it was not, but there was a close working relationship and the school's orientation was Marxist.[30]

Just before his departure for San Francisco, Jack Hall had moved back to Honolulu from Kauai. According to Hall's biographer Sanford Zalburg, he shared an old house behind the Royal Brewery on Queen Street with fellow labor organizer Koichi Imori. Hall referred to the house as "the Kremlin." Zalburg wrote: "Sometimes they used the place for beer parties and for Communist Party meetings. When bottling day came at the brewery, Hall often worked part-time. The job paid thirty or thirty-five cents an hour."[31] Hall was also a frequent visitor to the home of John and Aiko Reinecke, where he would get a decent meal and conversation about Marxism and the labor movement, and where he would meet his future wife, Yoshiko Ogawa.

It is important to remember that in 1939 Jack Hall was only twenty-four years old. He was still learning his trade. His base had been the *Voice of Labor* and the CIO. Not long after the Inter-Island strike, Hall's most natural rival for union leadership, Ed Berman, decided to go to the mainland to become a labor lawyer. When Berman returned to Hawaii after World War II, Hall was regional director of the ILWU.

Perhaps the most important part of Jack Hall's apprenticeship as a labor leader came during the years he spent on Kauai. From 1937 until 1941 Hall virtually commuted between Honolulu and Kauai. From his aid to the Port Allen longshoremen in 1937 to his organization of the nonagricultural sugar workers at McBryde Sugar Company in 1940, Hall developed a reputation among the locals for hard work and reliability. The five-to-one vote in favor of the United Cannery Agricultural Packing and Allied Workers of America (UCAPAWA/CIO) at McBryde was the first time sugar workers ever had a union recognized by their employer.

It was on Kauai that Hall first delved into local politics, forming the Kauai Progressive League on 28 August 1938. Hall was instrumental in getting John B. Fernandes elected to the territorial senate in 1938, defeating Lindsay Faye, manager of the Kekaha Sugar Company by 192 votes (3,204 to 3,012).[32] During the 1939 legislative session Hall drafted a "Little Wagner Act," which Fernandes introduced, but it did not pass. It would be six years before such a measure would finally be voted into law, opening the door for the organization of all plantation workers.

On 18 July 1940 the last big strike before the beginning of World War II began at Ahukini Landing on Kauai. Ahukini Terminal, Ltd., informed port workers that because of the new federal wage and hour law they would have to choose between working at the port terminal and losing their housing or working at Lihue Plantation and keeping their housing. The port workers offered to vacate their housing in exchange for a guarantee of $15 per week for thirty-one weeks a year. This offer was similar to an informal arrangement between C. Brewer and the Hilo longshoremen, but American Factors turned it down, and the longest strike in Hawaii's history, 298 days, was under way.[33]

The only positive note for the union was that the predominantly Japanese longshoremen at Port Allen refused to handle "hot cargo" that would normally have been handled by the predominantly Filipino longshoremen at Ahukini. The owners responded by closing down Port Allen and locking out the workers. Although Jack Hall opposed the Port Allen walkout on legal grounds, he was proud of the longshoremen for their demonstration of worker solidarity. "This was the first clear case," Hall declared, "of workers walking out in support of another group in the islands, even though it was made up of another race."[34]

Whatever virtue it may have had along the lines of worker solidarity, the Ahukini strike was vigorously opposed by top ILWU leaders. Harry Bridges told Ichiro Izuka that the Port Allen longshoremen had fallen into a company trap. Jack Kawano refused to allow Honolulu longshoremen to picket in support of the strike. Bridges finally dispatched Clifford O'Brien from San Francisco to bring the strike to an end with the aid of a Maritime Labor Board mediator. Sixty-five union jobs were lost, and those who kept their jobs received an average hourly pay increase of about four cents—little to show for their efforts.[35]

An important part of Jack Hall's training was as a journalist; he was a gifted writer and a firm believer in the power of the press. Hall had worked on the *Voice of Labor* practically from its beginning in 1935. When Ed Berman stepped down from the editorship in April of 1938 to devote more time to his responsibilities as CIO director, Hall became the editor. When the *Voice of Labor* failed financially in June of 1939, Hall was only temporarily out of the newspaper business. On 12 July 1940, just six days before the beginning of the Ahukini strike, Hall was back in business with the *Kauai Herald*. The nominal owner and publisher was Ichiro Izuka, but Hall was the editor and principal writer. When Hall returned to Honolulu on a more or less permanent basis, he brought the paper with him. On 30 June 1941 the *Kauai Herald* became simply the *Herald* and sought to serve the whole territory as a labor weekly.

From the time of the Nazi-Soviet nonaggression pact of 23 August 1939 until the Nazi invasion of the Soviet Union on 21 June 1941, the Communist party in Hawaii was under orders to lie low. This was not the problem for the party in Hawaii that it was on the mainland, because there was no open Communist party in Hawaii at this time. However, after 21 June 1941 favorable references to the Soviet Union began to emerge as World War II changed character, in the eyes of the communists, from another imperialist squabble to an antifascist crusade. Hall was not immune to this sentiment. On 10 November 1941 he presented his analysis of the Soviet political system in the pages of the *Herald*. "We have not grasped one fundamental fact," Hall wrote. "Russia is a democracy. Not our type of democracy. Some ways less democratic and some ways more democratic, but a democracy nevertheless."[36]

As U.S. participation in World War II approached, Jack Hall was by no means the acknowledged leader of the ILWU in Hawaii. Clifford O'Brien made these observations in a 20 September 1941 letter to Harry Bridges:

> Hall brings a real sincerity and a lot of ability to his work, but as a result of considerable experience in reference to our Port Allen and Ahukini troubles and other matters, I do not believe the CIO or any other trade union groups should entrust him with untrammeled powers, either in reference to organizational policy or with relation to negotiations and the possibility of economic actions to enforce demands. The only other specific suggestion is that if Hall is to be given CIO organizing responsibility, it is to be understood that they should be paramount to his relations to the newspaper. Frankly, with all his abilities, I do not believe Hall can do both effective organizational work and newspaper editorship.[37]

As matters turned out, a decision about the ILWU's Hawaii leadership was not required in 1941. The attack on Pearl Harbor ended all labor organizing for the time being.

After Pearl Harbor the employers of Hawaii presented a file "nearly a foot high" on Hall to Robert L. Shivers, special agent for the FBI, with the request that Hall be arrested "as a person dangerous to the security of the country." Instead, Shivers gave Hall a clean bill of health to accept a position as a Wage and Hour Division inspector for the territorial Department of Labor and Industrial Relations.[38] In that position Hall completed the last phase of his training for leadership of the ILWU.

Ichiro Izuka was not so lucky. On 11 April 1942 Izuka was taken into custody by the Kauai Office of Civil Defense and charged with having disrupted the war effort by distributing literature advocating strikes and slowdowns. In a somewhat naive defense, Izuka told the hearing board that the charges were preposterous; as a member of the Communist party, he was doing everything possible to defeat Nazi Germany. He was found guilty and held for 123 days. When Izuka was released, on 12 August 1942, it was, ironically, into the custody of Jack Hall. Izuka was ordered to report regularly to Hall, who was required to attest to Izuka's loyalty.

By and large, the issue of communism was quiescent during the war. The Soviet Union was now our ally. Employers were busy helping with the war effort and taking advantage of the opportunities for profit presented by the military government of the territory of Hawaii. Military orders froze workers in their jobs; employees could not leave their jobs without their employer's permission. Wages were also frozen. The Big Five took advantage of this situation by assigning a number of their workers, on a contractual basis, to other employers, paying the workers the "frozen" wage and pocketing the difference. These "indentured" workers might find themselves working side by side with workers imported from the mainland who were earning substantially more for the same work. Employers would pay for this practice when military rule ended, but under the military government the unions were powerless to help the workers. Union membership fell accordingly until the military government was terminated by presidential proclamation on 24 October 1944.

Another reason for union inactivity during the war was that so many of the union members were Japanese aliens or Japanese Americans who were intimidated into silence or convinced that silence was their patriotic duty. They had to overcome the kind of sentiment being expressed by people like William C. "Doc" Hill, a longtime legislator from the Big Island. "A Jap is a Jap, even after a thousand years," Hill said in a remark he was later to regret, "and can't become Americanized."[39]

While the Japanese-American population was treading softly, another phenomenon was taking place that would change the face of postwar Hawaii. Beginning with the One Hundredth Battalion in 1942 and the 442d Regimental Combat Team in 1943, young Japanese Americans came forward to volunteer for military service. One-third of all Japanese-American males who were of military age served their country. They represented 60 percent of Hawaii's fighting forces during World War II and suffered 80 percent of the territory's casualties.[40] These young men, armed with a new self-confidence forged on the battlefields of North Africa, Italy, and France, were not willing to return to Hawaii as second-class citizens. With this new found confidence and the aid of the G.I. Bill of Rights, these young men would create a social and political revolution in Hawaii—and they would lift their elders with them.

The most vocal of all labor leaders during the war was Art Rutledge, head of the AFL Teamsters Union. On 22 March 1944 Rutledge issued a "Memorandum on Military Control," in which he called the Labor Control Office antilabor. Among other things, he cited the Izuka case as an example of labor intimidation. Rutledge, never shy about speaking his mind, concluded: "We are convinced that the Office of the Military Governor is biased against unions and negligent of labor. . . . We consider the military incompetent to administer labor in Hawaii." In June 1944 a territorial War Labor Board was created, with civilian representation. Rutledge was named as labor's representative. But even Rutledge could go too far. When he threatened to picket some bar owners who were ignoring their contracts with his bartenders' union, a military aide warned Rutledge, "Do it and you'll get a bayonet up your ass."[41]

On 10 March 1943, when civilian authority was partially restored, unions began to stir once again. The ILWU, under the local leadership of Jack Kawano, began to restore union presence among the longshoremen of the territory. But when Jack Owens, an AFL representative, organized the nonagricultural workers at the Waiakea sugar mill, he got the ILWU's attention. Bert Nakano, secretary of the Hilo ILWU Longshore Local 1-36, importuned Kawano: "Come on down here. I think we can organize the plantations."[42]

In San Francisco the big question was who should become the regional director of the ILWU in Hawaii. There were three basic choices: they could send somebody from the mainland; they could name Kawano, who was virtually acting as regional director at the time; or they could pick Jack Hall. Lou Goldblatt decided to send Matt Meehan, ILWU international secretary from Seattle, to evaluate the leadership situation in Hawaii and make some recommendations. The first recommendation made was that the regional director should be somebody local. Meehan told Goldblatt that Kawano was the ILWU's "spearhead of the labor movement in Hawaii." Meehan continued: "I find him very capable. He is under a great handicap at the present time, however, because he is of Japanese ancestry; therefore, it will be necessary to have a *haole* (white, to you) to front for him."[43] Meehan was favorably impressed with Jack Hall because of his experience with the Hawaiian labor scene, the confidence he seemed to enjoy with the workers, and the knowledge he had picked up during his tenure with the Wage and Hour Division of the territorial Department of Labor and Industrial Relations. On 21 April 1944 Jack Meehan sent Goldblatt word that Jack Hall was his selection. By 1 June Hall had resigned his job with the territorial Department of Labor and was on the job with the ILWU.

It didn't take Hall long to get started. On 3 July he was back in the newspaper business with the first Hawaiian edition of the *ILWU Dispatcher.* But he was not working alone. On 8 July Frank Thompson arrived from the mainland to help Hall organize plantation workers. Thompson was sent by Louis Goldblatt, who referred to him in a 1978 interview as "a Wobbly right down to his toenails."[44] Thompson was a veteran of the ILWU's "March Inland" in California and had valuable experience in the organization of agricultural workers. Sanford Zalburg is quick to credit Thompson: "It was not Hall who did the big organizing of the ILWU in 1944 that suddenly made the union the most powerful force in Hawaii," Zalburg writes. "That credit belongs to Frank Thompson, from Sacramento, and to a host of local people on all the islands."[45]

But it was Jack Hall who got the ILWU into the territorial political scene. Drawing on his experience with the Kauai Progressive League in 1938, Hall started the ILWU political action committee (PAC) shortly after assuming his new position. He wanted to be ready for the 1944 elections, and he was. In November fifteen of the nineteen House candidates and six of the eight Senate candidates the PAC had endorsed were winners. They included local ILWU leaders Joe Kaholokula of Maui and Amos Ignacio from the Big Island. They also included Hall's old friend from Kauai, J. B. Fernandes. Hall's goal was to revive the "Little Wagner Act," which had failed in 1939. The passage of the Hawaii Employee Relations Act of 21 May 1945 was a major key to organizing the agricultural workers on Hawaii's plantations. As Fuchs pointed out, "From a mere 900 members in 1944, ILWU membership rose to an estimated 30,000 by 1947."[46]

As they organized in 1944 and 1945, Thompson and Hall pursued two key policies: First, they were emphatic about being racially and ethnically inclusive with regard to local leadership. Second, they sought to consolidate the locals into viable units. By December 1945 they had gone from thirty-three locals to three. In the process, many lost positions of leadership in the union. Frank Thompson controlled the organizational process with an iron fist. At a meeting on the Big Island, when a Japanese American had been nominated for president, followed by another for vice-president, Thompson declared the second nomination "out of order," demanding ethnic balance. As Lou Goldblatt recalled, "He damn near came to blows with Yasu Arakaki, but Frank is the kind of guy who says, 'Look, those are my instructions and that's the way it's going to be.' "[47] An example of Thompson's approach is captured beautifully in Zalburg's account of the following instructions to Local 148 on the Big Island in 1945:

> Thompson had ordered that two full-time business agents be appointed at a weekly salary of sixty-five dollars and insisted that they be of different races, "with the qualifications of office being secondary." Thereupon, with no discussion, Thompson presented his slate of officers—take it or else—for the new consolidated local: Amos Ignacio (Portuguese), president; Gus Nishihara (Japanese), first vice-president; Jacinto Conol (Filipino), second vice-president; and Henry Johnson (Hawaiian), secretary-treasurer.[48]

Thompson and Hall were more concerned with a democratic outcome than with purely democratic procedures. The distinction is one that a Marxist would understand clearly.

Matters came to a head in January 1946, when Arakaki wired Harry Bridges in San Francisco, demanding the dismissal of both Frank Thompson and Jack Hall. Bridges' reply came on 22 January: "Reurtel [regarding your telegram], Thompson's and Hall's execution international program justifies our complete confidence. We expect and insist upon full cooperation all ILWU members in performance of their work."[49] The ILWU's concerns about racial inclusiveness and consolidation were well placed. At a time when the union was approaching its first major test, it could ill afford to have individual units going out on strike or Japanese workers fighting with Filipinos. As Lou Goldblatt put it to the membership: "You either follow the directions of the union, or find yourself another union."[50]

Jack Hall's reputation as regional director got a boost in January of 1946 when he, with the aid of Lou Goldblatt and San Francisco labor lawyer Richard Gladstein, obtained a $1.5 million settlement for the ILWU from forty-nine Hawaiian sugar units for wartime violations of the Fair Labor Standards Act (FLSA). It was now "payday" for the years Hall had spent in the Wages and Hours Division. Despite the headaches involved in the division of this unexpected bonanza, Jack Hall had proven that he could take on the Big Five and win.

The year 1946 was a make-or-break year for the ILWU. On 31 August the sugar contract would expire, and all efforts were turned to obtaining a favorable new contract. The ILWU's initial demands included a sixty-five-cent minimum wage (an 18 ½ cent increase), a forty-hour work week, and a union shop. The industry was offering 6 ½ cents. On 1 August 1946 union members voted: 15,406 were ready to strike; 123 were opposed. The strike began on 1 September 1946 and lasted for seventy-nine days.[51] When the strike ended on 18 November, the union claimed a great victory. The minimum wage was set at seventy and one-half cents—5 ½ cents more than the original demand—and the paternalistic perquisite system, through which the plantations controlled so much of their workers' lives, was ended. The union did not achieve its goals of a forty-hour week and a union shop.[52] Management claimed victory as well, justifying the pay increase by its valuation of the perquisites it would no longer be required to provide—housing, water, medical care, and the like. But the plantations had lost an important source of their control over their workers, and the ILWU had proved itself a force to be reckoned with in Hawaii.

Philip Brooks, research director for the Hawaii Employers' Council, commented that the strike had frightened the employers: "For the first time in Hawaiian history, the employers had been soundly and definitely thwarted. The psychological value of this display of defiance of the employers could not fail to add immensely to union power."[53]

Lou Goldblatt saw the victory this way: "We had a new type of organization that helped make this the first successful strike against the Big Five. We had an industrial organization, from top to bottom, clear through from workers in the fields to the dock workers and longshoremen, and we added one thing—a direct line to the maritime workers, through the ILWU."[54] Goldblatt, however, was not complacent. Less than a month after victory in the 1946 sugar strike, he wrote a letter to Jack Hall, telling him, "They [the employers] were caught off-balance during the sugar strike and never got their footing, but they did lay some foundation for a counter-attack . . . especially with regard to red-baiting . . . which is now being thrown at the people full blast."[55] How right he was!

While Hawaii was going through the 1946 sugar strike, a new political season was under way. Hawaii, like much of the rest of the nation, was experiencing the impact of the CIO's political action committee. The success of the local PAC in 1944 had made friend and foe alike realize that organized union voting could have a powerful impact on the political process. The PAC was avowedly nonpartisan, although labor had more common interests with the Democratic party than with the Republicans. However, it was the endorsement of a Republican, Delegate to Congress Joseph R. Farrington, by the PAC that ignited the anticommunist flames in the 1946 election. The PAC endorsement was attacked by Republicans and Democrats alike. Many Republicans resented that the Republican incumbent to the territory's most significant elective office did not repudiate the endorsement. Roy Vitousek, chairman of the territorial Republican Central Committee, said, "We want a government run by and for the people of this Territory, instead of for the PAC, other organized minorities, communist front organizations and pressure groups."[56]

The Republican Campaign Committee passed a resolution that no Republican candidate could speak from a PAC platform but in deference to Farrington stopped short of asking any candidate to repudiate a PAC endorsement. Farrington spoke very little about the PAC endorsement, a fact regularly called to his attention by the *Honolulu Advertiser.* It was sometimes difficult to determine whether the *Advertiser*'s opposition was rooted in political philosophy or in the fact that Farrington was owner and publisher of the rival *Star-Bulletin.*

When Farrington did speak out on the endorsement, on the eve of the primary election, he made it clear that he accepted the support of all groups. He also made it clear that by accepting the endorsement of a group he did not endorse its principles. Farrington explained: "The action of this committee involves nothing more or less than an endorsement of the record I have made and the position I have taken on statehood for Hawaii.[57]

Farrington's benign approach to the PAC endorsement sustained a blow when *Time* magazine printed an article in its 28 October 1946 issue saying: "This week PAC got a kiss of death. Moscow radio, speaking in English, urged U.S. voters to cast their ballots for PAC backed candidates."[58] Beginning on 30 October and continuing through election day, the *Advertiser* printed a daily box with the heading "Moscow Supports These Oahu Candidates" with a list of the sixteen endorsed candidates of the PAC (thirteen Democrats and three Republicans). Although Farrington won the general election handily, with 55 percent of the final count (45,770 votes to 37,210 for his Democratic opponent, William Borthwick),[59] his margin had dropped substantially from the primary, in which he had polled 65 percent of the total votes cast (41,735 votes to Borthwick's 22,734).[60] Farrington was to carry the stigma of the PAC endorsement for the rest of his life. It is a sign of his popularity that he carried it as easily as he did.

The PAC endorsement of Farrington was an even more volatile and divisive issue on the Democratic side. William Borthwick, the Democratic candidate for delegate to Congress, was a political ally of Governor Ingram M. Stainback, who had appointed Borthwick to the position of territorial tax commissioner. The governor toured the islands with Borthwick in 1946, in support of his election. Both Stainback and Borthwick were bitter about the failure of the ILWU, through the PAC, to endorse the Democratic candidate. The most vocal critic of the PAC was Ed Berman, who had recently returned to Hawaii after completing his law degree at the University of San Francisco. After his return the personal antipathy between Berman and ILWU leaders Hall and

Kawano prevented his assumption of any significant role with the union —a fact Berman is alleged by many to have resented deeply.

Berman charged that a deal had been made between the ILWU and Joe Farrington. The morning before the general election, the *Advertiser* printed a photostatic copy of a report by Marshall McEuen, chairman of the PAC. In it McEuen said: "I am sure that all people have noticed that the *Star-Bulletin* gave the PAC every break in the news columns. They have been friendly to us and we should keep this situation in mind in future elections."[61] The McEuen report went on to predict a PAC victory in the territorial House of Representatives and talked of legislative planning. Here was proof for many that a deal had been made.

The failure to endorse Borthwick also created dissension within the ranks of the ILWU, especially on Kauai. In 1977 Jack Kimoto, head of the Communist party of Hawaii in 1946, wrote:

> I had to fly to Kauai in response to Robert McElrath's request that I talk to the comrades on that island to straighten them out on the matter of the ILWU's supporting Farrington for Delegate to Congress. . . . I told the Kauai comrades that although I had not been given any convincing explanation for supporting Farrington, I nevertheless felt that all ILWU members should, for the sake of unity, support Farrington because the ILWU had already publicly committed to support him. I told them that they shouldn't let politics split the ranks of sugar workers in the midst of a crucial strike. . . . Berman and Izuka, who were on Kauai to campaign for Borthwick, were naturally disappointed.[62]

Another bitter episode in the aftermath of the 1946 election was the request by Governor Stainback that Jack Hall resign his position as a member of the Honolulu Police Commission, a position to which Stainback had appointed Hall. Stainback said he demanded Hall's resignation because of a public statement the ILWU chief had made about Judge Philip L. Rice of Kauai. Rice had issued an injunction against striking workers of the Lihue plantation during the 1946 sugar strike. Hall had accused Rice of a conflict of interest, because he had represented the company and other Big Five companies as legal counsel. Such criticism of a judge by a member of the Police Commission was ethically incorrect, according to Governor Stainback.

Hall's response was quick and searing:

> While my statement regarding Judge Rice is ostensibly the reason for your requesting my resignation, I firmly believe that there exists a more compelling reason. . . . That reason is the refusal of the Political Action Committee to support the candidacy of Mr. William Borthwick for Delegate to Congress. It is common knowledge that Mr. Borthwick was your handpicked candidate to run against Delegate Joseph R. Farrington, against whom you are said to be carrying on a personal vendetta.
>
> While I am not an officer or official of the PAC, on many occasions you

> requested me to use my influence in obtaining PAC support for Mr. Borthwick, or at least to have PAC support withdrawn from Delegate Farrington. I am sure you knew at the time that had I been inclined to comply with your request, I should have been specifically in violation of the statutes which prohibit political activity by a police commissioner.
>
> Because of your continued pressure on me for support of Mr. Borthwick's candidacy, and because of the implication that I owed you such support in view of your appointing me to the police commission, I have for some time been giving serious consideration to the severing of my association with your administration.[63]

In addition to resigning from the Police Commission, Jack Hall resigned as a member of the Labor and Industrial Relations Appeal Board, although he was under no official pressure to do so. The credibility of Jack Hall's resignation statement might have been greater had he resigned before Governor Stainback's request, but there is no gainsaying the bitterness that existed between the two men after that time.

All in all, the PAC record in the 1946 election was mixed, especially in light of their stunning success in 1944. Throughout the territory of Hawaii, the PAC had endorsed thirty-four candidates, thirty Democrats and four Republicans. Twenty of their candidates won, while fourteen lost.[64] At the end of 1946 a precarious balance seemed to exist in Hawaii's political life. The territorial House of Representatives was evenly divided between Republicans and Democrats; in the Senate the Democrats fell one seat short of parity.

The stage was set for the counterattack Lou Goldblatt had warned Jack Hall about at the end of the 1946 sugar strike. The ruling oligarchy felt seriously threatened, both politically and economically. In their counterattack, the employers would reduce labor's legitimate demands to acts of subversion directed by leaders who were under the control of an enemy power. The motivation of those involved in the anticommunist crusade that would unfold over the next seven years can never be known with certainty, but many innocent people were painfully and needlessly hurt in the process.

PART TWO

THE SPECTER EMERGES

Chapter 3

The Stainback Battalion

On 15 November 1947 a letter appeared in the *Honolulu Advertiser*—an emotional response to a call for action. William H. George wrote:

> I admire forthrightness, courage, conviction, whereas I despise pussyfooting, dodging, hedging, hiding out like a skunk in a hollow tree. Dr. Stanley D. Porteus [in his book on Pearl Harbor] has pointed out effectively to us what happens if the watchman shall see the sword come, and "Blow Not The Trumpet." Our watchman on the battlements is Governor Ingram M. Stainback, and he has already sounded the trumpet, and he will continue to sound it. But what if those who hear the trumpet do nothing about it? Their blood shall be on their own hands; the watchman is in the clear.
>
> Hereby I enroll in the Stainback battalion, and am willing to stand up and be counted.[1]

Mr. George, a lifelong Republican, was responding to the Armistice Day declaration of war against communism in the territory of Hawaii made four days earlier by Governor Ingram M. Stainback, a lifelong Democrat.

On the twenty-ninth anniversary of the end of World War I, scarcely two years after the end of World War II, Governor Stainback lashed out against the communist threat to our national security. "We are facing a struggle for the very survival of our nation," he told his audience at the National Memorial Cemetery of the Pacific, located in the volcanic crater known as Punchbowl. "Totalitarianism in the form of communism is a threat to every democratic nation."[2] Governor Stainback, originally appointed to his position by Franklin D. Roosevelt in 1942, had been reappointed by President Harry S Truman in 1946. He served as governor until the spring of 1951, when Oren E. Long was appointed to replace him. Although he had been in the territory since 1912, Stainback was still considered something of an outsider in Hawaiian politics. His road to power had been achieved in the national Democratic party, not the local organization. In his anticommunism Stainback reflected the current sentiment of the Truman administration, which equated capitalism with democracy and communism with allegiance to the Soviet Union and which had, in March 1947, produced an elaborate set of loyalty procedures for federal employees. It was the growing sentiment of the cold war.

In November 1947 the military establishment in Hawaii was in the process of screening 26,000 civilian employees of the army and navy.[3] Governor Stainback, who had received his first warnings about the character of the communist threat in Hawaii from military intelligence, fully intended to do his part in purging the territorial government of any taint of communism. He made this point clear in his Armistice Day speech:

> I know there are many of our citizens of these Islands who refuse to see any menace to our nation in communism. Some of these people have gone to bed politically with the communists; others are fellow travelers. Others are well meaning people who decry as hysteria what they term as "red baiting."
>
> Now, as I have warned you many times of the dangers of communism in the Territory and of its active spread, I am going to read you just one paragraph from a plan of the communists under which they have operated in the Territory for many years, which is devised particularly for the Territory by one of its so-called brainiest leaders.[4]

As Governor Stainback indicated, he had warned the people of Hawaii about the dangers of communism on many occasions. Since his discovery of the "menace" in the early spring of 1947, the governor had sounded the alarm in speeches given on Navy Day, during Army Week, on the Fourth of July, on Labor Day, and again as recently as 24 October, before a gathering of the AFL. But in his Armistice Day speech he offered something new, something beyond a general warning. He submitted what purported to be the communist plan for the territory, and though he did not mention the name of the author, he made it clear that he was at large among the people of the territory of Hawaii. The governor quoted from this document views that were certain to be offensive to much of the community. The title was "What Must We Do?"—a title evocative of Lenin's famous pamphlet that was first published in 1902.

> Goals acceptable to liberal as well as radical elements in Hawaii should be set up and striven for (on the side) as a means of arousing popular support. For example:
>
> Anti-militarism: first attack ROTC in the high schools, then in the university; attack kowtowing to military in the local press and in public affairs; weaken the national guard units as much as possible and propagandize its members to make them sympathetic to unions; attack militarization of Boy Scouts.
>
> Education: wide extension of educational opportunities; removal of all

fees and rentals; aid to poor students (See Rex David, International Pamphlet Number 39). No discrimination in placement of teachers. It is highly important to win the teachers, and university and high school students.

Civil Rights: aim at legislation abolishing repressive legislation (present laws against "sedition," picketing, and curbing foreign press), and legalizing strikes and picketing.

Religion: as immediate objective, take the Christian religion out of the public schools, showing how the other religions are discriminated against in a subtle manner by use of Christian prayers, Easter, Thanksgiving, and Christmas exercises, use of schools by Catholic priests, etc. Go on to attack Mission board for its use of ministers and workers to *hoomalimali* [a Hawaiian word meaning to placate by the use of meaningless verbal massage] plantation employees. Attack Roman Catholics for interference in public affairs (as in attack upon sterilization bill). Attack exploitation of Mormons by Latter-Day Saints church.

Taxation, social legislation: work for change in incidence of taxation and outline a complete program of social legislation to be agitated for.

Press: arouse public to danger of "sugar coated" press.[5]

Governor Stainback concluded his speech with a request that all good citizens join him in the fight. He warned the audience that the communists saw Hawaii as fertile ground. He told them there were even communists in his territorial government. "I shall immediately take steps," Stainback promised, "to unearth these activities that are going on in this Territory and, where possible, expose and dismiss Territorial employees who are involved."[6]

Hawaii was primed for some anticommunist action. The board of supervisors for the city and county of Honolulu (called the city council since 1959) passed a resolution on 28 October 1947 calling for an investigation of communism in Hawaii. The resolution was sitting on the desk of Honolulu's Democratic mayor, Johnny Wilson, at the time Stainback was making his Armistice Day speech. Wilson, never one to be stampeded, ultimately refused to sign the resolution, although he did allow it to go into effect without his signature. The result, however, was nothing more than an expression of the sentiment of the board of supervisors.

The American Legion was quick to praise Stainback's speech and called on the governor to disclose the names of all communists working in the territorial government. The Legion quickly came up with its own answer to the problem of investigating communism in Hawaii. A. F. Wallace, chairman of the Americanism Committee of the American Legion, Department of Hawaii, met with the territory's delegate to Congress, Joe Farrington. The delegate, himself a member of the Legion, subsequently requested that U.S. Attorney General Tom Clark fully cooperate with the American Legion in their proposed investigation. The Honolulu Chamber of Commerce and the AFL quickly supported Farrington in his endorsement of the American Legion as the proper agency to carry on a "Red" probe in Hawaii.

The American Legion's offer had a short life. Tom Clark was not about to open security files for the Legion. Besides, Governor Stainback had plans of his own. The territorial attorney general's office had been investigating communism in the islands for nearly six months. The first fruit of their effort was about to come to light. On 25 November 1947 Dr. John E. Reinecke, a teacher at Farrington High School, and his wife, Aiko, a teacher at Waialae Elementary School, were suspended from their teaching positions without pay. John Reinecke had taught in Hawaii's public schools for seventeen years; Aiko Reinecke for twenty. The announcement was made by Dr. W. Harold Loper, superintendent of public instruction for the territory of Hawaii. Dr. Loper also announced that 18 December 1947 had been set as the date for a hearing on the charges against the Reineckes. The hearing was to be held by the territorial commissioners of public instruction. The charges, as published by the *Honolulu Advertiser,* were

1. That they are members, and have been for many years, of a secret, underground organization or society existing in the Territory of Hawaii calling itself the Communist Party.
2. That said secret society has existed in the Territory unlawfully without a license, contrary to the provisions of Chapter 281 of the revised laws.
3. That the Communist Party in the Territory follows a course of action which will be beneficial to the interests of the Communist Party of the Union of Soviet Socialist Republics.
4. That the policies of the Communist Party are the antithesis of and opposed to the principles of democracy.
5. That the said secret society is undemocratic. That some of the practices advocated by this secret society, and some of the activities in which it indulges, are highly dishonorable and reprehensible.
6. That the membership of Dr. and Mrs. Reinecke in the Communist Party has been exposed and publicized in the community, thereby bringing them into disrepute and causing them to lose the trust and confidence of the community.
7. That by reason of their membership in the Communist Party the conduct of the two teachers has not been exemplary.
8. That as members of said secret society they are not possessed of the ideals of democracy.
9. That as members of the said secret organization they do not bear undivided allegiance to the government of the United States.
10. That because of their membership in the Communist Party there is reasonable doubt as to their loyalty to the United States.
11. That their continued employment as school teachers will bring great odium and disrepute upon the department of public instruction. That their dismissal from service will be for the benefit of the department of public instruction.[7]

The Reineckes were represented by Harriet Bouslog, an attorney with strong ties to the ILWU. During World War II, while working for the War Labor Board in Washington, D.C., Bouslog met Harry Bridges. In 1944 Bridges made Bouslog the ILWU's Washington representative on the CIO Maritime Committee. In October 1946 Bouslog was brought to Hawaii during the sugar strike, along with Myer Symonds. Symonds was a lawyer with the San Francisco firm of Gladstein, Anderson, Resner, and Sawyer, the ILWU's West Coast law firm. The law firm of Bouslog and Symonds came to be be known not only as the ILWU's law firm in Hawaii, but as Hawaii's champions of the political left in general.[8]

The initial response to the charges against the Reineckes came from Harriet Bouslog. "The suspension of Mr. and Mrs. Reinecke," she charged, "is not only prejudicial to them, but is a denial of accepted standards of due process of law."[9] Calling the suspension tantamount to a conviction, Bouslog threw out a series of demands relative to the hearing that was scheduled for 18 December. First, she demanded that the Reineckes be allowed to plead their case before a body that was not already prejudiced against them (this meant a group other than the commissioners of public instruction); second, that the hearings should be public; third, that the names and addresses of all witnesses against the Reineckes be provided within five days; fourth, that all documents and other exhibits to be used as evidence against the Reineckes be made available to the defense within five days; fifth, that the defense be allowed to subpoena witnesses; and finally, that defense counsel be notified within five days of the rules of evidence to be utilized during the hearing. Territorial Attorney General Walter D. Ackerman, in a letter that read like a lecture in administrative law, dismissed Bouslog's demands as being without support in law.

But if the attorney general had been ready for Bouslog's first salvo, he was not prepared for her second. In a legal lecture of her own, Bouslog gave the Reinecke case a new twist:

> My clients are charged with violating a criminal law of the Territory prohibiting secret societies—a law which is unconstitutional on its face. If the Governor, Attorney General, or Superintendent of Public Instruction believe that this law is valid and that Dr. and Mrs. Reinecke have violated it, then these officials are duty-bound to turn over evidence to the proper prosecuting officials. The place to try criminal charges is in the regularly established courts with the customary safeguards of the criminal law.[10]

Bouslog's reference to criminal law was directed at a rarely used secret associations statute dating back to 1884. It somehow found its way into chapter 281 of the *Revised Laws of Hawaii* in 1945. Its inclusion in the charges against the Reineckes created a constitutional question that, in the eyes of federal judge Delbert E. Metzger, had sufficient merit to be presented to a three-judge federal court. Hasty efforts to amend the charges, deleting the reference to the criminal code, were unsuccessful, and the territory's plans for an 18 December hearing were dashed. It would be eight months before the hearings finally began.

John Reinecke, now exposed by Governor Stainback as the "mastermind" behind the "communist master plan in Hawaii,"[11] had also been named as a leading member of the Communist party in a pamphlet alleged to have been written by the former Kauai union leader Ichiro Izuka. The pamphlet was issued on 15 November 1947, just four days after Governor Stainback's speech.

Reinecke's first public response appeared in the newspapers on 29 November. It is presented here in its entirety:

> The charges against Mrs. Reinecke and myself amount to this—that we "are not possessed of the ideals of democracy," and that we do not "bear undivided allegiance to the government of the United States."
>
> The facts of our lives are to the contrary. In our hearings before the Commissioners of Public Instruction, we are prepared to prove both our good reputation as teachers and also our active devotion to the ideals of democracy. Mrs. Reinecke and I have never made any secret of our political views. We are ready to state them in public for the edification of the attorney general as in the past we have always been willing to state them in private conversations and letters to the local newspapers.
>
> Through our civic activities since 1927, we have constantly upheld the fundamentals of American democracy—political, economic, and racial. It is just because we have worked openly for our beliefs and perhaps more actively than most well-minded citizens, that we have incurred enmity and have been singled out to bear the first blows of a purge that is political in purpose.
>
> Although we are called undemocratic, no single instance of undemocratic conduct is stated. Nor can any be found.
>
> These charges against us include the statement that our supposed membership in the Communist Party "has been exposed and publicized in the community." This "exposure" comes from the governor's Armistice Day speech and from a recent pamphlet that names us as Communists and attacks Joseph R. Farrington as a tool of the Communist Party. The political issues are greater in importance than our two jobs.
>
> In these two publications—the speech of the governor and the pamphlet—the final political aims lie right on the surface. It is no accidental matter that the pamphlet appeared immediately after the governor's speech was made. Nor is it a coincidence that both the speech and the pamphlet are now in heavy use to prejudice visiting members of Congress against statehood.
>
> It is probable that our hearing will be of value to the community. If the hearing is held in a fair and judicial manner, we have complete confidence that we shall be teachers in the public schools for another 20 years.[12]

Governor Stainback was clearly not interested in the "facts" of the Reineckes' lives. He was concerned with one fact alone. "Mr. Reinecke," the governor wrote in response to the school teacher's press statement, "carefully sidestepped the only question: Is he or is he not an enrolled Communist?" Stainback continued: "Instead of answering this question, he says that the charges against him are a plot by me against statehood. Quite the contrary, it is obvious that the greatest service I can render statehood will be to clean the Communists out of our Territorial government and certain local labor unions."[13] In this revealing statement, Governor Stainback was hinting at an idea that he would shortly make more explicit when he stated that the investigation of communism by the territory was primarily for the purpose of setting a good example for the ILWU, so that union might "clean its own house."[14]

In another statement the governor indicated that he was simply trying to follow the lead of the Truman administration in the area of loyalty procedures. This certainly was one of the motivations of the governor, who was an appointee of the president. The establishment of loyalty procedures by the Truman administration in the spring of 1947 corresponded almost exactly with the first revelations to the governor about communism in Hawaii. This information was provided to Governor Stainback by military intelligence sources. Stainback had developed a fairly friendly relationship with labor during the first five years of his service as governor. He had appointed both Jack Hall and Jack Kawano to public commissions. Now the names of Hall and Kawano were coming before him as members of the Communist party in Hawaii. This embarrassment to the governor undoubtedly confirmed him in his present course, a public demonstration of his own loyalty and patriotism.

There were many besides the governor who wanted a straight answer from Reinecke to the question "Are you a communist?" When asked this question directly by a reporter from the *Honolulu Star-Bulletin*, Reinecke replied: "It is very well known that I share a number of opinions with the communists, but that doesn't say that I am one." The reporter persisted: "Then are you denying that you are a communist?" Reinecke refused to answer directly, saying that he had been smeared with the label so often that he did not see any point in talking about it.[15]

The *Honolulu Advertiser* was quite clear about its view of the constitutional rights of a man who is charged with being a communist. "Persons under investigation should not," the paper editorialized, "be allowed to take refuge in silence."[16] Only the day before the *Advertiser* had printed a column by the firebreathing columnist Westbrook Pegler that seemed to capture the editorial feeling of Honolulu's morning daily with regard to American communists: "When Congress asks a man whether he is a communist," Pegler wrote, "the question actually means 'are you a sworn enemy of the United States?' "[17]

Governor Stainback was not alone in speaking out against the communist menace. The *Advertiser* had been carrying on an anticommunist campaign since 1946. As a matter of fact, the *Advertiser* had been critical of Governor Stainback, himself for not speaking out against the CIO's political action committee, an organization the *Advertiser* considered a communist front.[18] Stainback could also be assured of support from the business community. In a speech given before the Hawaiian Sugar Technologists shortly after Governor Stainback's Armistice Day speech, Philip Spaulding, president of C. Brewer & Co., Ltd., one of the Big Five firms, warned three hundred assembled members: "Our own communists are endeavoring in every way to keep production down and achieve personal success on a foundation of chaos and misery."[19] From 28 December 1947 through 2 January 1948, the *Advertiser* published a series of articles by attorney Alfred L. Castle, a missionary descendant intimately related to the Big Five, titled "There Can Be No Compromise with Communism."

Nor was membership in the Stainback battalion restricted to people living in the territory of Hawaii. The governor's papers contain extensive correspondence with the virulent anticommunist labor writer Victor Riesel. One letter, dated 25 March 1948, from Riesel to Stainback is particularly revealing:

> You will remember that sometime ago you were good enough to send me some information on Communist activities in your territory. I used this to very salutary advantage when I found that none of it was known here in the United States.
>
> I passed some information on to Lieutenant Governor Arthur W. Coolidge of Massachusetts, and, as I gather it, he contacted you. In a speech subsequently delivered by Mr. Coolidge, he discussed a set of instructions issued by the Communist Party to its agents, and he said that he had received these documents from you. I wonder if I couldn't get a photostatic set. My outlets now are in 102 cities, and we can do some good in telling the story.[20]

The reference to Lieutenant Governor Coolidge dealt with a speech made in Quincy, Massachusetts, on 24 February 1948. There is a letter in the Stainback Papers from Coolidge to Stainback dated 17 December 1947, requesting information about "Communist infiltration in Hawaii and on the rumor that the Reds plan to stage a general strike in your territory in February."[21] In his reply, dated 11 February 1948, Stainback told Coolidge: "Communism has made great headway in the Territory, particularly in some of our labor organizations. The ILWU . . . is completely dominated by the Communists. . . . We also have some in our University and among our school teachers. I am enclosing a copy of an article written by one of the communists entitled, 'What Must We Do?' "[22] Stainback added that his recent exposure of the communist threat in Hawaii had averted the general strike that had been threatened. The source of the rumored "general strike" is unclear, and this writer has seen no evidence that any such action was contemplated. Still, Stainback was more than willing to take credit for having "averted" it.

Coolidge's speech reminds one of Joe McCarthy when he declared to the Quincy assemblage: "I have in my possession a photostat copy of orders issued by the Communist Party, outlining a program . . . to make Hawaii the most completely communist area under the Stars and Stripes. This document was sent to me by the Governor of Hawaii, Ingram M. Stainback."[23] Thus, this document of undetermined date, purpose, and circulation had developed a life of its own—growing in infamy as it went.

In time, Stainback found that he needed to take a less conspicuous role in his anticommunist crusade. When Victor Riesel asked Stainback to appear in his space as a guest columnist in the spring of 1948, the governor declined, saying: "I find that discussion of Communism in the Islands has been a rather ticklish proposition as so many of our advocates of statehood seem to try to conceal its presence here and are very resentful of any disclosures or comments. However, I plan to discuss the whole problem with Washington authorities and hope to get the green light."[24]

There is evidence in Stainback's papers that he fed information to Senator Pat McCarran, the staunch anticommunist and foe of Hawaiian statehood. McCarran had been in Hawaii at the time of the revelations of November 1947. On returning to the mainland, McCarran told a Los Angeles reporter: "I told them to clean out their Communists. They have infiltrated deeper than on the Mainland. They seek to make it a Red outpost, just as they would like to do with Cuba."[25]

The governor was active in bringing Jack B. Tenney, chairman of the California Senate Fact-Finding Committee on Un-American Activities, to Hawaii in 1949. Tenney had originally proposed the visit to address the territorial legislature in a letter to Governor Stainback on 26 January 1949. Tenney told Stainback: "I have been concerned over the growing Communist menace in the Islands. We learned several years ago that Communist activities in the Islands are largely directed from California."[26] Stainback could not have agreed more. In making the arrangements for Tenney to speak before the territorial legislature, Stainback turned to William C. "Doc" Hill, a fiercely anticommunist Republican from the island of Hawaii. Shortly thereafter, on the recommendation of Jack Tenney, Stainback sent two of his assistant attorneys general, William Blatt and Robert Griffith, to a work session on communism in San Francisco put on by a privately sponsored right-wing group called the National Americanism Committee.

Governor Stainback maintained his vigorous anticommunist views in the face of severe criticism from those who resented his tactics and the disunity they created in his own party, and from those who felt the governor's approach represented a serious roadblock to Hawaiian statehood. Stainback was never able to capture the people's imagination as the leader of an anticommunist crusade, and the Stainback battalion was never more than a small platoon. But what Governor Stainback started in November 1947, others were quick to continue.

Chapter 4

The Truth

Less than a week after Governor Stainback's Armistice Day speech, a sensational thirty-two-page pamphlet entitled *The Truth about Communism in Hawaii* was released to the public. It was purported to have been written by Ichiro Izuka, former vice-president of ILWU Local 135 on Kauai and a self-confessed former communist. In a prefatory note Izuka explained why he had written this document, which named no fewer than forty-seven alleged members of the Communist party: "Because of all that I did to strengthen the Party in the days of my blindness, I now desire to tell you the truth of my experience whatever the consequences may be to myself. You must know what is among you before it is too late. This is my warning."[1]

The Izuka pamphlet contained a story that would be told many times, in various forms, during Hawaii's struggle with the issue of communism. One of the most important questions about the document was whether or not it was actually written by Izuka. That and other questions about the veracity of his account will be dealt with later at some length, but for now *The Truth about Communism in Hawaii* will be treated as Izuka's own story, as it was presented to a public still aroused by Governor Stainback's Armistice Day speech.

Ichiro Izuka was thirty-six years old at the time his pamphlet was published. He had been born at Hanapepe, Kauai, on 5 June 1911, the sixth of nine children born to parents who came to the islands from Japan as contract laborers in 1900. Izuka left the plantation when he was sixteen years old to work as a boatman at Port Allen. Working conditions were harsh and dangerous, and Izuka soon found himself caught up in the growing labor movement on his island of Kauai.

Izuka explained that it was during the 1937 strike of the Independent Longshoremen's Union of Kauai that he first heard about the Communist party. During the strike the Kauai dock workers were assisted by many people in the labor movement, including two who made a very strong impression on Izuka: Jack Hall and George Goto. "Hall and Goto were members of the Communist party," Izuka stated. "They had brought with them plenty of communist literature and distributed it secretly. . . . I devoured it, and for the first time thought I had discovered a party that really had something to offer the workers."[2]

Within a year Izuka was ready to join. The pamphlet described the excitement the dock worker felt as he became a member of the Communist Party. Izuka named Jack Kimoto as the individual directly responsible for his induction into the Party. Kimoto was characterized as a "direct representative" of the Communist party in Hawaii, whereas Hall and Goto were depicted as "union Party members."

The pamphlet placed great importance on the secret nature of the Communist party and developed a detailed exposition of the relationship between the Communist party and the ILWU:

> At our secret meetings, sometimes held in my home, sometimes in my automobile in lonely spots, we were taught how to control union meetings, parliamentary procedure, and, of course, Party principles. We were taught, too, that the Big Five was a fascist organization, and that both [political] parties were like a coin—heads or tails, it's the same coin. These lessons were given to us by Hall and Kimoto, sometimes together, sometimes separately.[3]

Izuka assured his readers that the same tactics were still being used in the ILWU, "and the union members still do not realize what is happening to them."[4]

The influence of the Communist party on Kauai did not stop with the union, Izuka explained. The Progressive League of Kauai was alleged to have been controlled by the Party without the knowledge of its members. The communists, through the Progressive League, were credited with the defeat of Kauai's conservative Republican territorial senator Lindsay Faye in 1938. The pamphlet implies but does not state that the beneficiary of this alleged communist support, Democrat J. B. Fernandes, knew the character of this aid. Izuka also contended that Jack Hall had personally extended the influence of communism into Kauai politics through his control of Senator Clem Gomes. Gomes, for whom Hall acted as a speech writer, was unaware of Hall's communist affiliation, wrote Izuka. The author added that he had recently been told that Hall still boasted of having Senator Gomes under his control.

Izuka next described how he became involved with recruiting for the Communist party on Kauai. He said the Party's method was "to recruit only the strongest and most fanatical elements who knew how to obey orders."[5] Izuka told of having been sent to the Party's school in San Francisco in 1939 as a reward for his efforts and as an investment in his future usefulness to the Communist party. The decision to send him was made, he said, by the central committee of the Communist Party of

Hawaii. The chairman of this committee was identified as Jack Kimoto. The other members were Dr. John E. Reinecke, Jack Hall, Jack Kawano, and Ah Quon Leong (the future Mrs. Robert McElrath). Izuka indicated that Jack Hall had attended the Communist party school with him in San Francisco. While attending the school, Izuka first met Robert McElrath, whom he described as "one of the greatest advocates of extending Communist power throughout the unions."[6]

In the eyes of the general public, one of the most damning allegations in the Izuka pamphlet was the description of Communist party efforts to subvert the American effort to aid the Allies after the beginning of the war in Europe in 1939. Izuka said that he was attending the California Labor School in San Francisco at the time the war in Europe broke out. He said that he and Jack Hall were called into the office of Louise Todd, one of the instructors at the school, and told "to destroy all evidence, including books and other literature, important Party papers, membership books, etc., because after the Soviet-Hitler pact the Party expected raids from the FBI."[7] Upon his return to the Islands, Izuka indicated that he had actively engaged in antiwar work until the German invasion of the Soviet Union (which was erroneously dated 5 July 1941 in the pamphlet). He did not mention his own arrest and detention during World War II.

The pamphlet's sharpest attacks were reserved for Jack Hall. Izuka sought to belittle the role played by Hall in the development of the ILWU in Hawaii. At one point Izuka charged that Hall had urged the Kauai longshoremen to affiliate with the ILWU, rather than the AFL, because "the Communists had trouble working through the AFL."[8] Hall was later described as having taken the Kauai dock workers out on a needless ten-month strike in 1940–1941, a strike in which the workers "took a real beating." Izuka continued: "This was the first time I seriously doubted the Communist plan for 'helping' the laboring men of Hawaii. At this time Jack Hall was a Communist representative and adviser to the union, although not many members realized his true character."[9] Izuka was referring to the Ahukini Strike, which Hall and virtually all of the top ILWU officials had opposed.

The Truth about Communism in Hawaii continued with a description of the reactivation of the Communist Party of Hawaii at the end of World War II. It began, Izuka wrote, with informal discussion groups at which unwary middle-class people were indoctrinated with communist literature. The leading lights in these discussion groups were John Reinecke, Mr. and Mrs. Robert McElrath, Peter and Alice Hyun (brother and sister), Eileen Fujimoto, Jack Kawano, Jack Kimoto, and Izuka himself. When orders came to reactivate the Party, Izuka said, the discussion groups were dropped.

The pamphlet then offered a detailed description of the various cells, clubs, or fractions (all terms meaning the same thing) that were formed primarily according to occupational groupings or geographic location. It was in this section that Izuka built his list of forty-seven Party members. Many of these names were to appear over and over again—in the press, at hearings, and in a variety of reports—on the strength of their having been present in the Izuka pamphlet.

The most striking feature of Izuka's membership lists was the connection between the Communist party and the ILWU, from the secretarial level (Elizabeth Bristow, Peggy Uesugi, Jeanette Nakama, Pauline Rosenthal, Eileen Fujimoto) all the way to the top ILWU staff members in Hawaii (Jack Hall, David Thompson, Jack Kawano, Robert McElrath). In all there were at least twelve groups identified in the Izuka pamphlet in what appeared to have been a rather fluid organizational structure.

In an interesting aside to the general description of the Party organization, Izuka described the manner in which the Communist party used one member, Koichi Imori, to infiltrate the AFL Teamsters Union. Imori, who had worked his way into the confidence of Art Rutledge, head of the Teamsters, was assigned to assist Robert Mookini in raiding the ILWU pineapple workers. Mookini, formerly president of the ILWU pineapple local on Oahu, had been suspended by the ILWU for openly breaking with union policy in May 1947. The raid was not successful. In his pamphlet Izuka implied that Imori was effective in his quiet efforts to subvert the drive that was being led by Mookini. Imori, denounced by Rutledge, resigned from his position in the Teamsters Union on 23 May 1947. Izuka indicated that Rutledge had openly attacked Imori after he discovered that he was soliciting subscriptions from AFL members for the West Coast communist newspaper *People's World*.

Another interesting characterization in the Izuka pamphlet was that of Yasuki Arakaki, president of ILWU Local 148 at Olaa. Arakaki was reputed to have been converted by Jack Kimoto and Mr. and Mrs. Charles Fujimoto. "The argument that won him over," Izuka asserted, "was that joining the Party was the only way to control Hall and Thompson because they, too, were subject to Party discipline."[10]

Izuka's examination of the organization of the Communist party in Hawaii concluded with the following description of the Party's central leadership structure:

> Each cell group elects a delegate to the Executive Board which is the supreme authority in Hawaii, but in turn responsible to California. Before I resigned in November 1946, the Executive Board of the Communist Party in Hawaii was as follows: Denichi "Jack" Kimoto, chairman; Dr. John E. Reinecke, treasurer; James Freeman; Mrs. Ah Quon (Robert) McElrath; Jack H. Kawano; Charles Fujimoto; Eileen Fujimoto; Ralph Vossbrink; and David Hyun.[11]

This group was supplemented, from time to time, by the addition of Yasuki Arakaki and Harry Kamoku from the island of Hawaii and Yoshikazu Morimoto of Maui, according to Izuka. In addition, the pamphlet asserted, Jack Hall, Robert McElrath, and Henry Schmidt, an ILWU official from San Francisco, were called in for important problems. "We might say," Izuka summed it up, "that the union feeds the Party and in return the Party controls the union in the interests of Party policies and objectives . . . geared to the policies and objectives of the Soviet Union. If one changes, the other changes."[12] Izuka offered no evidence of the alleged link-up with Moscow.

In the next segment of the pamphlet, Izuka's message became more strident as the cause of his departure from the Communist party was treated. He charged that the ILWU-PAC was dominated by the Communist party and worked against the best interests of the working person in Hawaii. It was over the PAC endorsement of Delegate Joseph R. Farrington instead of his Democratic opponent, William Borthwick, that Izuka quit the Communist party. "The Communist leadership," Izuka charged, "had decided to crucify Borthwick for "thirty pieces of silver."

The "thirty pieces of silver" the PAC sought and got, according to Izuka, was the neutrality of the *Honolulu Star-Bulletin* in the 1946 sugar strike. Farrington, the major stock holder of the *Star-Bulletin*, was either bought or duped into this evil bargain, Izuka speculated. Izuka did not deal with the possibility that the ILWU may have had substantial pragmatic justification in securing the neutrality of the *Star-Bulletin*, Hawaii's most widely circulated newspaper, during the historic 1946 sugar strike. The whole matter was treated as an episode in a sinister international conspiracy rather than as a rational political decision.

Izuka, the narrative continued, had openly challenged the decision to endorse Farrington. His support of Farrington was made a matter of Party discipline. The following day, on 12 October 1946, Izuka submitted his resignation from the Communist Party of Hawaii. Izuka insisted that there were others in the Party who wanted to support Borthwick in the delegate's race: Wilfred Oka and his wife, Koichi Imori, and Charles and Eileen Fujimoto were mentioned. These people were willing to follow Party discipline, whereas Izuka was not. Izuka commented on Borthwick's loss to Farrington by 8,500 votes: "He lost because a conspiratorial Communist Party deceived the workers of Hawaii, who did not know they were Communists, into following their leadership in simple trust."[13]

Izuka closed with a flourish:

> I quit the Communist Party because it is not honest with the workers. With Adolph Hitler, the Party believes that the lie is a very useful means

> for gaining its ends. The bigger the lie, the better it works. . . . Moreover, the Communist Party is not interested in the workers in Hawaii as human beings or individuals. . . . Its loyalty is not to Hawaii or America, but to the Soviet Union.[14]

The Izuka pamphlet served two important immediate purposes: First, it underscored Governor Stainback's warning about the menace of communism in the territory of Hawaii. Second, it set the stage for events that were to follow in rapid succession. Ten days after the pamphlet was issued, the Reineckes were suspended. A little more than a month after the Izuka pamphlet was made public, the ILWU had a revolt on its hands.

Chapter 5

Trouble in the Ranks

Writing for the U.S. Department of Labor in 1948, University of Hawaii professor James H. Shoemaker commented on the phenomenal growth of unions, particularly the ILWU, in the territory of Hawaii in the years immediately following World War II: "Until 1944, Hawaii was one of the least organized areas in the United States," Shoemaker pointed out, "but within two years it had become one of the most highly organized areas."[1]

With this rapid growth, internal stresses were inevitable. Within the ILWU the issue of communism became a significant cause for stress and, for some, a convenient tool for the achievement of personal goals. The causes of the so-called Ignacio revolt were complex, probably involving a mixture of personal ambition and genuine anticommunist concern. Whatever its purpose, the Ignacio revolt threw the ILWU seriously off balance during the days immediately following the appearance of the Izuka pamphlet.

On Sunday, 14 December 1947, Amos Ignacio, vice-president of the Hawaii division of the United Sugar Workers, ILWU Local 142, announced to the executive board of that division that he was leaving the ILWU and that Unit 6 at Pepeekeo was leaving with him to form what would be called the Union of Hawaiian Workers. The minutes of the board meeting quote Ignacio, who was also a member of the territorial legislature, as follows: "I want to be a free man and want no part of communism. In the interest of the workers in the plantations we will set up an independent union. I realize that we are going to run on rough sailing with the ILWU out to destroy us. I realize that there are other units that would like to take the same stand."[2] Asked if there was any proof of communist domination of the ILWU other than the Izuka pamphlet, Ignacio said that he had been approached to join the Communist party and had refused. David Thompson spoke for the ILWU:

> This comes as a great shock to me. Rumors have been going around about communism, but in spite of these rumors that I have heard, I, as Interna-

> tional Representative, have been working here trying to help the people of this island. I have not given these rumors much credence. I have had differences of opinion in the past with Brother Ignacio, but I thought we were working along an honest program. . . . This action is going to destroy the Labor movement in the Territory, if you are successful. The ILWU is not going to sit down. This is going to be taken to the membership. . . . As an independent union your units will have favors for a couple of years, until the Employers can succeed in destroying the Union here. You must realize the power the International has given you. I don't see how you can take this step in honesty. You are not representing the wishes of the rank and file. . . .
>
> Communism is not the issue. It is a weapon that the bosses are using to destroy the Unions in the Territory. But, if that is the issue, you are off the beam. The ILWU is not a communist organization. It may be that some ILWU members are communists, but the program of the ILWU is what people make it.[3]

As the meeting proceeded, the discussion grew more personal and Thompson became more agitated. "If Amos asks me if I am a communist, I will tell him it's none of your business," Thompson declared at one point. "Do you think that if I'm a communist, then I'm not a good American? I fought in the last war for America and have a wooden leg now."[4]

The meeting of the executive board took three hours and twenty minutes that Sunday morning in December of 1947. Ignacio was unshakable. He refused even to hold off his announcement until the International representatives might have a chance to talk with the rank and file, as requested by Yasuki Arakaki. "We will," Ignacio concluded, "operate as an independent union as of tomorrow morning."[5]

In a 1975 interview, David Thompson, for many years the ILWU's educational director, commented on some of the reasons for Ignacio's bolt from the ILWU. Thompson posited that Ignacio, as a member of the territorial legislature, was living under the "pressure of respectability," that he wanted to be well thought of by the "best" people in the community. In addition, Thompson stressed that Ignacio's personal pride had been assaulted when the ILWU sugar locals were consolidated. In the process, he lost his position as president of his local, having to settle for a vice-presidency in the newly consolidated local.[6]

The next morning's *Hilo Tribune-Herald* told the story, in somewhat exaggerated form, under the banner headline "4,000 Bolt ILWU Ranks." Where that number came from was not discussed in the article that followed. The story stressed that Ignacio was a highly respected union leader and a two-term member of the territorial House of Representatives. Ignacio was quoted as saying, "There have been no denials of communism in the ILWU."[7] Ignacio struck another responsive chord for many by denouncing the kind of thinking represented by International vice-president J. R. Robertson, who, on a recent visit to the Big Island, had been quoted as saying to the rank and file, "There are smart bosses, but there are no good bosses."[8]

On the Big Island, where the Ignacio revolt took place, ILWU leaders such as David Thompson, Harry Kamoku, and Bert Nakano were seriously worried. In Honolulu ILWU leadership played down the Ignacio revolt while planning their strategy. On the island of Kauai, Ignacio found an ally, and it appeared to some that the Union of Hawaiian Workers just might become a viable, territorywide organization. The ally was George Aguiar who, in the spring of 1947, had achieved notoriety when, as a newly elected Democratic member of the territorial House of Representatives, he broke an eighteen-day organizational deadlock by voting for the Republican candidate for speaker of the House. Now Aguiar was announcing his resignation from the Democratic party, and he said he chose 15 December 1947, the day after Ignacio's announcement, in order to support his fellow legislator's bold act. Aguiar protested the control of Kauai's Democratic party organization by ILWU leaders such as "Slim" Shimizu and Robert Kunimura. "They are only interested," Aguiar charged, "in controlling the local party for their ends, and for those of their leaders in Honolulu."[9] Those same leaders were the ones responsible, Aguiar revealed, for his decision in the last legislature: "I have never made any statement regarding how I reached the decision to vote to break the deadlock in the recent legislature. I can say now that the reason I did resulted from my being given unquestionable proof that the Democratic delegation in the House were Communists. I might add that as the result of being presented with the facts regarding Communism in Hawaii, the Izuka pamphlet was no surprise to me."[10]

Amos Ignacio followed up on the opening Aguiar had given him as rapidly as possible. In the next day's *Hilo Tribune-Herald* he was quoted as saying, "I have always considered Kauai the stronghold of the ILWU in the territory, and I believe the desire of Kauai workers to withdraw from the ILWU is proof that the union has outlived its usefulness in Hawaii."[11] Either Ignacio was trying to "fill an inside straight," or he did not realize how totally isolated George Aguiar was on Kauai. Robert Kunimura, president of ILWU Local 149, called Ignacio's statement a "boldfaced lie" and produced a statement to that effect signed by every local unit official on Kauai, including Ichiro Izuka's brother Fred, who was president of the American Factors unit at Hanapepe.[12]

The *Honolulu Advertiser* saw a great future in Amos Ignacio's handiwork. The *Advertiser* saw the dawn of a new era in Hawaii's labor relations "in which employer and employee meet on a basis of mutual respect and trust, each realizing that one is necessary to the other."

According to the paper, "It should mean that, together, the employer and the employee may go forward to the ultimate goal of security for all in a future the possibilities of which we do not dream in the present."[13]

The ILWU did not waste time in reasserting itself. Returning from a three-day executive board meeting of the International in San Francisco, Jack Hall, on 19 December 1947, announced that the union had reversed its decision of July 1947 and would now comply with the anti-communist provisions of the Taft-Hartley Act. "It will not be our purpose to be isolated from the mainstream," the ILWU's regional director told reporters.[14] In a letter to the rank-and-file membership of the ILWU, Hall stated flatly that he was not a member of the Communist party, adding, "The writer's denial that he is a member of the Communist Party . . . will not put a stop to the circulation of the lies and our membership must expect it to continue."[15] Hall's enemies, however, were demanding that he state not only that he was not a member of the Communist party at that time, but that he had never been one, a statement Hall could not and would not make.

A decision on what to do was made by Lou Goldblatt, with no hesitation. They would take the matter to the rank and file. The ILWU chose the Hilo Armory for a "Unity Conference" from 3 to 5 January 1948. International president Harry Bridges suggested a variety of issues for discussion, only one of which was whether Hawaii's sugar workers preferred to be represented by an independent union. Bridges suggested a secret ballot to resolve that issue.

At first Ignacio accepted Bridges' offer, with certain conditions: The conference must be for sugar workers only. There should be no interference from San Francisco. The secret ballot should be supervised by the National Labor Relations Board, not the ILWU. Ignacio was also skeptical about a Bridges move to open the conference to the press. Finally, the president of the Union of Hawaiian Workers wanted the issue of communism to be debated openly at the conference.

Clearly, the ILWU did not plan to run the Unity Conference for the benefit of Amos Ignacio and the Union of Hawaiian Workers. Ultimately, Ignacio did not attend the conference, although the vice-president of the UHW, Akoni Pule, did. Louis Goldblatt was on hand from the International office in San Francisco. Leaders of other, nonsugar unions, such as Harry Kamoku and Bert Nakano, of Hilo's longshoremen, and Ernest Arena, president of ILWU Local 150, were very much in evidence. Before the conference began, an ILWU team that included another Filipino, Rick Labez, to offset support for Ignacio, were sent out to talk to workers from those plantations on the Big Island and Maui that were most likely to defect.

Goldblatt was responsible for one of the most important decisions of the Unity Conference. He convinced many reluctant union leaders that Izuka should be allowed to appear before the delegates to plead his case. In a letter requesting the right to appear, Izuka had stated:

> As author of the pamphlet, "The Truth About Communism in Hawaii," I have been slandered and lied about by certain ILWU officials who are attempting to discredit me and the facts contained in my pamphlet in the eyes of rank and file sugar workers. I have been called "a moron, renegade, self-confessed liar," and other uncomplimentary names.
>
> I believe sincerely that the real issue facing the sugar workers of Hawaii is Communist domination, both here and on the west coast, and no smokescreen should be raised at this time to becloud the issue.
>
> I am in Hilo to present my side of the story to the Unity Conference, and to answer the lies and slander directed at me. Your International officers have publicized the ILWU as "the most democratic union in the United States." Now is the time to prove whether this is true or false.[16]

Assessment of how well or how badly Izuka performed at the Unity Conference is largely dependent on the prejudices of the observer. One thing is certain: Izuka was operating in hostile territory. The *Maui News* reported that Izuka "stood alone facing a constant barrage of questions, accusations, catcalls, laughs and mockery."[17] He spoke to the delegates for about forty-five minutes on global communism over the preceding twenty years, making little reference to his pamphlet or matters of local concern. When he did get around to mentioning his pamphlet, he admitted that a ghost writer had worked with him but refused to divulge his identity. This response was clearly not satisfactory to the delegates.

At one point during the question-and-answer session, a delegate jumped to his feet and asked, "Mr. Izuka, do you know my name?" Izuka replied that he recognized the face but could not remember the name. "My name, Mr. Izuka, is Thomas Yagi and I was one of those mentioned in your pamphlet." Yagi, a sugar worker from Maui, was reported in the Izuka pamphlet as having been asked to join the Communist party by a fellow union member but having declined on religious grounds. Yagi denied that he was ever asked by anyone to join the Communist party. He challenged Izuka to tell the delegates how he had come by the story he told in the pamphlet. Izuka replied that he had been told the story by Yoshikazu Morimoto, whereupon Morimoto rushed to the podium and denied having told it.[18]

In the eyes of Tom O'Brien, an observer friendly to Izuka with a patronizing view of the delegates, Izuka's performance looked this way:

> Frankly, most of his discussion about Communism itself was far over the heads of the delegates. He spoke of the Communist Manifesto, about Karl

Marx, and the international intrigue of the Kremlin. It was all above the grasp of the little delegates, and the big ones pretended they did not understand.

When Izuka asked for questions, the real railroading started.

"Is it legal to be a Communist?"

"Will the Communists overthrow the U.S.A. by force?"

"When you were a Communist, did you plan any sabotage?"

The questions came tricky and fast. . . . It was soon obvious that both Jack Hall and Louis Goldblatt were engineering the entire inquisition. . . .

I left the Hilo Armory that rainy evening with the conviction that Izuka had really won. He had stood up in the midst of his enemies, unafraid, and had done a good job.[19]

Few of the delegates shared O'Brien's view. Izuka's credibility suffered its greatest setback when he was asked to name a Communist party program in the ILWU. When he responded that a strike could disrupt the government and destroy the democratic system, the boos were deafening.

In a 1973 interview Ichiro Izuka repeated his complaints that the question-and-answer session during his presentation at the Unity Conference had been manipulated by Goldblatt, McElrath, Hall, and Steve Murin, who, according to Izuka, had been admitted into the conference by means of fraudulent press credentials from the Japanese-language newspaper *Nippu Jiji*.[20]

Steve Murin was not directly associated with the ILWU, but he was very close to many union members. Murin had arrived in Hawaii in 1947, at the age of twenty-nine, from Boston, where he was a student at Boston College. Still living on the G.I. Bill, he had become a full-time student at the University of Hawaii, where he received a Bachelor of Arts degree in 1951. Murin had achieved a degree of notoriety in the community owing to his leading role in the establishment of the Hawaii Civil Liberties Committee (HCLC) in response to the plight of John and Aiko Reinecke. In a 1973 interview Murin described himself as having been a "radical left-winger." In the 1930s he had been a member of the Young Communist League in Pennsylvania, where he grew up. His first wife, Bessie Steinberg, was once identified before HUAC as an officer of the Communist Party of Pennsylvania. Murin was unwilling to comment on whether he had been a member of the Communist party in Hawaii, but there is no doubt that he was at least sympathetic with the Party's philosophy and objectives. After graduating from the University of Hawaii, Murin went to work for the United Public Workers of America. In 1953 that union was expelled from the CIO for "communist influences" and operated as an independent union for several years before establishing its present affiliation with the reformulated AFL/CIO.[21]

Izuka had come to the Unity Conference for the purpose of defending himself, not to support Amos Ignacio. Izuka claimed that the first time he had spoken with Ignacio about the Union of Hawaiian Workers was at lunch on the day he appeared before the Unity Conference. Izuka saw no driving ambition in Ignacio, who had ignored the positive appeals that the ILWU could honestly make to the workers, offering an entirely negative program in its place. Izuka was never associated with the UHW.[22]

There were propaganda efforts on both sides during the Unity Conference. The ILWU distributed a twenty-three-page pamphlet titled *The Mysterious Stranger*, which told of a retired newspaper editor from San Francisco named Lee Ettleson. A product of the Hearst organization, Ettleson was, according to the ILWU pamphlet, "an expert at red-baiting, race-baiting and labor wrecking."[23] Ettleson's advice to the bosses, it was charged, was to weaken the union from within, to praise responsible unionism and seek to isolate the workers from their leadership. "Find some ex-Communist, give him some money and put his name on a pamphlet and be sure to 'expose' every militant leader as a 'red.' "[24] On the story went, a transparent explanation for the events of the past month and a half. It was all a bosses' plot.

The concluding section of *The Mysterious Stranger* was subtitled "Nailing the Lies." One of the "lies" it sought to "nail down" was that "the International officers are outsiders, 'reds,' and agitators."[25] The pamphlet's response to this question dealt only with whether the International officers were "outsiders." The question of whether they were 'red' was ignored, an omission that did not elude the ILWU's critics. Woven into the overblown rhetoric about the bosses' plot was an effective account of the progress of Hawaii's workers under the ILWU.

Among the organizations supporting the Ignacio revolt was the American Legion. The Legion distributed five hundred copies of an "open letter" to the delegates at the Unity Conference. The subject was Jack Hall. The letter asked the rank and file:

> Has he ever told you, during the nearly six years since the Roberts Report on Pearl Harbor was published, that this report lied when it called Mr. Hall a Communist? Has he ever told you that he is fearful of your learning what the Roberts Report said about him? . . . Mr. Hall, in his letter to you, has denied he is now a member of the Communist Party. However, the day after the letter was reported in the newspapers he refused to answer a news reporter's question: "Have you ever been a member of the Communist Party?" He stated that he would only answer that question "at the proper time." . . .

> Isn't this the "proper time" for Mr. Hall to explain to you his connection with the Communist Party—a party whose avowed purpose is to *destroy our unions* in order to successfully *destroy our United States.*[26]

References to the Roberts Report, like John Reinecke's statement "What Must We Do?", keep coming back, throughout the period covered in this book—always out of context. Under the leadership of Supreme Court justice Owen J. Roberts, a special commission had met in Honolulu from 22 December 1941 through 9 January 1942. They reconvened in Washington, D.C., from 16 to 24 January 1942. The purpose of the commission was to determine responsibility for America's inadequate response to the Japanese attack on Pearl Harbor on 7 December 1941. The Roberts Report, itself, is only twenty-one pages long, and it was submitted secretly to President Franklin D. Roosevelt. The report said absolutely nothing about communism.

In the spring of 1947 the United States government declassified and released thirty-nine volumes of material related to the proceedings, including an enormous amount of raw data that had been accumulated by the FBI. Most of these data were given no consideration by the members of the special commission. Volume 25 of that material included a chart, prepared by the FBI, that listed the members of the central committee of the Communist Party of Hawaii. Those named were Jack Hall, Jack Kimoto, John Reinecke, Robert McElrath, and Ah Quon McElrath. The chart also listed twenty-four organizations that were deemed to be sympathetic to communism, several communist front organizations, and two ILWU locals that were alleged to be infiltrated by communists.[27]

The American Legion statement that the Roberts Report had been published for six years was obviously intended to mislead. Governor Stainback said in December 1947, "I doubt if prior to early this year anyone in Honolulu, outside of the various intelligence departments and their superiors, knew that the Roberts Report contained a list of communist-dominated organizations and the so-called executive committee of the communists in Hawaii."[28] The executive committee members may well have occupied those positions at that time, but the list contained in the Roberts Report was not an official government finding. When it came down to the organizations named, many innocent people were implicated as the frequent mention of the Roberts Report gave the document additional currency in the community.

An ILWU pamphlet titled *The Big Lie* sought to deal with the Roberts Report in an interesting fashion, as the rank and file were being urged by anticommunists to rid themselves of Jack Hall on the basis of his mention in the infamous document:

Should they follow this course, their next move must be to seek the dismissal of Circuit Court Judge A. M. Cristy. Judge Cristy is listed in the "Roberts Report" as being a member of a German propaganda agency. He is listed in FBI Chart XVI and his FBI code number is (100-1559).

They must ask for the Chamber of Commerce to drop from membership several prominent individuals in the Territory's business world. For example, there is Guido Giacometti, Mill Superintendent of the Olaa Sugar Company, and his son, Luigi. These individuals are listed in FBI Chart XVII as being members of Italian "observation and listening posts." The senior Giacometti's FBI number is (100-1538), his son's number is (100-1539).

Has Ingram Stainback suggested that the American Legion remove from its membership rolls a man listed by the FBI as being an "advisor" to the Japanese Consul in Honolulu immediately prior to Pearl Harbor? He has not. FBI Chart III lists an ex-Legion official and high officer of the Boy Scouts, Wade Warren Thayer, as a member of the "Advisory Council" of Nagao Kito, Consul of the Imperial Japanese Government. Mr. Thayer's FBI number is (100-617).

Has the Governor requested that the Royal Brewery fire its brewmaster, Walter Glockner. Herr Glockner's name appears on FBI Chart XVI. His number is (65-15).[29]

The charges and countercharges continued, but the ILWU left the Unity Conference in Hilo intact. One week later, in a secret ballot taken at the union members' place of work, 98 percent of the members voted. The result was 5,908 in favor of remaining in the ILWU, 122 opposed.[30] Amos Ignacio was later tried by the union *in absentia* and was found guilty of dereliction of duty and expelled, a gesture referred to by the *Honolulu Advertiser*, with justification, as "a farce."[31] In July 1948 the Union of Hawaiian Workers was welcomed into the American Federation of Labor as Sugar Workers' Union, Federal Local 24405, with John Owens, AFL territorial representative remarking, "The workers of Hawaii realize ILWU-CIO leaders have not answered the big $64 question about communism."[32]

The Union of Hawaiian Workers was never a viable organization. Not even the AFL could breathe life into it. On 10 December 1948, nine months after recognition, the UHW was suspended by the AFL after losing a representation election at Laupahoehoe. Less than one month later, on 4 January 1949, the union Amos Ignacio had started scarcely a year before had died a quiet death.[33]

Chapter 6

The Waiting

Eight months and nine days passed between the December 1947 suspension of John and Aiko Reinecke as teachers in the public schools of Hawaii and the beginning of their hearing in August 1948. Much of the delay was caused by legal procedures of no relevance to the substantive issues of the case, but an understanding of the mood of the public during the waiting period is important to an understanding of the events of 1947–1948.

There were some immediate manifestations of support for the Reineckes. Even before they were suspended, there was much speculation about the authorship of "What Must We Do?" the statement Governor Stainback had offered as the "Communist blueprint for Hawaii" in his Armistice Day speech in 1947. An enterprising *Honolulu Star-Bulletin* reporter, guessing or having been tipped off that John Reinecke was the author, interviewed Walton M. Gordon, Reinecke's principal at Farrington High School. The interview took place on 14 November but was not printed in the newspaper until 26 November, the day after the Reineckes' suspension. Gordon called Reinecke "a very good teacher—one of the best we have at the senior level." Gordon continued: "There has never been any intimation whatever of Dr. Reinecke's flavoring his own teaching with whatever his political beliefs are. I think he reserves that entirely as an out of school activity. I believe the other teachers would say the same thing."[1] Gordon was unwilling to give similar testimony by the time the hearing began in August 1948.

Immediate support also came for the Reineckes from within the ranks of labor. On 15 December 1947 a meeting was held at the Honolulu YMCA to discuss the Reinecke case. Marshall McEuen, head of the CIO-PAC, served as chairman. Harriet Bouslog spoke to an audience of roughly two hundred about the civil rights aspects of the case. Most of those assembled were sympathetic to the Reineckes, but not all.

Hal Lewis, better known in later years as the acerbic radio personality "Aku," generated some heat when he accused those assembled of merely "throwing jeers at the attorney general."[2] Myer Symonds, who was speaking at the time, dismissed Lewis by charging that he had come solely to disrupt the meeting. With that, a lady jumped up and demanded the civil rights of Hal Lewis be respected. McEuen responded by giving Lewis the floor. Lewis used the opportunity to begin talking about the Ignacio revolt, which was declared out of order.

It is interesting to note that Lewis had worked for the ILWU when he first came to Hawaii. His boss was Robert McElrath. In an interview, McElrath said that Lewis had done radio work for the ILWU during the 1946 sugar strike. After the strike was over, Lewis is purported to have come to McElrath saying that "the big boys" were interested in him and that he would not be working with the ILWU any longer. Lewis told McElrath that he would remain committed to the union's cause and remained in contact for "a couple of months." Soon, however, Lewis became an active spokesman for the Elks Club's "Spearhead for Freedom," whose vigorous brand of anticommunism frequently put him in the position of attacking the ILWU.[3]

A rump session of the meeting of 15 December continued after an intermission. About seventy-five members of the original crowd remained to organize what came to be known as the Hawaii Civil Liberties Committee (HCLC). It was decided that the scope of the committee's activities would go beyond the Reinecke case, although that case was the proximate issue for which the HCLC was being formed. The HCLC supported the Reineckes through their ordeal, both financially and morally. It was to earn a reputation as a communist front organization in the eyes of many.

Unexpected support came for the Reineckes from a group of clergymen on the island of Maui. A letter to the editor of the *Maui News* indicated that the ten undersigned ministers believed that the Reineckes had been denied their civil rights:

> As ministers and citizens we hold no brief for Communism. If the Reineckes are members of the Communist Party as alleged, we feel they are misguided and are in serious error. But the present issue is not that of Communism as the governor insists. The present controversy involves the rights of citizens to believe what they see to be true; to act on those convictions within the law; and to associate with whomever they please.[4]

The letter went on to say that if the Reineckes had broken the law, as the original charges asserted, they should be given those protections afforded by the judicial process.

This letter was the product of a resolution proposed, but not formally prepared, in the closing minutes of a Maui ministerial meeting. The actual author was the Reverend Mineo Katagiri, who would subsequently experience extreme pressure from local church supporters. In a 1974 interview with another of the signatories, the Reverend Abraham

Akaka, I was told that it had taken a great deal of patient explaining to convince an aroused group of prominent citizens that the position taken by the ministers was "an expression of our patriotism" rather than an attack on American institutions.[5]

Four days after the original letter, another appeared over the names of five of the ten original Maui ministers. Neither Katagiri nor Akaka was among them. The five explained the way the original letter was written, absolving themselves of any direct responsibility for its contents. They also protested the use of the letter by one Honolulu newspaper, where it was juxtaposed to an advertisement seeking financial aid for the Reineckes. They concluded with an oblique allusion to the fact that the references to the Secret Associations Statute had been dropped from the charges against the Reineckes: "We feel that persons whose ideologies are in conflict with American principles should not be teaching in our public schools. Our sole concern in this case is one of civil rights. If these rights have been granted, and we are now informed that they have been, then we have no further issue."[6]

In a final exchange with the editors of the *Maui News*, who had been critical of the original letter written by Reverend Katagiri, the beleaguered minister asserted: "I still maintain that the way to fight the communists is to create here a land of freedom and equal sharing of the earth's goods, and to bind its people by a common love for the rich blessings of liberty." The editors got the last word, in the form of a question: "Does Rev. Katagiri have any recommendations as to how the United States can fight an enemy within its own borders and thus protect the Bill of Rights and maintain the freedom which all Americans should love above life itself?"[7] Their question was purely rhetorical, as the editors announced that no further letters would be published on this subject.

The social disadvantage of being associated with an accused communist made itself evident shortly after the Reineckes' suspension. Ray Jerome Baker, noted lecturer, photographer, writer of frequent letters to Honolulu newspapers, and a forty-year resident of Hawaii, took John Reinecke to a meeting of his Lions Club as a guest. Shortly thereafter, Baker was dropped as a member of this club to which he had belonged for ten years. A lawsuit was threatened, but nothing came of it. As a sign of the times, Baker felt obliged to declare to the press that "I am not now and never have been a member of the Communist Party."[8]

By the end of February 1948 the HCLC had raised $1,500 for the Reineckes and had collected 5,500 signatures on petitions asking for their reinstatement. The HCLC voted $500 for the support of a tour to the neighbor islands by John and Aiko Reinecke. In March they were on their way. They faced generally friendly crowds, mostly union people, and got predictably unfavorable editorial comment in the local newspapers.

In the papers of Governor Stainback there is a letter that poignantly demonstrates the emotional response to the issue of communism in Hawaii at this time. The letter was written by a teenager named Marian Lai. Lai met the Reineckes during their tour of the neighbor islands. She was drawn to the couple and was initially sympathetic regarding the plight of the two suspended teachers. She asked the Reineckes to sign her autograph book, which they did. Aiko wrote: "All men may be cremated equal if we don't learn to live in peace. Let's do our bit for humanity wherever we are." John wrote: "As Paul Robeson sings, 'I've got to keep fightin' until I'm dyin' '—and so must we all, if we are to keep our heritage as Americans and continue to go forward." The more Marian thought about these statements, the more they seemed to be a badge of shame. She turned to Governor Stainback in her guilt:

> I do not have anyone to confide in at home, first, because my father is a union man and cherishes the union as an ideal, while the snakes creep under the hollow trees. . . .
>
> May you receive the greatest abundance of fortitude to combat this menace to Americanism and may the Lord keep us both physically and mentally fit to combat communism without falling into it.[9]

Communism in the schools was a matter of concern to many. Even before the Reinecke case, the *Advertiser* was writing editorials on the subject that displayed alarm, if not always accuracy:

> An Island high school teacher's study of his pupils leads him to believe they are being made receptive to Communism. This is being done by adroit propaganda that pictures Hawaii's industrial history as being akin to the feudalism of Czarist Russia. It is decorated with a heroic picture of Russia's bravery in battle in World War II. Then the question is put, "If Communism hasn't given them something superior to inspire them, why then did the Russians fight? They failed under the Czar in World War I."
>
> The teacher made an intelligent and perceptive analysis of an effective method that is being applied diligently by Communist propagandists here and throughout the United States. The answer, of course, is simply that it was not until after they had assassinated the Czar that the Russians collapsed in World War I.[10]

The collapse of the Russian army, in fact, was almost complete by the time of the Czar's abdication in March 1917. Indeed, the Kerensky government fell, in large part, owing to its efforts to reestablish an eastern front in July 1917. Immediately following the Bolshevik revolution of October 1917, Lenin took Russia out of World War I permanently. Czar Nicholas II was not assassinated until July 1918, and there is no evidence to support the assertion that he could have kept the Russian people fighting. With regard to World War II, there is no gainsaying the valor of the Soviet forces, although it can be argued that they were fighting more against Nazi Germany and for "Mother Russia" than for any abstract political ideal.[11]

How were the schools to deal with the thorny issue of communism? Indeed, the matter was much discussed after the suspension of the Reineckes. On 16 March 1948 the superintendent of public instruction, W. Harold Loper, advised his principals in a circular introducing a special issue of *School Life*. The issue was titled "Zeal for Democracy." In his instructions to the principals, Loper offered explicit guidelines on how the communist issue was to be handled:

> The professional obligation of the teacher to remain neutral on controversial issues, to present impartially the facts and arguments on both sides of any question, may result in some uncertainty on the subject of Communism. . . . The Communism we are talking about is not just another political party. It is a dictatorship which demands unswerving loyalty and uncritical obedience. . . . It tolerates no disagreement, no freedom of thought or action, crushes all opposition. . . .
>
> A wise teacher, in the discussion of any controversial issue will not use his position nor his classroom to spread propaganda for either side. . . . However, where the question of Communism is concerned, such academic impartiality is a sign of uncritical thinking. There is no middle ground on this issue.[12]

In the final months before the Reinecke hearing, there was a flurry of activity involving the controversial Mundt-Nixon bill. In support of the Mundt-Nixon bill, a group called "We, the Women" held a panel discussion at McKinley High School. Eight hundred people came to hear attorney Daniel G. Ridley, AFL leader John A. Owens, former Office of War Information and State Department official Norbourn Smith, and Ichiro Izuka. Izuka did not show up. The three speakers who did appear interpreted the Mundt-Nixon bill as a measure that would, for all intents and purposes, outlaw the Communist party in the United States, and all supported it warmly.

The sponsoring group, "We, the Women," was first established as a loose coalition of women's groups to protest a threatened general strike of all public utility workers that was scheduled for 1 July 1946. They succeeded in causing great embarrassment for the leader of the proposed strike, the anticommunist union leader Art Rutledge. The strike was called off. "We, the Women" then turned their attention to anticommunism. In an interesting episode, a small group of ILWU-related women tried to "crash" an organizational meeting of "We, the Women." Aiko Reinecke asked, from the floor, why the wives of labor leaders had not been invited to participate when the wives of business leaders were so abundantly represented? This impertinence was overlooked, but when an attempt was made to add the names of Ah Quon McElrath and Pauline Rosenthal to the slate of candidates for the executive committee, that motion was declared out of order. "We, the Women" proceeded to elect Thelma Akana, Mrs. Mona Hind Holmes, Mrs. Elizabeth St. John, Mrs. E. E. Black, and Julia White Brown to the executive committee. All were "pillars" of the community. "We, the Women" continued to be a highly visible foe of communism in Hawaii for years to come.

In opposition to the Mundt-Nixon bill, the ILWU sponsored a concert tour featuring Paul Robeson, the controversial "negro" baritone. The tour was alternately praised and criticized, depending on speakers' loyalties. The Hawaii Civil Liberties Committee sponsored a rally against Mundt-Nixon at Aala Park in downtown Honolulu. John Reinecke, helping out by distributing leaflets and encouraging passers-by to attend the rally, was accosted by two thugs, John Lewis and Mike Danguvich. When he refused to leave the corner on which he was standing, they punched Reinecke in the mouth and scattered his leaflets to the wind. The two assailants were subsequently found guilty of assault and received one-year suspended sentences. There is no evidence that Lewis and Danguvich were acting other than on their own, but there were many who suspected that the men had been urged on, perhaps even paid, by others.

During the summer of 1948 the Communist Party of Hawaii was actively producing propaganda, much of which was directed against the Mundt-Nixon bill. This propaganda so enraged the *Honolulu Advertiser* that the paper demanded that this "faceless underground force," seeking to seduce the people of Hawaii "into a revolution that would have as its objective the overthrow of the American government," come out into the open.[13] There was little chance of that, especially when the top twelve leaders of the Communist Party of the United States had been arrested in July 1948 for violation of the Smith Act. All twelve were listed as coconspirators in the 1951 indictment against Hawaii's Smith Act defendants.

On 2 August 1948, the day before the Reinecke hearing began, the *Star-Bulletin* published a national Gallup poll directed at the issues of the proceedings that were about to begin in Honolulu. Responses to four questions were printed:

1. Would you favor or oppose a law requiring all members of the Communist party in this country to register with the Justice Department?

Favor	77%
Oppose	12%
No Opinion	11%

2. In general, do you think most American citizens who belong to the Communist party in this country are loyal to America or Russia?

	December 1947	*August 1948*
Loyal to U.S.	19%	16%
Loyal to Russia	59%	65%
No Opinion	22%	19%

3. Should American citizens who are members of the Communist party be forbidden to hold civil service jobs or should they have the same rights as others to hold government jobs?

Forbidden	67%
Allowed	19%
No Opinion	14%

4. Should an individual accused of being a Communist have the right to a hearing before being dismissed?

Yes	68%
No	19%
No Opinion	8%[14]

On the following day, the day the Reinecke hearing began, Whittaker Chambers began his portentous testimony before the House Committee on Un-American Activities.

Chapter 7

The Ideals of Democracy

When the Reinecke hearing did begin, on 3 August 1948, it was with great fanfare. The territorial government flew in one of the nation's leading former communist witnesses, the "hero" of the Owen Lattimore case, Louis Budenz. Budenz had held several key positions as a member of the Communist party, the most significant of which was managing editor of the *Daily Worker*, a position he held from 1941 until his departure from the Party in October 1945. Herbert Packer, in his valuable work *Ex-Communist Witnesses*, pointed out that Budenz was the "leading interpreter of Communist theology in the many proceedings in which he has testified, partly because he has been so prolific a source of accusations against persons prominent in American political and intellectual life."[1] Budenz had no personal experience with the Communist Party of Hawaii on which to base any accusations; he was in Honolulu to demonstrate the general proposition that no communist could possess "the ideals of democracy."

Budenz' appearance brought the following headline in the *Honolulu Advertiser:* "Hawaii Red Target: Budenz." The most dramatic statement in the article was this comment from Budenz: "The infiltration effort [in Hawaii] met with some success. But it was not as successful as the party leaders hoped."[2] When it came to the purposes of the Communist Party in America, Budenz was more forceful: "The whole reason for the Communist Party in America is the overthrow by force of the republic—when Moscow wants that to be done."[3] This was a revealing preview to the character of Budenz' testimony before the territorial commissioners of public instruction.

Before Budenz actually took the stand, there was the inevitable round of legal motions and challenges from Richard Gladstein, a colorful ILWU attorney from San Francisco, and from the Reineckes' local counsel, Harriet Bouslog and Myer Symonds. In a 1976 interview, Aiko Reinecke stated that legal assistance from the ILWU was not immediately forthcoming. She asserted that Jack Hall had initially tried to have the Reineckes resign rather than force a hearing. Only when that attempt failed did the ILWU provide the Reineckes with legal support.[4] The most interesting, if quixotic, challenges were those leveled at the commissioners themselves. A review of those challenges will serve as an introduction to those who were to sit in judgment of John and Aiko Reinecke.

The first challenge was directed at Mrs. Ruth E. Black, wife of E. E. Black, president of Honolulu Gas Company, director of Castle & Cooke, secretary of Hawaiian Gas Products, Inc., and president of E. E. Black, Ltd., contractors. Mrs. Black was vice-president of E. E. Black, Ltd. Myer Symonds charged that Mrs. Black should be disqualified because her business background would necessarily make her biased; because she had openly displayed an antilabor bias during the pineapple strike of 1947, during which John and Aiko Reinecke had both walked the picket lines in support of the strikers; because Mrs. Black was one of the prime movers in the vocally anticommunist group "We, the Women" and had addressed that organization on the subject of a fifth freedom—the freedom to hold a job without being obliged to join a union; and because on 25 April 1947 Mrs. Black had entered John Reinecke's classroom at Farrington High School and openly challenged his method of presenting an outline of the Taft-Hartley Act to his social studies class.

Next, Wayne Ellis was challenged because his business and social connections on Kauai were mostly with plantation owners and management and because in March 1948 he had denied the Reineckes, illegally the defense contended, the right to use a schoolroom for a public and lawful meeting on Kauai.

The third challenge was lodged against E. Stanley Elmore of Maui. Elmore was ill at the time and subsequently removed himself from the panel of commissioners hearing the Reinecke case.

John A. Owens, territorial representative of the AFL, was Symonds' next target. Symonds pointed out that there was a well-known split within the AFL. Owens led one faction, Art Rutledge the other. Not only had John Reinecke worked in behalf of the ILWU, but he had also helped Rutledge on many occasions. These activities would make him double-damned in the eyes of Owens, Symonds contended. Furthermore, Owens had openly opposed the ILWU's 1946 sugar strike; during the 1947 pineapple strike, he had sought to raid the ranks of the ILWU; he had testified at a statehood hearing on 8 January 1948 that the ILWU was a communist-dominated union; he made the same charges in a forum held by "We, the Women"; he had guided Amos Ignacio's Union of Hawaiian Workers into the AFL; and, finally, Owens was well known as a whole-hearted supporter of Governor Stainback's anticommunist program.

The last challenge was to the chairman of the commissioners of public instruction, Edward N. Sylva. In March 1948 Sylva had been appointed as a deputy attorney general for the territory of Hawaii. His associates were presenting the case against the Reineckes. Sylva had helped prosecute the case known as *ILWU v. Ackerman*, a case in which John Reinecke had been deeply involved in the preparation of a challenge concerning the representative character, or lack thereof, of the grand jury that had brought the original indictments. "The Reineckes . . . see no difference between Mr. Sylva sitting as chairman of the commission than if he was to go down and sit at [Attorney General] Ackerman's table, and one of the deputies were to take Mr. Sylva's place," Symonds concluded.[5]

Commissioners Goo and Falconer were not specifically challenged, but the entire board was challenged for being antiunion, because they were subject to appointment and removal by Governor Stainback, and because in approving Principals' Circular 943 in March 1948, they had demonstrated that their minds were closed to the issue at hand. The commissioners, after a short executive session, determined that they were fit to hear the charges against the Reineckes—to the surprise of no one.

Gladstein, knowing that Budenz had to return to Washington, D.C., quickly, sought to have Superintendent W. Harold Loper called as the territory's first witness, on the basis that it was he who had brought the charges against the Reineckes. Sylva said no. Gladstein then threatened to demand separate hearings for John Reinecke and Aiko Reinecke, which would have made it necessary for each witness to testify twice. Sylva rejected that request as well.

As Gladstein was being obstructive regarding Budenz' testimony, Attorney General Ackerman offered a plan that he suggested would help the hearing go more smoothly. Ackerman suggested that, while each side questioned its own witnesses, the other side would refrain from raising objections until the testimony of that witness had been completed. Gladstein nearly exploded:

> I think it is bad enough . . . that an effort is being made to "gag" those in the teaching profession . . . but I have yet to hear, until this morning, the idea that when those teachers, imposed on as they are, are brought before a supposed bar of justice . . . that their attorneys are subjected to a similar gag rule so that when Mr. Ackerman and Mr. Budenz play a little game here, back and forth, passing the ball, we sit here silently and be prevented by rule of this commission from calling attention to what is being done.[6]

On this rare occasion, Sylva found for the defense.

Louis Francis Budenz, when not testifying for the United States government—or the territory of Hawaii—was employed as an assistant professor of economics at Fordham University. Before that he was on the faculty at Notre Dame University, having received a faculty assignment there within forty-eight hours of his official resignation from the Communist party in 1945. Budenz' renunciation of the Communist party came in conjunction with a new assertion of the faith of his childhood, Roman Catholicism. After a brief interlude, Budenz came forward as a prize government witness, an expert on the nature and purposes of the communist conspiracy.

On 5 August 1948 Louis Budenz launched into an account of the nature and purposes of the Communist party in the United States for the benefit of the commissioners of public instruction of the territory of Hawaii. His testimony bore no direct relationship to the Reineckes, and it was replete with hearsay evidence. Attorney Gladstein objected to both aspects of Budenz' testimony, particularly to the latter. Sylva disposed of Gladstein's objections regarding hearsay testimony in a perfunctory fashion: "In the taking of testimony, both by the attorney general and the defense, hearsay, and even hearsay upon hearsay, will be allowed. . . . This is a hearing before this board. The technical rules of evidence do not strictly apply."[7]

The chief function of Budenz' testimony was to paint a picture of the Communist party in the most conspiratorial tones. The exchanges between Budenz and Gladstein were bitter and often personal. Hamilton Ware of the *Honolulu Advertiser* commented on the atmosphere in the hearing room:

> At times the carnival sideshow aspect of the hearing is so marked that a witness walking in for the first time would not realize the seriousness of the issues before the commission. . . .
>
> From the line of questioning by Reinecke counsel, led by Richard Gladstein, it was apparent that it was the intention to smear Mr. Budenz with everything that could be found. Attorney Gladstein accused the witness of framing his answers as speeches. Territorial Attorney General W. D. Ackerman, Jr., accused Mr. Gladstein of framing his questions as speeches. The average spectator would agree with both accusations.[8]

At one point Budenz grew angry at Gladstein's pronunciation of his name, drawing a cutting response: "I thought it was more in harmony with the nature of your testimony to put the accent on the 'Boo' and that's why I have been using it."[9]

The most telling aspects of Budenz' testimony came in exchanges such as the following:

> SYLVA: In light of your experience as a Communist up to the fall of 1945, and from what you know today, and speaking just for yourself, and if you were still a Communist, what would be your attitude in the event of a shooting war?

> BUDENZ: As a Communist I'd do what ever the Soviet Union wanted done, as Communists in the Communist Party have always done under orders. I would, therefore, do anything that would advance the victory of Soviet Russia over the United States.[10]

This was damning testimony, from a man who should know. The willingness of Americans, at this time, to give special consideration to the testimony of former communists was one of the special features of what came to be known as the McCarthy era. Herbert Packer, who studied most of the important former communist witnesses, indicated that they were generally unstable people with a tendency to go to extremes. They were "true believers" by personality type. This trait may account for some of the unshakable assurance with which they testified. Ichiro Izuka certainly fit into the true believer mold, but Budenz was a master. He had a celebrity quality that helped to reinforce the predispositions carried into the hearing by the commissioners.

When asked about teachers, Budenz pointed out that a communist teacher might well be instructed to maintain a low profile. "The Communist Party might consider a teacher," Budenz said, in a thinly veiled reference to the Reineckes, "more valuable as a member of the community, operating in certain organizations, and not wanting the teacher to expose himself."[11] Budenz added, for the record, that every member of the Communist party was a potential espionage agent.

In his cross-examination, Gladstein tried to establish a monetary motive for Budenz' new profession as an "ex-communist." Budenz remained cool, even when Gladstein pointed out that the witness was not only collecting witness fees from the government, but was receiving invaluable free publicity for his recently published book, *This Is My Story.*[12] It was not established at the Reinecke hearing how much profit there was in being a professional ex-communist, but in 1953 Budenz boasted of having earned $70,000 for his ex-communist activities—in that year alone.[13]

Gladstein made even less headway when he went into Budenz' married life, seeking to depict him as a bigamist, adulterer, and family deserter. This line of questioning actually became counterproductive when Budenz pointed out that he had, indeed, done all of those reprehensible things—while under the influence of communism. His three-day stint in Honolulu over, Budenz hurried back to Washington, D.C., where he was to testify before the senate investigating committee chaired by Republican senator Homer Ferguson of Michigan that was looking into alleged World War II espionage activities by American communists who held sensitive government positions.

The territory's second witness was W. Harold Loper, superintendent of public instruction. Loper, with the Department of Public Instruction since 1921, came to this position in 1946, when he replaced Oren Long, the future governor of the territory of Hawaii. Loper opened his testimony with an account of a meeting with John Reinecke and Walton Gordon, Reinecke's principal at Farrington High School. The meeting took place in April 1947, just after the limited release of the documents associated with the Roberts Report. Loper had asked Reinecke if he was a member of the Communist party. He recalled that Reinecke had hedged the question but was firmly negative when asked if he advocated the overthrow of the U.S. government by force or violence. When Loper asked Reinecke if he would be willing to come before the commissioners of public instruction to express himself on the matters they had discussed, Reinecke is reported to have demurred.

Loper then reviewed the charges against the Reineckes. Deputy Attorney General Griffith posed the big question: "Have you formed an opinion, Dr. Loper, as to whether a member of the Communist Party is possessed of the ideals of democracy?"

> LOPER: Well, it's my opinion that it would be impossible for a person of any considerable education to believe in the principles and practices of the Communist Party as we see it operating in the world today, and at the same time be possessed of the ideals of democracy. . . .
>
> GRIFFITH: Would your answer be any different . . . if it were shown that there was an absence of any obvious act . . . of the teaching of principles of communism in the public schools?
>
> LOPER: I think not. That is, I think, even apart from teaching Communism in the schools, that such a teacher would be unfit for service in the public schools. If we may assume that acceptance of the principles of Communism means loyalty to the party line and accepting dictatorship from above as to what a party member must do at any time, even though such a teacher had not, up to the present time, talked Communism, advocated the practices and principles of Communism to the boys and girls in the school, such a teacher might at any time be ordered to do so by the authorities, or the dictator in the Communist Party. I have another reason for my opinion on that point and it is this: That a teacher of children influences their lives almost as much by what the teacher is as by what he says. To have a known Communist continue as a public school teacher would be, in effect, saying to the boys and girls and to the parents of those children, "It is quite all right for you to join the Communist Party, too."[14]

There, in brief, was the heart of the territory's case against John and Aiko Reinecke.

In cross-examination Gladstein hammered away at the concept of guilt by association, quoting U.S. Supreme Court Justice Frank Murphy: "The doctrine of personal guilt is one of the most fundamental principles of our jurisprudence. It partakes of the very essence of the concepts of freedom and due process of law. It prevents persecution of the innocent for the beliefs and actions of others."[15] Gladstein also quoted Chief Justice Charles Evans Hughes: "It is the essence of the institutions of liberty that it be recognized that guilt is personal and cannot be attributed to the holding of opinion or to mere intent in the absence of overt acts."[16] Loper seemed, in his response, to agree with Gladstein in theory, if not in practice.

Gladstein questioned Loper extensively about his circular to the principals and the implied threat to the rights of Hawaii's teachers contained in that document. Loper took the position that a teacher's rights were not as broad as those of other citizens, citing the fact that a teacher could not hold a political office or hold a seat as a delegate to a political convention. This anomaly existed because territorial employees were treated as federal employees and were subject to the restrictions of the Hatch Act. This situation changed after statehood.

In a more philosophical discussion it became apparent that Loper equated the terms "capitalism" and "democracy." This confusion of economic and political terms was characteristic of most proceedings concerning the nature of communism. Loper conceded that capitalism could exist under a dictatorship, with Hitler's Germany being the prime example. But he would not concede that communism could exist in a democratic setting.

When the line of questioning turned to John Reinecke, Gladstein asked: "Has there ever been any evidence . . . of Dr. Reinecke's ever teaching what you called doctrines or principles of the Communist Party in the classes?" Loper's response: "There is no evidence that has been brought to my attention."[17]

Gladstein, seeking to discover just how much controversial discussion Loper was willing to tolerate, asked the superintendent about a hypothetical debate between William Z. Foster and Governor Stainback on communism versus capitalism. "Do you think, Doctor," Gladstein asked, "that such a debate would be in the interest of the people?" Loper responded: "I think that such a debate would certainly draw a big crowd."[18]

Gladstein continued his cross-examination, setting a trap for Loper. He engaged in a very close inspection of the 1945 Constitution of the Communist Party of the United States of America. Ackerman, growing restive, told Gladstein the territory would concede that the document was "quite innocuous." Gladstein rejoined that there was nothing innocous about the document, but that he would continue anyway. When he concluded reading the preamble, he asked Loper if there was anything he had read that was inconsistent with the ideals of democracy. Loper said no, not on the face of it. Then he fell into the trap:

LOPER: There is a place in the Bible that says, "By their works ye shall know them." So I would take what you are reading here as a statement that looks fine and supplement it by other information and evidence as to what they actually believe by what they do.

GLADSTEIN: I am not opposed to that. In fact, I have been insistent that what we judge people by is their conduct and not what they believe, Doctor.[19]

The preceding exchange notwithstanding, the commissioners of public instruction continued to hear a case against John and Aiko Reinecke that was entirely based on their assumed beliefs. No instance of classroom misconduct was charged by the territory.

The territory's third witness was Ichiro Izuka. Public reaction to Izuka's testimony was mixed. The ILWU was not impressed. "That's the same old stuff from the same old source," Robert McElrath barked. "Izuka was thoroughly exposed at the ILWU Hilo conference last January. All his charges have been rejected."[20] Hamilton Ware was more sympathetic: "Exceptionally interesting is the similarity of thought processes which led him first to embrace the Communist philosophy and then caused him to reject it at some personal risk. In both cases he was motivated by a desire to help the cause of the ordinary man. When he found out he was being fooled, he got out."[21] This generous interpretation of Izuka's motivations is possible, but it is also possible to make the assumption that neither side was above fooling Izuka or using him for their own purposes, and that he was only too willing to be used in exchange for a moment in the limelight and a sense of belonging, however transient that might be.

The testimony of Izuka on direct examination was essentially from *The Truth about Communism in Hawaii*, with some augmentations to highlight the participation of John and Aiko Reinecke in the activities of the Communist Party of Hawaii. The most dramatic addition was a story of buried communist literature that fell into the hands of U.S. military intelligence during World War II.

At the outset of the war, members of the Communist party were ordered to maintain a low profile and to destroy any literature in their possession that might link them with the Party. Rather than destroy the literature in their possession, Peter and Alice Hyun decided to bury a box of books and newspapers in a field on some land they were leasing near Koko Crater. The Hyun family subsequently moved, leaving the books and newspapers behind. Some of the buried newspapers belonged to John Reinecke and bore his name.

Izuka said that he was drawn into the affair when he was called to a meeting at the home of Robert McElrath on Sunday, 30 May 1943. Also in attendance, besides Izuka and McElrath, were Ah Quon McElrath, Alice Hyun, and Jack Kimoto. Izuka was told that the new tenants of the former Hyun leasehold at Koko Crater had called to say that they had discovered a box of buried books while plowing. They asked the Hyuns to come by and pick them up. The group at the McElrath house did not know that the tenants had called military intelligence before calling the Hyuns and that a trap had been set. When Izuka, Kimoto, and Alice Hyun went to pick up the books, they were arrested and detained by military intelligence for several hours. The three were released at 10:30 P.M. that evening, and nothing more was ever said about the matter by the authorities. But the story, revealed five years later in Izuka's testimony, smacked of communist intrigue, and the press gave it special attention.

Izuka added to the story's newsworthiness when he revealed that, after he and Kimoto were released by military intelligence, they went to Jack Hall's house, where Hall "just raised hell with Kimoto and myself."[22] Izuka also indicated in his testimony that John Reinecke had taken part in the burying of the books, a charge that Reinecke denied, vehemently, when he took the stand.

The territory called three witnesses to corroborate Izuka's testimony on the buried books. Charles Gilliland of Hawaiian Trust Company was called to give testimony showing that the Hyun family had, indeed, leased the property in question. Everett Afook, one of the arresting officers, who had subsequently joined the territorial attorney general's office as an investigator, verified Izuka's story about the arrest and told how it had been planned. Finally, Elaine Young, daughter of the man who then held the lease on the property in question, testified that she had seen Aiko Reinecke and Alice Hyun looking about the premises, presumably for the spot where the books were buried, a couple of weeks before the arrest. Miss Young also corroborated Afook's testimony on how Izuka, Kimoto, and Alice Hyun had been set up for the arrest.

The rest of Izuka's direct examination included long and involved descriptions of organizations and procedures, an extensive list of names, few of which were new, and a largely self-serving description of his departure from the Communist party.

Sandwiched between Izuka's direct testimony and his cross-examination, the territory's last witness was presented. He was Dr. K. C. Leebrick, acting president of the University of Hawaii. Leebrick, whose specialization was political science, argued with attorney Gladstein about Jefferson and Lincoln and their interpretations of the right to revolution. But when the defense counsel asked Leebrick whether it was possible for socialism to exist in a democratic society, the professor begged off, saying, "You are going way aside from political science when you take that line."[23] Just how such a question fell outside the scope of political science Leebrick did not explain.

Leebrick's short testimony concluded, the main event began—the cross-examination of Ichiro Izuka. It was not an equal match. Gladstein was relaxed, sophisticated, and extremely articulate. Izuka was ill at ease and inarticulate, at times to the point of incoherence. Izuka's testimony was living proof that somebody else had prepared the prose, if not the substance, of his now famous pamphlet. In a 1973 interview, Izuka confirmed this fact. The original draft had been prepared by Paul Beam, a Honolulu advertising and public relations expert who was paid by the American Federation of Labor. His services had been arranged for by John A. Owens, territorial representative of the AFL—the same John Owens who was sitting in judgment of the Reineckes. If that weren't enough, the final draft of *The Truth about Communism in Hawaii* had been revised and edited by Arnold Wills, the head of the National Labor Relations Board's office in Hawaii. Wills, once a close friend of Jack Hall's, had split with Hall and the ILWU over the issue of communism.[24]

Whatever help Izuka may have had with the pamphlet, he was alone before the territorial commissioners of public instruction. The following dialogue gives a sense of the exchange between Gladstein and Izuka:

GLADSTEIN: During the last forty-five minutes—not last year, not ten years ago—but within the last hour this morning, at one point you said here under oath in the record that while you were in the Communist Party, neither did you believe in force and violence, nor did you regard the Communist Party as believing in force and violence. You gave that answer one time. Later, you gave the answer here today that when you gave such answers—similar answers—on your application for a job to the Army, you were telling a lie. Now these are two opposite statements. They cannot both be true. I want you to say here and now which time you were testifying falsely under oath this morning; the time that you said you've never believed in force or violence or the time you said you were lying when you said "no" on that very question in the Army application blank?

IZUKA: I can't understand the question; it's confusing me. . . .

GLADSTEIN: (after once again reviewing Izuka's earlier testimony) Please, now, that's your testimony. Now those two are just opposite. I want you to tell me which is correct? Which one is right and which one is wrong?

IZUKA: I didn't say those things.

GLADSTEIN: What's that? Say that out loud. You say you didn't say those things? Why, there are 500 people in the room that heard you say those things.

IZUKA: I cannot understand.

GLADSTEIN: Are you confused, Mr. Izuka?

IZUKA: You're confusing me plenty. Really confused.

GLADSTEIN: You know, there's an old saying, confusion of the mind comes from corruption of the heart.[25]

At times Izuka broke out in giddy, nervous laughter. One of the more humorous, if pathetic, moments of the hearing took place when Gladstein asked Izuka why he would not look at him while he was attempting to interrogate him. It turned out that Deputy Attorney General Blatt had instructed Izuka not to look into Gladstein's eyes—in order to avoid their hypnotic effect.

Izuka was caught in a number of minor discrepancies in his testimony. He said none of his family knew of his having been a member of the Communist party until the release of his pamphlet, only to admit later that he had brought his own brother, Kame, into the Party in 1938. He characterized a PAC meeting in Hilo as a Communist party meeting, although one of those in attendance was Sam Stevens, a foreman at Mutual Telephone Company, whom he admitted was not a communist. He placed John Reinecke at a Communist party meeting at a time when Reinecke could prove that he was not even in the territory. He testified that John and Aiko Reinecke were on Kauai during the 1946 sugar strike, when only Aiko had been there. Such errors were undoubtedly damaging to Izuka's credibility, but the overwhelming bulk of his testimony worked in his favor, as did the sympathy many felt for this simple man who was being so brutally browbeaten by the carpetbagger attorney from San Francisco. One other point worked in Izuka's favor—the majority of what he said was true. Perhaps the manner in which it was characterized was false and the conclusions derived from his testimony were not justified, but there was a Communist Party of Hawaii and Izuka had been a member of it, as were most of those he named as members—including John Reinecke.

Gladstein's fruitless probing of the relationship between Izuka and Ed Berman was interesting but essentially superfluous. At this time many people in the ILWU assumed that Berman was the one who had helped Izuka with his pamphlet. Izuka himself refused to discuss who had assisted him in the writing of *The Truth about Communism in Hawaii*. In the end, Gladstein could only attack Izuka himself:

GLADSTEIN: Mr. Izuka, isn't it a fact that the reason or one of the reasons that you have been giving the kind of testimony you have given here is that you hate men like Jack Hall, Jack Kawano, McElrath; isn't that right?

IZUKA: I don't hate them individually. The only thing I don't like is the Communist discipline—what the Communist Party says—what the Communist Party thinks.[26]

By the end of his nearly five days of cross-examination, Izuka was in the mood to retaliate. He implied that the deal between Jack Hall and

Joe Farrington in 1946 involved Hall's well-known penchant for alcohol.

GLADSTEIN: Wait a minute. Jack Hall was in favor of supporting Mr. Farrington because he likes to have a drink? Is that your testimony? Is that your testimony?

IZUKA: That's one part. Maybe the *Star-Bulletin* has something to do. . . . [27]

Finally, Izuka got his chance to strike out at Gladstein. Izuka was complaining about something the attorney had said about him that appeared in the newspaper:

GLADSTEIN: What did I say about you?

IZUKA: I think you said something—demise.

GLADSTEIN: Do you know what the word "demise" is?

IZUKA: I don't know, I don't know and another thing followed up saying that I'm one of the biggest liars in what—what you say?

GLADSTEIN: . . . that it has been my good fortune to meet.

IZUKA: I would like to make one good remark against you too, just so we'll be even. (laughter)

GLADSTEIN: Go ahead—make a speech.

IZUKA: I was going to tell you this: that you is one of the racketeering, professional liars defending the Commies in the Territory. Now we're even. (laughter)

GLADSTEIN: You want to say more?

IZUKA: That's all. That's all.

GLADSTEIN: That's all you want to say? Just so you won't feel bad, do you want to know what the word "demise" means?

IZUKA: I don't know.

GLADSTEIN: Well it simply means . . . that by the time we're finished with you in cross-examination, Mr. Izuka, the record of this case . . . would stamp with unquestionable permanence the fact that the things you have said on direct examination were not true and that the real reasons why you have been acting the way you have, the motives behind your conduct, will have come out so that people can pass [judgment] on whether or not you are the savior of the rank and file in this Territory or whether you are one of its worst enemies.

IZUKA: The meaning is a long meaning. First time I heard that "demise" had a long meaning like that. (laughter)[28]

Moments later, Izuka left the witness stand and Richard Gladstein announced that he would have to withdraw from the case to meet an ILWU obligation in San Francisco. Before he left, he made a motion to have the charges against John and Aiko Reinecke dismissed. In support of that motion, he offered a definition of loyalty taken from Mark Twain's *A Connecticut Yankee in King Arthur's Court:*

> You see, my kind of loyalty is loyalty to one's country, not to its institutions or officeholders. The country is the real thing, the substantial thing; it is the thing to watch over and care for and be loyal to; institutions are extraneous, they are its mere clothing, and clothing can wear out, become ragged, cease to be comfortable, cease to protect the body from winter, disease and death. To be loyal to rags, to shout for rags, to worship rags, to die for rags—that is the loyalty of unreason.
>
> I was from Connecticut, whose constitution declares that all political power is inherent in the people, and all free governments are founded on their authority and instituted for their benefit; and they have at all times an undeniable and indefeasible right to alter their form of government in such a manner as they may think expedient.
>
> Under that gospel, the citizen who thinks he sees that the commonwealth's political clothes are worn out, and yet holds his peace and does not agitate for a new suit is disloyal, he is a traitor. That he may be the only one who thinks he sees this decay does not excuse him, it is his duty to agitate anyway, and it is the duty of others to vote him down if they do not see the matter as he does.[29]

Having built their case around the testimony of two former communists, Louis Budenz and Ichiro Izuka, the territory then proceeded to offer exhibits designed to tie the Reinecke case in to the national scene. First, President Truman's Executive Order 9835 was offered as evidence. This order established that the United States government could deny employment or remove from employment anyone who was in violation of the standards set forth in part 5 of the order, which included

> membership in, affiliation with or sympathetic association with any foreign or domestic organization, association, movement, group or combination of persons designated by the Attorney General as totalitarian, fascist, communist or subversive or as having adopted a policy of advocating or approving the commission of acts of force or violence to deny other persons their rights under the Constitution of the United States or as seeking to alter the form of the Government of the United States by unconstitutional means.[30]

The order had established the attorney general's list of subversive organizations, a copy of which was also submitted as evidence by territorial Attorney General Ackerman.

The territory next offered as an exhibit a letter from the attorney general of the United States, dated 27 May 1947, concerning the Hatch Act and the Loyalty Review Board's relation to it. The Hatch Act, which regulated the political activities of federal employees, contained in section 9-A a requirement that any federal employee found to be a member of an organization declared subversive by the Loyalty Review Board must be dismissed.

The two final territorial exhibits came from reports of the House Committee on Un-American Activities. The first made it clear that HUAC wanted to dispel the idea that the Communist party was a legitimate domestic political party. The second was from the testimony of J. Edgar Hoover, director of the FBI, before HUAC on 26 March 1947. In tone and content the Hoover testimony was characteristic of much of the anticommunist sentiment being heard throughout the nation, including the territory of Hawaii:

> The Communist movement in the United States began to manifest itself in 1919. Since then, it has changed its name and its party line whenever expedient and tactical. But always it comes back to fundamentals and bills itself as the party of Marxism, Leninism. As such, it stands for the destruction of our American democracy. It stands for the destruction of free enterprise and it stands for the creation of a Soviet of the United States and ultimate world revolution. . . .
>
> The communists have been, still are, and always will be a menace to freedom, to the democratic ideals, to the worship of God and to America's way of life. . . . Communism in reality is not a political party. It is a way of life—an evil and malignant way of life. It spreads like an epidemic and, like an epidemic, a quarantine is necessary to keep it from infecting the nation.[31]

Chapter 8

In Their Defense

The main line of defense for the Reineckes was an effort to show the reputation they enjoyed as teachers and as members of the community. The point was to prove that the Reineckes were indeed possessed of the "ideals of democracy" and that their lives demonstrated this fact. The Reinecke case was unique among the anticommunist proceedings discussed in this book in that the accused were willing to testify in their own behalf.[1]

During the first two days of the Reineckes' defense, fifteen character witnesses took the stand. A few examples will suffice to show the kind of testimony that was offered in behalf of the suspended school teachers.

John C. Luiz, principal of Central Intermediate School, had known Aiko Reinecke since 1927, when they had worked together for two years, and John Reinecke, casually, since 1936. Luiz told the commissioners:

> I believe they are possessed of the qualities of democracy, and I say this: basing my judgment on the way they have lived their lives, I've never heard it stated anywhere that the Reineckes have been convicted of any crime. I have not heard it stated anywhere that the Reineckes were not good neighbors. I have not heard it stated anywhere that the Reineckes have not been good members of the community. On the contrary—I've heard that they've done a lot of good. I have known for a fact that they have helped others under unfortunate circumstances.[2]

Edith Keen, a counselor at Farrington High School since 1943, first knew John Reinecke in the 1920s, when he was teaching on the Big Island. She told the commissioners a long story related to Reinecke's ability as a teacher and his decency as a man. She concluded:

> I can say quite emphatically that Dr. Reinecke is one of those rare teachers who has no problem children, but is able to discover children with problems in his classes—there's quite a difference. . . . I know of no class-cutting of his classes, no disciplinary problems in his classroom, at all times have his classes proceeded in an orderly fashion, democratically conducted

and yet he is known as a teacher who makes his students work and produce.[3]

Louis Inagaki and Richard Hirakami were students of John Reinecke's at the time of his suspension. They took the lead in circulating a petition in Reinecke's behalf. At the hearing Louis spoke of Reinecke as "unbiased and unprejudiced." He said Reinecke was a good teacher "because he respected the students."[4] Richard said, simply, "He was the best teacher I've ever had,"[5] a sentiment echoed by Thomas Suzuki, a former student of Reinecke's at Kalakaua Intermediate School. Thomas told of how, when he was forced to drop out of school owing to illness, Reinecke had brought him books during his convalescence. He also told how Reinecke had bought both his ticket to the ninth grade graduation banquet and his class picture when his family was unable to afford them.

Maxie Santiago, another witness, was a bellboy at the Royal Hawaiian Hotel. He told of problems he had been having with his daughter Simone, who had taken to stealing. Santiago, a father of five, then told how Aiko Reinecke, Simone's teacher at Waialae Elementary School, had helped his daughter overcome her problem. "What she taught my daughter in six months," Santiago told the commissioners, "I couldn't do in six years."[6]

Hisayuki Sakaguchi, an insurance agent, told how his daughter, Yukino, had been a student in Aiko Reinecke's class at Waialae Elementary School in 1942. Sakaguchi had been president of the Parent-Teacher Association and had found Aiko Reinecke to be the most helpful teacher in the school. When Sakaguchi went into the U.S. Army for three years, Aiko continued to be helpful. "Mrs. Reinecke made it a point," Sakaguchi testified, "to see to it that at least my daughter wrote to me regularly while I was in the Army and in those letters she wrote and said how much Mrs. Reinecke tried to ease the separation and that she took both my daughter and my son to the beaches, to picnics; she even went to personal expense getting photographs of the children taken and sent to me."[7]

Mrs. Juliette Ballenti, a taxi driver and mother of six, told the commissioners that her son, Abraham, had been in Aiko Reinecke's class at a time when the family was having serious difficulty. Abraham had been sent to the Salvation Army Home and had, when he most needed it, received the loving attention of his teacher. When Abraham read about the Reinecke case, Mrs. Ballenti said, her son had come to her and insisted that she "help Mrs. Reinecke as much as I can if I do love him."[8]

The most dramatic testimony about Aiko Reinecke came from Mrs. Ito Isosaki. There were eight children in the Isosaki family. Aiko Reinecke had deeply touched the life of Mrs. Isosaki's daughter Martha, who had been one of Aiko's students. "One summer," Mrs. Isosaki recalled, "my daughter was very sick and her fever won't come down for two, three days, she had 103 temperature. But Mrs. Reinecke sent a postcard from Mexico and I showed to my daughter the card, she can't even open her eyes to look at the card, but she hugged the card, and then the fever was off. When three o'clock came she had no fever, she was all well."[9] Aiko Reinecke also provided timely help for Mrs. Isosaki's son Kiyoshi when he needed legal assistance. Deputy Attorney General Blatt asked who had been obtained as legal counsel for the boy. Symonds stipulated that it had been Symonds and Bouslog, without fee. "Congratulations," Blatt responded, "you will find your reward in Heaven, counsel."[10]

Discounting any special healing powers, there is little doubt that the Reineckes had made a profound impact on the lives of many in the community. Counsel for the territory of Hawaii grew restive with the line of testimony described here in its barest outlines. The community had its skeptics as well. A letter to the *Advertiser* from John Blanding Mason of Wahiawa illustrates:

> I am following very closely the newspaper accounts of the Reinecke trial. It would not be just to assume that all these wonderful things done by the Reineckes . . . were not done out of pure charity or at least through natural humanitarianism. However, the pattern seems so typically Red that one is almost forced to doubt the Reineckes' sincerity. . . .
>
> May I strongly urge the readers of this letter to obtain a copy of the July 1948 issue of the "American" and read the article entitled, "THE REDS ARE AFTER YOUR CHILD," by Harry Gideonse, L.L.D., president of Brooklyn College, New York. In this article, speaking about the Communists in our American public schools, Mr. Gideonse says, "They have a thorough knowledge of young people and know just how to go about winning their sympathies and they know how to exploit the weaknesses of our educational organizations.[11]

Having made the point that there were those in the community who admired, even loved, the Reineckes for their seemingly selfless acts as good teachers and good neighbors, the defense next turned its efforts to the destruction of Ichiro Izuka's testimony. It was not difficult to show that Izuka had testified erroneously on a number of points, but the sheer bulk of his testimony and the plausibility of much of it made him a difficult witness to dismiss. The legal dictum *falsus in uno, falsus in omnibus* merely means that if a witness is proven to have given false testimony in one area, the remainder of his testimony may be doubted, not that it must be.

The first rebuttal witness, Constantine Samson, was dismissed without being allowed to testify because he had been present at some earlier sessions of the Reinecke hearing. He was prepared, had he been allowed to testify, to contradict some of Izuka's testimony relating to the ILWU Unity Conference at Hilo in January 1948.

Next was Masaru Shimonishi of Hanapepe, Kauai. He and Izuka had been children together. Both were involved in the organization of ILWU Local 135 at Kauai Terminals in 1937. Shimonishi was the president of the local for four years, during three of which Izuka was vice-president (1938–1941). Shimonishi contradicted Izuka's testimony on the character of a labor dispute at Port Allen in 1938. Izuka had called it a strike and had said that it was dictated to the local by Jack Hall. Shimonishi said it was a lockout and that Hall, although he supported the union men, had nothing to do with the basic decisions made by the local. These, Shimonishi insisted, had been democratically arrived at among the membership.

Shimonishi also testified that Izuka had developed a reputation for having "wild ideas" by the latter part of 1938 and in 1939. He brought up an allegation, to which Blatt objected, that Izuka had been suspended for one month from Kauai Terminals in 1935 for pilfering cargo. Shimonishi also indicated that both before and after Pearl Harbor, Izuka had been behind a deliberate attempt to slow down on the job. "We even had to call meetings," Shimonishi testified, "to tell Mr. Izuka, who was vice-president of the union, not to read pamphlets during work hours regardless the cargo was coming down on his head."[12]

Justo de la Cruz was the defense's twentieth witness. As vice-president of ILWU Local 142, he testified that Izuka's challenge regarding the accuracy of the ILWU's minutes for the Hilo Unity Conference was not justified. Conceding that Izuka's remarks had been condensed in the version of the minutes the union had released, de la Cruz assured the commissioners that the full text of Izuka's remarks was on file at the ILWU office for any union member to read. This testimony came as a surprise to Myer Symonds, who admitted that he was unaware that Izuka's remarks had been condensed in the minutes.

The final rebuttal witness to deal with the Izuka testimony was Tony Kunimura of Kauai. Kunimura testified that he had first met Izuka in October 1946, shortly after the primary election. Izuka had convinced Kunimura to support William Borthwick in the general election. The second time he saw Izuka was at the home of Ed Berman. At this meeting, Kunimura said, Izuka called Jack Hall "a labor racketeer" who "wanted only power" and "didn't give a damn for working people." Kunimura testified that Izuka continued with the assertion that Ed Berman "was more responsible in building the ILWU in the Territory than anybody else" and that "Jack Hall should be removed as International representative here."[13] Ed Berman was then alleged to have entered the conversation with the comment that Jack Kawano "was just a stupid labor racketeer too and he just wanted power." Berman is then asserted to have said that Izuka was "a more capable labor leader [than Kawano, and] should be leading the longshoremen."[14]

In a 1977 letter, Jack Kimoto, former chairman of the Communist Party of Hawaii, made the following related observation:

> Curiously enough, I had a very similar experience with Izuka and Berman in approximately the same period [1946]. By Berman's request, Izuka persuaded me to meet Berman at the latter's home. There, Berman denounced Jack Hall and Jack Kawano for their "lousy" leadership given the ILWU members, and for their "shameful" support given to Farrington, a Republican unfriendly to labor. Berman said he and Wilfred Oka would make an excellent team to lead the ILWU. He even expressed his desire to rejoin the Communist Party of Hawaii, as a formal request. When I mentioned Berman's request to Jack Hall, the latter said he was very suspicious of Berman's motive for picking that crucial moment in the sugar strike for rejoining the Party. He felt that Jack Kawano's reaction would also be unfavorable. Since objection by one member was enough for me to reject Berman's request, I dropped the matter at that, and Berman never brought it up again.[15]

John Reinecke, in a 27 December 1947 letter to his and Aiko's "friends," said that Berman had sought his support for a leadership role in the ILWU. Reinecke described a scene in which Berman is alleged to have stopped him on the street and said: "Jack Kawano and McElrath have no use for you, because you are an intellectual. They say, 'Comes the revolution, Reinecke will run like a rabbit, pissing in his pants at every step.' But there *is* a place for us intellectuals, don't you agree? *I* can work all day on the waterfront and then write a pamphlet. Can Kawano do that?"[16]

Clearly, Ed Berman played a significant role in the 1947 defection of Ichiro Izuka from the Communist Party of Hawaii. As many assumed that Berman had been Izuka's ghost writer, the matter of Berman's alleged membership in the Communist party became a matter of hot dispute. Kawano said that it was Berman who took him to his first Communist party meeting in 1937. But Bill Bailey, who was running that meeting and working with Berman, in his roles as CIO director and editor of the *Voice of Labor*, said in 1992 that he had no indication that Berman had ever been a member of the Communist party.[17] Kimoto's comment that Berman had wanted to "rejoin" the Party in 1946 would certainly seem to indicate that he had been a member at an earlier time. During a 1973 interview, Berman vehemently denied that he had ever been a member of the Communist party.[18] If Berman was not a member of the Communist Party of Hawaii in the years 1937 and 1938, he was at least in sympathetic and knowing company with a number of Party members during this time.

Kunimura's testimony was intended to show that Izuka had acted selfishly and under the influence of a man with an axe to grind—Ed Berman. In cross-examination Deputy Attorney General Blatt sought to show that Kunimura's testimony was itself selfishly motivated. Tony's brother Robert was vice-president of the Kauai division of ILWU Local 142 and one of those named by Izuka as a member of the Communist party. Until his move back to Kauai, Tony Kunimura had been very active in the Hawaii Civil Liberties Committee and had worked actively in behalf of the Reineckes. What was more, Blatt revealed, Tony Kunimura had been brought to Honolulu to testify in the Reinecke case at HCLC expense. When asked by Blatt whether he or his brother was a member of the Communist party, Kunimura refused to respond.

The final witness for the defense, before the appearance of John and Aiko Reinecke themselves, was Celeste Strack, the thirty-three-year-old education director of the Communist Party of California. Strack was a Phi Beta Kappa graduate of the University of Southern California and had a Master of Arts degree from the University of California at Los Angeles. She had a long record of involvement in the communist movement, dating back to 1933, when she had joined the Young Communist League. Her task in Hawaii was to counter the testimony of Louis Budenz. To that end, she discussed her job, which she held openly, hoping to defuse some of the negative feeling that existed for the Communist party. Strack's testimony was measured and thoughtful but seems not to have won many converts for the Reineckes. To some observers her mere presence was an affront and a confirmation of every suspicion they held against the Reineckes.

Louis Budenz had testified that authors of Communist party publications were given absolutely no freedom of expression; they did nothing more than reflect the "party line." Celeste Strack took issue with that viewpoint, citing examples of her own work that had been published in party organs. "I could not claim," she contended, "that the articles I had written were the official expression of the Party's viewpoint."[19] Strack asserted that a close examination of party publications, particularly the theoretical journal *Political Affairs*, would reveal a significant amount of open debate among members of the Communist party.

Strack went on to testify about social issues within the mainstream of American political life that had been, according to her, the primary object of Communist party activity in the United States. The Party had supported social security, unemployment insurance, antilynching laws, anti–poll tax legislation, price supports, and the cause of the underprivileged in general; it had opposed the Taft-Hartley Act and the proposed Mundt-Nixon bill.

Strack's testimony next turned to the role of the Communist party in organized labor in the United States. The defense chose to deal with the concept of "class struggle" directly. The young California Communist party official used an analogy to depict the position of the communists:

"One may observe an earthquake and state that there is an earthquake or that an earthquake is liable to occur under certain conditions, but that doesn't mean that one is advocating earthquakes."[20]

On the more volatile issue of the "inevitability of force and violence," Strack read from the Constitution of the Communist Party of the United States of America:

> Any member shall be expelled from the Party who is found to be a strike breaker, provocateur, one who advocates force and violence or terrorism or who adheres to or participates in the activities of any group or party which conspires or acts to subvert, undermine, weaken or overthrow any or all institutions of American democracy through which the majority of the American people can maintain their right to determine their destinies to any degree.[21]

She went on to cite a specific case in which a Communist party member named Humphreys had been expelled for just such cause.

A substantial part of Strack's testimony consisted of introducing into the record quotations by communists that directly contradicted those offered by Louis Budenz. Her efforts pointed out the difficulty in a hearing that sought to measure the motives of the accused in terms of the words of others. It was a difficulty that afflicted virtually all such proceedings in the United States during the late 1940s and early 1950s.

Richard Gladstein had earlier pointed out the problems of what he called "literary" proceedings by quoting passages from the *Casa editorial de arte católico* (17th revised edition, 1944). This antiliberal Spanish catechism supported state censorship "because [the government] must prevent the deception, calumny and corruption of its subjects, which harm the general good." It warns that a man should not buy a liberal paper "because he contributes his money to evil, places his faith in jeopardy, and gives others a bad example." The document concluded with a warning: "Do not read any newspaper without the previous consultation and approval of your confessor." Gladstein pointed out that to hold all Roman Catholics responsible for such writing would be both an absurdity and an injustice. Similarly, to hold any communist responsible for the utterances of another would be equally untenable.[22]

Celeste Strack's appearance in Hawaii had an impact far beyond her appearance before the territorial commissioners of public instruction. This attention was due to her participation in a speaking tour of the neighbor islands, under the sponsorship of the Hawaii Civil Liberties Committee, during the Labor Day break. The purpose of the tour was to generate popular support for the Reineckes and to show people that an open, practicing member of the Communist party was not a monster. Strack was given a generally friendly reception from the people she met and a generally unfriendly reception in the press.

The *Honolulu Star-Bulletin*, tired of being chided regularly by its morning rival, the *Honolulu Advertiser*, for failing to become actively involved with the communist issue, sent the following telegram to Roger N. Baldwin, director of the ACLU in New York:

> Hawaii Civil Liberties Committee announces that it is sponsoring a territorial tour by Miss Celeste Strack who is education director of the Communist Party of California.
>
> Miss Strack was brought here as a defense witness on behalf of Dr. and Mrs. John E. Reinecke, public school teachers suspended on charges they were Communist Party members, have Communist leanings and associations, and do not possess democratic ideals essential to school teachers.
>
> No concealment whatever that Miss Strack is Communist Party member. In fact, she so testified under oath before the territorial school board which is holding the hearings.
>
> Has Civil Liberties Committee of Hawaii any connection or affiliation with the [American] Civil Liberties Union?
>
> Does [American] Civil Liberties Union approve or oppose speech tours by avowed Communists under auspices of civil liberties organizations?[23]

Baldwin's reply to the *Star-Bulletin* appeared in the same edition of the paper:

> Replying to your telegram, the Hawaiian Civil Liberties Committee is only tentatively affiliated with the American Civil Liberties Union, pending completion of its personnel. We would not affiliate any organization taking a political partisan position or engaging in partisan activities.
>
> The proposed tour of a Communist official by the Civil Liberties Committee is entirely out of line with our principles and practices.
>
> Whatever its purpose, the impropriety of such a relationship would be obvious, particularly in connection with an educational case whose interest for defenders of civil liberties is solely one of principle.
>
> No Communist is in a position to defend any such case on principle, or, indeed, any principles of civil liberties.[24]

Stephen Murin, president of the Hawaii Civil Liberties Committee, was infuriated by the exchange between the *Star-Bulletin* and Roger Baldwin. In a letter to the editors of the *Star-Bulletin*, Murin vented his anger:

> After reading your article I have arrived at these conclusions: 1) You have attempted, by wiring the American Civil Liberties Union, to confuse the issues involved in this case. 2) You have attempted to create the impression that the Hawaii Civil Liberties Committee is an affiliate of the ACLU and that the HCLC has encouraged the impression.
>
> This is not the case. By consulting with any active member or officer of the HCLC, you could have ascertained the truth. . . .
>
> Regarding your quoted reply from the ACLU, I wish to point out that the ACLU had a long and respected record for work in its field. Because of its valuable work in defense of minorities, it too earned the hatred of the

> most reactionary sections of the press. After years of "red-baiting" attacks, the leadership of the Civil Liberties Union surrendered to the baiters' pressure and dismissed the Communist members of its own board of directors. This fact must have been known to you. As a man of intellect you knew that it is unnecessary to wire an organization that forbids Communists to sit on its board of directors to find out if that organization would sponsor a tour by a Communist Party official. . . .
>
> The decision to send Miss Strack to the outer islands to speak on her organization's position on civil liberties was made at a membership meeting held September 7. . . . The membership of our committee has as much right to sponsor such a series of forums as had the members of the Republican Club, who exercised their right to have Miss Strack speak at their forum last Friday evening.[25]

Strack had her own reaction to press criticism of her tour. "It appears," she wrote in a letter to the *Advertiser*, "that certain elements in Hawaii believe that such debates and discussions represent 'too much' democracy, and are prepared to oppose any opportunity for a frank statement by the Communist Party." Strack concluded with a warning: "If they are prepared to deny the right of free speech to the Communist Party, which is a legal political party, they are also capable of restricting or denying that same right to others with whom they disagree."

The editor's comments left no doubt about the *Advertiser*'s opinion of Strack and her letter: "The *Advertiser* has no apologies, Celeste, to make for anything it has said, or may say in the future, against Communism or Communists. . . . It is a mockery for a Communist to even mention 'democracy.' "[26]

While the argument raged over the propriety of Strack's tour, the Reinecke hearing moved on. The defense had only two witnesses left: John and Aiko Reinecke. John Reinecke was first to take the stand.

Chapter 9

I neither Deny nor Affirm

John Reinecke's testimony began as defense counsel Myer Symonds led the dismissed teacher through a biographical review of his life. It showed how a young man from Kansas had come to Hawaii and made it his home. It showed something of the intellectual development of a young teacher with vaguely socialistic leanings, portraying him as a school teacher in a plantation economy, as a sociology student in a Chinese university, as the young husband of a Japanese-American wife, as a returning visitor to the mainland during the depths of the depression of the 1930s, as a tenacious student who earned his Master of Arts degree at the University of Hawaii in summers and so impressed a visiting professor from Yale that he was given a scholarship to do graduate study and earn a doctorate in the sophisticated intellectual environment of New Haven, as a radical young instructor at the University of Hawaii, whose outspoken commitment to controversial issues resulted in his not being rehired, as a volunteer who gave freely of his time to aid the cause of organized labor in Hawaii, and finally, as a man who had returned to teaching in the public schools, only to be suspended for lacking the "ideals of democracy" necessary to retain such a position of public trust.

Myer Symonds provided the backdrop for an exposition of John Reinecke's political philosophy. The most important part of Reinecke's testimony was a textual analysis of the so-called plan of the communists, his paper, written in late 1934 or early 1935, titled "What Must We Do?" This was the paper from which Governor Stainback had quoted in his 1947 Armistice Day speech. Stainback, however, had quoted only one section of the text, representing about 20 percent of its total length, which had been written by Reinecke shortly before his departure for Yale University to study for his doctorate. The parts Stainback used were, without question, the weakest and most assailable sections of the document. Symonds sought to have the paper placed into its proper context.

The paper was, essentially, a set of reflections about conditions John Reinecke perceived during the time he was teaching at Honokaa, on the island of Hawaii. It focused on the harsh realities of plantation life in Hawaii in the 1930s. John Reinecke was, by this time, at least in sympathy with communism. However, he was very troubled by a pamphlet written by a communist writer named Samuel Weinman. The pamphlet was called *Hawaii, a Story of Imperial Plunder.* While Reinecke agreed with the Marxist orientation of the work, he was disturbed by the many errors of fact and interpretation he found in it. Weinman had never been to Hawaii and was deeply burdened by stereotypes gleaned from some extremely superficial writing done in the 1920s by the Japanese Marxist Sen Katayama.

Reinecke testified that his concern over the Weinman pamphlet led him to engage in correspondence with the author and even to visit him in New York, while traveling from Hawaii to New Haven. It also led him to write "What Must We Do?" in order to "straighten out my own thinking, such as it was then, on the subject of Hawaiian social, political and economic structure . . . and how, in my opinion, it should be changed."[1]

Reinecke testified that, at the time he wrote "What Must We Do?" he knew no communists or any person he had any reason to believe might be a communist. He stated that he might have sent copies of the paper to two friends in Honolulu, Kenneth Sano and John K. Akau, Jr., men he had met in Honolulu during the summer of 1934, but the idea that the document could be looked on as a Communist party directive was, he contended, ludicrous. Furthermore, Reinecke said, he had not seen a copy of "What Must We Do?" for fourteen years.

In interviews with John K. Akau, Jr., in 1975, I found corroboration for John Reinecke's speculation that Governor Stainback had received his copy of "What Must We Do?" from Akau. Akau described himself as having been a "fellow traveler" in the 1930s, but was most emphatic that he had never been a member of the Communist party. Akau supports Reinecke's assertion that there was no Communist party in Hawaii in 1934 and 1935. Akau felt that Governor Stainback had misrepresented "What Must We Do?" in his Armistice Day speech for reasons of political expediency.[2]

Jack Kimoto also denies the existence of a Communist party in Hawaii in 1934 and 1935. In a letter dated 15 April 1977, Kimoto asserted:

> The Party was formed in 1938 [Kimoto apparently did not count Bill Bailey's 1937 efforts to start a Communist party in Hawaii], after my return to Hawaii from the mainland. Governor Stainback should have known that from Izuka's story. At the time I returned to Hawaii, I didn't know that John had written such a paper [as "What Must We Do?"]. That paper shows John's ideological immaturity at that time, and it certainly wasn't reflecting the views of the Communist Party of the United States.[3]

Symonds led John Reinecke through the complete text of "What Must We Do?" The first section dealt with the creation of militant industrial unions in the sugar and pineapple industries, with an eye to the "domination" of those industries. Reinecke told the commissioners of public instruction: "That statement I should have to change very materially because of the word 'domination.' At that time I had a very vague idea of the functioning of trade unions and of the limitations of trade unions, particularly within our capitalistic economy."[4]

The document continued, dealing with practical matters such as an eight-hour work day, a forty-hour work week, overtime pay, and the guaranteed right for workers to organize. Reinecke pointed out that, at the time he was writing, the sugar mills were on a twelve-hour day, there was no overtime pay, and the legislation that would enable all plantation workers to organize, the "Little Wagner Act," was eleven years away.

Section 2 of "What Must We Do?" dealt with organizing smaller industries. Reinecke made special reference to the coffee growers of Kona and recommended that they "be organized into cooperatives to try and break the power of the factors." He also pointed out the value of organizing workers in the "subsidiary" industries in and around the plantations: "the Honolulu Iron Works, the railways, the Inter-Island, the trucking service. These are necessary to help win major strikes and to build up supporting morale."[5]

Section 3 discussed racial antagonisms. Reinecke was particularly concerned about the isolation of the Filipinos:

> The Filipinos can see clearly enough how they are discriminated against in favor of the Latin and Oriental workers, and probably will be willing to cooperate in any effort to better the lot of all workers if no racial distinctions are made. But the young Orientals, Latins and Hawaiians will require the greatest pressure of propaganda and of the logic of events to make them see that . . . the present trend against alien labor must be redirected. Instead of hostility to the Filipinos (divide and rule of the sugar barons) there must be hostility toward the system which has imported foreign labor. The Young Americans must be shown that only by bringing the Filipinos up to their own economic and social level can they be free from their competition.[6]

Reinecke struggled mightily with the ongoing question of organizing people of disparate backgrounds. His answer was "in the cultural field there is room for the widest diversity of national activities; in the economic field, none." He closed section 3 with the plea "if there is to be racial hatred, let it come from outside the movement."[7]

Section 4, only a short paragraph, continues with the theme of racial harmony. In it Reinecke praises "the public schools for having made a good beginning we must follow up." The paragraph also included a reference to "radical labor," which Reinecke urged to "stand uncompromisingly against all forms of racial and intra-racial discrimination."[8] Reinecke was asked just what he meant by "radical labor." "At this time, I don't really know exactly what I meant," Reinecke told the commissioners. "To the best of my recollection, I must have had in mind . . . a labor party in opposition to the political control of the Islands by the Big Five. I don't think I had any concrete ideas what form it should take."[9]

Further reading in the document supports John Reinecke's testimony here. In section 7, Reinecke tentatively suggested that it might be desirable to "organize a radical political party aiming to drive the Democrats and Republicans together and so expose their identity."[10] When questioned as to whether he still favored such a party, Reinecke replied, "I would not be opposed, certainly, to having a truly radical political party, that is to say a Marxist party operating here, but I fear that it would not draw very many votes."[11] One reason, he explained, was that the Democratic party had, in recent years, become morally and financially independent of the Republican party.

Section 5 dealt with the youth of Hawaii and their lack of awareness about economic and political movements in the world. "Every effort should be made," Reinecke wrote, "to bring them into a full class consciousness, to read understandingly and to see where they stand." He suggested: "Radical literature should be distributed and a book stand established in Honolulu. Probably, as soon as possible, a newspaper should be established to express radical views."[12] Reinecke's candor in analyzing this section of "What Must We Do?" is remarkable:

> The first sentence, I think, was quite true at the time and I should say that it is, to some extent, true today, although it is my impression that the young people of Hawaii are somewhat more aware of what is going on in the world than they were then. Now, as for the second sentence—as I said at the time that I wrote this, I considered myself a Marxist although I had a very imperfect idea of what Marxism was. I still consider myself one. I consider that socialism is a goal which should be striven for and therefore I still subscribe to the idea that young people should be brought to full class consciousness.[13]

The remainder of John Reinecke's explanation of the passage was lost in the resounding echo of the "admission" he had just made. He qualified his view on the distribution of radical literature to refer to literature that was "progressive in general." He qualified his statement on a "radical" newspaper to a general plea for competition in the marketplace of ideas. But he had said he was a Marxist and that he felt that young people should be "brought to full class consciousness." If John

Reinecke had any hope of keeping his teaching position, it ended with this testimony. He had just pleaded "guilty."

The next paragraph of section 5 merely tightened the noose, as Reinecke wrote of establishing "close contacts between Hawaiian comrades and mainland centers."[14] His explanation of his use of the code word "comrades" was as follows: "Presumably I meant by 'Hawaiian comrades,' people in Hawaii who were militantly in favor of building up a radical labor movement. . . . So far as I knew then and so far as I know at present, there were, in Hawaii, no members of a Socialist or Socialist-Labor, or Communist Party—the three parties which, I believe, use the word 'comrade' in referring to their members."[15]

Section 6, the section quoted by Governor Stainback, was the part with which the John Reinecke of 1948 took the greatest exception: "At that time, my ideas were very immature. One can see that a number of points . . . have little or no relevance to the building of a strong—shall we call it anti-monopoly or anti-big business movement in Hawaii, so that much of what follows I would consider now has no place in any such movement and would not represent my views at present."[16]

Reinecke testified that his experience teaching at McKinley High School had taught him that the Reserve Officers' Training Corps (ROTC), which he had attacked in "What Must We Do?" could be a "useful institution." With regard to the military in general, Reinecke pointed out that his paper was written shortly after the infamous Massie rape case of 1931–1932, which had led a small, powerful group of local citizens to support a move by the United States Navy to replace what representative government then existed in Hawaii with government by a military commission.[17] Reinecke's 1948 view was that a military presence in Hawaii was acceptable as long as the military remained subordinate to civilian government. He explained that his opposition to the National Guard in the 1930s was mostly owing to the manner in which Guard units had been used as strike breakers. He indicated that he no longer objected to the National Guard because their use for this purpose seemed to have ended. Reinecke admitted that his expressed concern over the "militarization" of the Boy Scouts had been silly, adding that he had served as a scout master from 1927 to 1928, while teaching at Konawaena School on the Big Island.

Reinecke stood behind his observations on education in Hawaii in the 1930s, offering a long explanation. "It is highly important," Reinecke had written, "to win the teachers and university and high school students."[18] He explained at the hearing:

> I thought that teachers and university and high school students would see rather clearly how the welfare of Hawaii—democracy in Hawaii—were

[*sic*] held back by the big business men. Today, I am not at all so hopeful that they can be brought to see that. . . . Nevertheless, I should say that any labor or progressive group should aim at winning teachers and university and high school students to at least see their point of view and that the point of view of the labor unions should be presented just as fully and effectively in the schools as the point of view of big business.[19]

Reinecke also defended his paragraph on civil rights, although he was critical of his own lack of understanding at the time "What Must We Do?" was written:

The shortness of that paragraph shows my ignorance of conditions. If I knew as much then as I know today about the history of repression of civil liberties in Hawaii, I could have written several pages instead of three lines.

At the time I wrote this, picketing was absolutely forbidden by one of the most stringent anti-picketing laws on the books of any state or territory. I think *Fortune Magazine* characterized it as "penalizing anyone who lurked about any establishment with the idea in his mind of picketing." This has been repealed, thanks to the pressure of organized labor.[20]

Regarding his attack on religion, Reinecke said that by 1940 he had "come to the realization of the useful purposes which the religious institutions played in the lives of people."[21] While making a strong plea for freedom of conscience and separation of church and state, John Reinecke praised the social work done by Buddhist religious organizations for the Japanese and the Catholic church for Filipinos, Puerto Ricans, and the Portuguese.

Reinecke deemed his section on taxation and social legislation "all right as far as it goes," adding that "its brevity shows my ignorance at that time." Regarding his statement about the danger of the "sugar coated press," Reinecke responded, "Well, I don't think that I need to add anything to that."[22]

At the beginning of the second day of John Reinecke's testimony, Myer Symonds fed John Reinecke a question that allowed him to make a statement about how the document had,in his opinion, been misused by Governor Stainback:

The Governor's charge [that it was a plan for the communists of Hawaii] is preposterous and a complete lie. It has absolutely no foundation. The document which he terms the plan is a plan only in the sense that More's *Utopia* and Bellamy's *Looking Backward* are plans. [It was] an intellectual exercise, wishful thinking. . . . Had the Governor, instead of seizing upon the document with the opportunism of an irresponsible politician, examined it critically as a man who has been a judge might be expected to, he would have seen from its form and content that it was written in an organizational vacuum. Governor Stainback has acted dishonorably and

> meanly using this writing as he had done; first, to create odium against me; second, to slander the Communist Party; third, to aid the enemies of statehood for Hawaii. . . .
>
> The Attorney General, Dr. Loper and the Commissioners of Public Instruction must also bear a share of the blame. First, the Governor foisted upon the Communist Party a document in which it had no part—

At this point, Chairman Edward N. Sylva broke into John Reinecke's prepared statement, asking, "Would you mind telling us whether you are a communist or not?" Myer Symonds registered a strong objection, both to Sylva's question and his interruption. After the dust had settled, John Reinecke continued reading his prepared statement, beginning at the exact point where he had been interrupted:

> and of which it was ignorant in order to create odium against it. Then, he or Mr. Ackerman indicated me to the press as author of the supposed plan, but without naming me so that I had no way of coming forward to explain the document. Finally, when odium had already been aroused against the unnamed author of the manuscript, Dr. Loper filed charges against me based in part on my presumed authorship and the odium arising from its exposure.
>
> Mr. Stainback, Mr. Ackerman, Dr. Loper, or the Commissioners could have confronted me with the document at any time and asked me for an explanation and I would have been glad to tell them the truth of the matter. Had any of these persons given me an opportunity to explain what the document was and the circumstances under which it was written, before the Armistice Day speech was delivered or the charges against me were drawn, I should never have had to face much of the odium which I have faced from certain uninformed persons during the past ten months. One week after my suspension, on December first, I pointed out in the *Star-Bulletin* that Mr. Stainback's speech . . . contained long and specific charges against an individual who he was not man enough to name but who was later identified by the press as myself. . . .
>
> The Governor did not answer my statement or seek to discover if he had been mistaken or misled. To have done so would have deprived him of an effective if dishonorable weapon. Instead he distributed copies of the document. One was reprinted in a local magazine [*Hawaii Digest*, March 1948]. Another was used by Mr. Norborn Smith of the Spearhead for Americanism in his forum address to "We, the Women." Mr. Stainback sent a third copy to Lieutenant Governor Arthur W. Coolidge of Massachusetts who used it over a national hook-up to harm Hawaii and to help create anti-Russian war hysteria by making it the basis of his fantastic statements. Finally, I am informed that Senator Hugh Butler used this same document—this same "Communist plan" in quotes—to help kill the statehood bill.
>
> Mr. Stainback and Mr. Coolidge have illustrated perfectly how a Red scare can be built up from a basis of pure imagination.[23]

Having thus attacked the governor of the territory of Hawaii as well as the commissioners of public instruction, John Reinecke turned to a more positive exposition of his views. He now offered a statement by the American Law Institute, running to eighteen articles and titled "Statement of Essential Human Rights," as best reflecting his view of the "ideals of democracy."[24] The statement goes beyond constitutional rights but is no more radical than New Deal rhetoric. Franklin D. Roosevelt's "Four Freedoms" speech of January 1941, for example, made many of the same points. John Reinecke did have one modification to make in Article 10 of the statement. This article declared, "Everyone has the right to own property under general law." Reinecke's amendment pointed out that "those who believe in socialism would interpret 'property' as personal property not . . . coming under the means of production."[25]

As John Reinecke's testimony continued, inevitably it turned to the question of force and violence. His response was that "if the will of the people can be applied through normal democratic channels, there is certainly no need for the use of force and violence to preserve the democratic rights of the people or to extend them."[26] A fair interpretation of these words would be that socialism was the democratic wave of the future and that it would come peacefully, unless the reactionary elements, seeking to retain capitalism, precipitated violence.

Reinecke continued on the subject, making reference to Hawaii's history:

> In 1893 the business centers, by *coup d'état* overthrew the established government. . . . They not only overthrew the established government but they set up what was openly an oligarchy of a small section of the Caucasian population. . . . A number of native Hawaiians, abetted by some of the Whites, rose in rebellion against the oligarchy in 1895 and did their best to overthrow the government by force and violence. It seems to me that this was a futile and anachronistic movement but I certainly could not blame them. If I had been living in Hawaii at that time and had been of an age to join them, I think I would have. . . . However, looking at it from the vantage point of history now, I should say that they would have done better to have waited for annexation.[27]

Then Reinecke was asked whether it would now, in the present, be proper to use force and violence to overthrow the government of the United States:

> I should say most decidedly not, unless that government had become an openly fascist government, in which case I would consider it the duty of every democratic citizen and resident of the country to oppose the fascist government just as it was the duty of every democratically minded Italian, for example, to rise up against the government of Mussolini when the

> opportunity offered itself, and just as thousands of Italians did rise in the partisan movement. Only under those circumstances, those very extreme circumstances, would an American citizen be justified in exercising force and violence, it appears to me.[28]

Before the conclusion of direct examination, Reinecke was asked to evaluate his own loyalty to the United States:

> I think that my whole life speaks . . . as a testimonial to my loyalty; that within the limits of my capacity, I have taken an active part in community affairs . . . in movements and organizations which have tried to extend democracy in a Territory which had a very imperfect democracy. . . . During the past war . . . I believe that my conduct was equally loyal and patriotic to that of any other citizen of the Territory. It seems to me that the charge was drawn with one eventuality in view—a war between the Soviet Union and the United States.
>
> Now, just as the loyalty of the Japanese-Americans of Hawaii was suspect before 1941 and there was nothing they could do about it in the face of prejudice, I suppose there is nothing which I can do affirmatively in the face of the charges that have been aimed at me except to demonstrate my loyalty in everyday life . . . as a citizen of the community.[29]

The defense concluded its case by asking the same question of John Reinecke that the territory's counsel had asked so many times before: "Are you a member of the Communist party?" The question was asked to enable John Reinecke to read into the record a statement by Ring Lardner, Jr., to the House Committee on Un-American Activities in 1947:

> I do not wish to answer this question at this time for what seem to me to be cogent and compelling reasons. They are based upon my conviction that the right to hold any political belief, including that of communism, carries with it as a natural corollary the right to choose for one's self the time and occasion to make a public statement of one's opinions.
>
> As the question stands now, if I am a member of the Communist Party, I would be exposing myself to the bigotry and inspired hysteria which is forcing not only the communists but all left-of-center political groups into semi-secret status. . . .
>
> If I am not a member, I would be exposing other men to the same bigotry and blacklist by contributing to the precedent that all non-communists must so declare themselves in order to isolate the actual offenders. . . .
>
> The communists declare themselves to be loyal Americans and they propagandize in favor of democracy, tolerance and higher living standards. Their critics say that they don't really believe in these things. I'm not trying to prove here which side of the argument is right. I simply maintain that it is not sound Americanism to prosecute or persecute people for what they think or what we think they think. Only an act—only an act can be a crime—never an idea. As Jefferson put it, "It is time enough for

> the rightful purposes of civil government for its officers to interfere when principles break out into overt acts against peace and good order."
>
> I am withholding my answer at this moment, then, because I am in the middle of a fight for my right to keep silent about my political beliefs. Freedom of speech has no practical reality unless it includes the freedom to associate and to act in concert with others of a like mind and the freedom to keep to himself those opinions and associations a man doesn't feel ready to communicate to his neighbors.[30]

Still not satisfied, Deputy Attorney General Blatt pressed John Reinecke for a definitive statement about his membership in the Communist party—in his own words. Reinecke responded that whether he was a member of the Communist party or not was irrelevant to the question of whether he possessed "the ideals of democracy." Sylva countered that Reinecke was usurping the authority of the commissioners by stating what was relevant and what was not. The chairman pressed on: "I would like to put the question this way," Sylva said. "Do you deny that you are now or ever have been a member of the Communist Party of the United States? And what is your answer then to that, Doctor?"

"I neither deny nor affirm," John Reinecke responded, "that I am now or ever have been a member of the Communist Party of the United States, and my answer is based upon the same reasons I have already given."[31]

During cross-examination one piece of new and dramatic evidence was introduced against John Reinecke. It was a letter that Samuel Weinman, author of the pamphlet *Hawaii, a Story of Imperial Plunder,* had written to John Reinecke. It was dated 29 May 1935 and opened with the salutation "Dear Comrade Reinecke." Weinman asked a number of questions about Hawaii, prompted by the critique John Reinecke had written about Weinman's pamphlet. He also made a reference to "the group" that seemed to be related to John Reinecke's earlier correspondence. Weinman went on to ask whether "the group had formulated their ideas as to what is the next step in Hawaii." Weinman's conclusion left no doubt that he assumed "the group" to be a cell of the Communist party: "We have discussed linking the Hawaiian movement to the one in the United States. We plan to do something definite about it shortly. It would be well if you could get this letter into the hands of the Communist Party group and have them communicate with us directly telling us what we can do specifically to aid them." The letter was signed, "Fraternally, S. Weinman."[32]

With regard to the major question raised by the letter, the existence of a Communist party in Hawaii in 1935, John Reinecke insisted that Weinman had jumped to this conclusion. The group, which had a definite Marxist orientation, was identified as the Committee on Youth Opinion, led by John K. Akau, Jr., whom John Reinecke had identified as one of the two men to whom a copy of "What Must We Do?" was given.

In an interview in 1974, John Reinecke described Weinman as a "sanguine young man in his early twenties who had arrived at his conclusions and did not want to be confused by facts."[33] In 1948 the following exchange took place in front of the commissioners of public instruction:

> REINECKE: Well, Mr. Weinman was a resident of New York and there's an old chestnut about leaflets being issued back in the 20's addressed to "the workers and peasants of Brooklyn." Maybe he was one of them. . . . I think that this is further evidence that Mr. Weinman had a stereotype of what a colony should be like—peasantry and all—and this was after I had written to him telling him specifically that we had no peasantry here but that we had plantation agriculture, but he still couldn't get it through his head that there wasn't a peasant class.
>
> BLATT: So you had to go to New York to edify him?
>
> REINECKE: No. I did not go to New York to edify him. I went through New York on the way to edify myself [at Yale University].[34]

Blatt knew he had valuable evidence in the Weinman letter, and he worked it assiduously. There can be no doubt that it hurt John Reinecke's case.

Another piece of damaging evidence was the disclosure that John Reinecke had written articles for the *Kauai Herald* just prior to World War II under the assumed name of N. K. Jui. Dr. Reinecke revealed in 1973 that the name derived from the Chinese phonetic spelling of his last name, Jui (= Rui) Ni-k'e.[35] N. K. Jui could be categorized as a fairly radical malcontent. He was against martial law. He wanted to stop fascism abroad, but not at the expense of fascism at home. He attacked racism in the military. As late as 2 June 1941 he was taking the position that the United States should not enter the war in Europe, a position taken by the Communist Party of the United States from the time of the Nazi-Soviet nonaggression pact of 23 August 1939 to the time of the Nazi attack of the Soviet Union on 22 June 1941. John Reinecke admitted that his thinking on the matter had substantially followed the Communist party line but contended that, unlike the party line, the transitions in his thinking had come gradually. There is no doubt that the N. K. Jui articles were another blow to the defense.

Nor did Reinecke win any points with the commissioners when he was questioned by Chairman Sylva about the Fifth Amendment to the U.S. Constitution. Sylva was not talking about self-incrimination, but about the confiscation of property without just compensation. When John Reinecke was asked how he could reconcile that amendment with his views about property, he replied, "I don't think it is necessary to reconcile it because I have always been under the impression that the Constitution of the United States can be amended."[36]

Commissioner John Owens continued with the property theme, using a different line of attack. He asked John Reinecke if he had ever read the Bible. After an affirmative reply, Owens asked Reinecke if he remembered reading the Ten Commandments. John Reinecke grew wary:

REINECKE: I have some faint recollection of reading it.

OWENS: I was wondering in carrying along with your line of reasoning there about what I will call confiscation of property, especially in those circumstances where they are the means of production, how you would reconcile the seventh commandment: thou shalt not steal, to your line of reasoning of taking these means of production without compensation?

REINECKE: I don't suppose that you want me to go into a long lecture on the history of morals, but I should say that the concept of theft and the concepts of property have changed a great deal from time to time. For example, unless I am greatly mistaken, it was at one time thought to be confiscatory to take property as an inheritance tax, or as a gift tax, and I am afraid that some people who would like to inherit or receive large sums of money as gifts still think that. In other words, the concepts of property and concepts of theft that exist among the Americans in 1948 are somewhat different.

OWENS: Well would you say then that the concept of religion—there has been a change in the meaning or the application of the Ten Commandments then?

REINECKE: Oh, undoubtedly. Anybody who has the slightest smattering of history and of sociology knows that.[37]

When Sylva reminded John Reinecke that he had been the recipient of a Carnegie Foundation fellowship and asked him what he would do about the Carnegie Foundation if the United States became a socialist nation, he responded that he would be happy to do some research for the commissioner on student financial aid in socialist countries.

And so the cross-examination of John Reinecke continued. Interspersed with Reinecke's witty, if self-defeating, remarks were a number of heavy-handed efforts on the part of the territory's counsel to get John Reinecke to commit himself or an associate on the matter of membership in the Communist party. Asked about his unwillingness to discuss fully his political beliefs with the commissioners, Reinecke was quick to reply, "I should say . . . that I have given a much fuller summary of them than I feel the board is in right entitled to."[38]

John Reinecke's cross-examination ended on a note of near absurdity. Blatt insisted that Reinecke was being hypocritical in withholding information about his possible association with the Communist party on the grounds that his politics were his own business. After all, reasoned Blatt, hadn't John Reinecke freely admitted being a member of the Democratic party? Seeing the logic, or the absurdity, of the statement, John Reinecke retracted his earlier admission and declared: "I will neither affirm nor deny that I am a member. I would say that if the Board came around with a set of charges to show that by reason of my membership in the Democratic Party, alleged membership, I was not possessed of the ideals of democracy and that I was of doubtful loyalty to the government, I should certainly decline to discuss my alleged membership in the Democratic Party."[39]

Before putting Aiko Reinecke on the stand, Myer Symonds decided to edify Jack Owens with a Marxist interpretation of the Ten Commandments. He quoted from a book called *Socialism and Ethics,* by a onetime philosophy professor from Brooklyn College, Howard Selsam. Some of the moral questions raised included whether or not the confiscation of American oil properties and subsoil rights in Mexico had been stealing on the part of the Mexican government, whether or not the Emancipation Proclamation was stealing, whether or not the Russian revolutionaries had stolen the private property they had confiscated, whether or not stealing was involved in the Protestant Reformation, when the property of the Roman Catholic church was confiscated. "Were such acts as these contrary to God's eternal law as expressed in the Eighth Commandment? Selsam asked. "Either a yes or no answer to this question requires the interpretation of the commandment in terms of more fundamental moral principles and thus reveals their limited and relative moral character."[40] Symonds continued with the assertion that the commandment "Thou shalt not kill" had always been treated relatively, that no society of any historical significance had ever literally observed it. He also cited Selsam's contention that monogamous marriage originated more as a means of orderly property inheritance than out of a timeless moral principle. With this, Chairman Sylva could stand no more and ended the discussion thus: "I'm sure that everyone in this room has been taught since the cradle that it's wrong to steal. It was wrong to steal in the days of the Israelites and it's wrong today."[41]

When Aiko Reinecke finally took the stand, there was a sense of anticlimax, a realization that she was there only because she was married to John Reinecke. First, she was led through her direct testimony by Harriet Bouslog. Aiko Reinecke described her early life, a life distinctively shaped by Hawaii's plantation economy. Aiko Reinecke, born Aiko Tokimasa of immigrant parents, went to work in the fields at the age of eleven for fifty cents a day. She described the rustic camp conditions; the loving influence of a teacher, Mrs. Sisson, who had a great impact on her subsequent life; the family and personal sacrifice involved in gaining a high school education; the ultimate success of graduation from the Territorial Normal and Training School, where she trained to become a teacher; the struggle to support her family when her father was laid off by Libby, McNeill, and Libby after fifteen years of service, without a pension of any kind, at the age of sixty-six. One year after her father was laid off, Aiko Tokimasa married John Reinecke and began a life very different from that she had known before.

With her new husband Aiko Reinecke visited the mainland for the first time in 1932. She was impressed with the vastness of the continent, while being deeply shocked by the ravages of the Great Depression. When John and Aiko Reinecke went to New Haven in 1935, Aiko savored an intellectual climate she had never imagined. Together they went to the South and learned something of the racial injustice that then prevailed in that part of the country. And together the Reineckes went to Mexico in 1941, broadening their social perspectives still further.

In 1938 Aiko Reinecke had learned that being married to a radical had its hardships. The decision of the University of Hawaii not to rehire John Reinecke was a heavy blow for the family. The couple gave up their home and moved in with Aiko's family. Now, in 1948, Aiko Reinecke was discovering anew the hardships of life with a radical. If John Reinecke was considered guilty by association with the Communist party, Aiko Reinecke's guilt came from her association with her husband.

Over time and through her own experiences as well as the influence of her husband, Aiko Reinecke had made her own political observations. When Harriet Bouslog asked her about them, she responded:

> Well, that's a very difficult question. . . . I haven't really done a great deal of reading and thinking to have formulated a philosophy, but I have been . . . puzzled by the contradictions that I have run into and the problems that I have met in my private life as well as in the lives of my students.
>
> As I said earlier, I've experienced the layoff of my father, his unemployment, my husband's unemployment, and I have lived through two World Wars. Also, I vividly remember the depression . . . the poverty and the squalor and worry of the period. And so, for many years I've been trying to get at the root of all this evil: poverty, unemployment and insecurity. . . .
>
> I feel that these things are part of the system under which we live and that if we had a different kind of system which would give people better livelihood, more security and the good things of life, that it would be better than what we have today. . . . I feel that if we socially owned the things that must produce the necessities of life, then perhaps we would have a happier life on this earth.[42]

After Celeste Strack's tour, the Reinecke hearing had received little attention in the newspapers. Aiko Reinecke's testimony, however, seemed to release a torrent of latent hostility. Debate focused on a letter written by a woman named Alice Carlson. The letter, shown below, appeared in the 22 September 1948 edition of the *Honolulu Advertiser:*

> Aiko Reinecke and I have quite a lot in common. She is a schoolteacher; so am I. She taught school for $119 per month. My first year teacher salary in Hawaii was $120 per month. Her parents, I assume, came from Japan; mine came from Sweden, though not as contract labor. . . . According to her testimony, when a child, Aiko worked in pineapple fields for 50 cents a day. I, when a child, picked mustard in Minnesota grain fields for exactly 50 cents per day.
>
> She went to the Mainland in 1932, the depression period, and "learned there were beggars in our America." She didn't say she saw the beggars. In 1933 I went to Japan and saw many beggars. Old women and old men and children at temple doors with thin outstretched hands. That wasn't the depression in Japan; merely a normal condition. In December 1933, after a tour around the world, I traveled the Mainland coast to coast on my return to Hawaii. I saw no beggars. Pan-handlers, yes, but they're a different breed. But I saw a huge relief program in full swing, our America doing its utmost to help the unemployed. Didn't Aiko Reinecke on her mainland trips in 1932 and 1935 see the PWA, the CCC, the WPA, and NYA and still other employment-relief projects in full swing? Strange that she mentions only the bad she saw, not a word of the good. . . .
>
> Regarding her work in plantation fields, Aiko stated: "I should like children to be children while they are children and not forced to earn wages in order to go to school." Apparently Aiko still harbors a resentment that she had to work for wages when a child. I have no resentment. I know that the all-day picking mustard in the grain fields put health and strength in my growing body. And the many jobs I worked at all through high school and college gave me rich experience, better character, and deep appreciation that in America school doors were not closed to me. In many countries, you know, Aiko, no matter how ambitious you are, no matter how hard you work, you wouldn't have a chance at even a high school education, much less a college education.
>
> If today anyone should ask me my political beliefs or party allegiance, I would not, like Aiko, refuse to answer on the grounds that my constitutional right to keep silent is being transgressed. I can answer in a firm and proud voice. In that, Aiko Reinecke and I have nothing in common.[43]

The statements of Aiko Reinecke and Alice Carlson demonstrate the subtle complexity of contending philosophies at a time when polarities prevailed. They capture the tension of the period while revealing the relativity of moral codes, an issue defense counsel had raised the very morning Aiko Reinecke began her testimony.

The cross-examination of Aiko Reinecke demonstrated nothing more than that she had been suspended from her teaching position for being the wife of John Reinecke. After more than six weeks, after thirty-two days in session, the Reinecke hearing was ended. The transcript of the proceeding ran to 3,934 pages when it was completed. The Reineckes, who had waited almost ten months after their suspension, waited once more. Final arguments were set for 13 October 1948 in order to give defense counsel time to study the transcript and to allow Myer Symonds to meet a commitment in San Francisco. And so they waited.

Chapter 10

Teachers No More

The end of the Reinecke hearing was anticlimactic. It had been so many months since the Reineckes' suspension and the hearing itself had dragged on so long that there was little public interest left as counsel for both sides prepared closing arguments. The decision was such a foregone conclusion that there was little drama attached to that remaining detail.

As final arguments began, the *Honolulu Advertiser* announced its approval of the way in which the hearing had been conducted:

> The Reineckes have had their "full and complete" hearing on charges of being Communists and with having principles opposed to democracy, as is required by Hawaii law before school teachers may be dismissed. The case has been dragged out for long weeks; has been a springboard for Communist propaganda. Lawyers for the Reineckes even went to the extent of importing an admitted Communist propagandist, a paid agent of the Party, to come to the aid of the accused teachers. The community has been deluged with smooth-tongued attacks on American democracy; false pictures of the delights of Communist totalitarianism.
>
> The result has not been favorable to the Communists, although the opportunities they have been given to air their views may have netted them a few more gullibles. . . .
>
> Now the "full and complete" hearing is finished. The Communists—and the Reineckes in whom they seem to be very much interested—have had their field day. Hawaii's people hope that the commissioners of education will reach an early and definite conclusion.[1]

The *Honolulu Star-Bulletin* was somewhat more analytical in its discussion of the "importation" of a communist by the defense. "By bringing Louis Budenz to the Territory as an expert witness," the editors observed, "the Territory set the example. . . . Once the door was opened, in came a real, live Communist, Miss Strack of California." But if the *Star-Bulletin* was more understanding than the *Advertiser* about how Strack came to testify, it was even more vehement about the alleged effect of her having been in Hawaii:

> Then ensued the spectacle of Communism being paraded before the school board and Territory dressed up in its most alluring colors—not the deep red of armed revolt, blood, flame and devastation, but delicate mauves and pinks and pastels with which Communism in the United States is painted to attract and deceive the unwary and inexperienced eye. Against this parade of plausibility and persuasion the Territory was powerless to interfere.[2]

Almost a month after testimony had been completed in the Reinecke case, final arguments were offered. Each side was limited to three hours. Deputy Attorney General Griffith opened for the territory, reviewing the history of the case. He then dealt with the question of bias, which had been raised by defense counsel. Griffith told the commissioners that the common law governing administrative proceedings decreed:

> Administrative officials, even though otherwise disqualified, may still act if their failure to act would necessarily result in a failure of justice. . . . In this instance you are the only Commissioners of Public Instruction. There is no provision for calling in substitutes. If at least a quorum, which is five Commissioners, does not act there would be a failure of justice by preventing the determination of the proceeding. You can see, therefore, that you must make a decision in this hearing.[3]

For the good of the Department of Public Instruction, Griffith contended, the Reineckes had to be dismissed. He also indicated that it was the recommendation of the attorney general's office that the Reineckes' teaching certificates be revoked, although he did point out that it was possible for the commissioners to dismiss the teachers without revoking their certificates. Griffith concluded his portion of the territory's summation:

> One cannot show possession of the ideals of democracy merely because one is kind to children or works to alleviate discrimination or to gain new working conditions or wages for labor. Possession of the ideals of democracy cannot be based on the double talk of belief in economic democracy and its superiority to the extent that individual civil liberties may be suppressed to achieve it. . . .
>
> Can one be possessed of the ideals of democracy and advocate the overthrow of our present government by force and violence or be a part of a party which is acting as the agent for Soviet Russia? Can one be possessed of the ideals of democracy and its principles of free thought and free speech when he invokes the protection of the Constitutional freedoms in the aid of the struggle of his party to achieve power, being all the while intent upon suppressing the exercise of those very freedoms by others as soon as his party comes to power? . . .
>
> A teacher must be possessed of the ideals of democracy to teach democracy. His or her beliefs and convictions must and do color his conduct and

> affect the presentation of the subject to his pupils. . . . The teaching of doctrines opposed to those of American democracy by teachers as skilled as the Reineckes could not be expected to be open and apparent and evident to all. On the contrary, their teaching would be clever and difficult to detect. Communists are merely preparing the ground and sowing the seeds of their faith. Even Communists do not expect to reap the harvest overnight. . . . Should the party at any time require that teachers exert all their influence in converting school children, the attitude of the Reineckes as loyal and longtime members can readily be predicted.[4]

Thus did the territory of Hawaii portray the cunning and subtle way in which John and Aiko Reinecke sought to purvey an insidious foreign doctrine to the unwary youth of Hawaii. They were, indeed, so subtle that no witness for the territory was provided to give an example of the manner in which they practiced their evil arts.

After Griffith had concluded his summation of the legal aspects of the case and had recommended the Reineckes' dismissal, Deputy Attorney General Blatt summed up the territory's evidence in the case. Blatt contended that the evidence, particularly that provided by Ichiro Izuka, proved conclusively that John Reinecke was a member of the Communist party. Blatt pointed to "overt acts—and acts they were—[that] clearly prove Dr. Reinecke to be, and to have been for years, a member of the Communist Party and one of its principal officers."[5]

The "acts" Blatt referred to, other than those contained in Izuka's testimony, included the Weinman letter; John Reinecke's visit to Weinman's office in New York; the fact that there was an open Communist party in New Haven while Reinecke was studying there; a letter written by Reinecke to his department chairman at the University of Hawaii explaining his Marxist orientation; John Reinecke's teaching of courses about Marxism at the Labor Canteen at the end of World War II; the selling of communist literature by the Reineckes; and, finally, "the action of the Communist Party of California in voluntarily dispatching Celeste Strack to testify here in the Reinecke case to the high purposes of the Communist Party."[6]

Resolving that John Reinecke had been a member of the Communist party was not a difficult task. Most would have concluded that he was. But whether this membership automatically disqualified him from possessing the "ideals of democracy" is not the same question. In the minds of the territorial commissioners of public instruction, however, it clearly was.

During my first interview with John Reinecke, in the spring of 1973, I put the question to him, "Were you a member of the Communist party?" His response was "Sure, I was a member." He insisted, however, that he had not been a member of the Communist party at the time he wrote "What Must We Do?" and that there was no Communist party in Hawaii at the time it was written. Reinecke said he joined the Communist party while studying at Yale University, during the 1936–1937 academic year. He added that he knew of no Communist party in Hawaii until the spring of 1938. He joined that summer.[7]

As to Aiko Reinecke, who had neither "denied nor affirmed" her membership in the Communist party, Blatt told the commissioners: "We contend that her answer—I do not deny it—is in and of itself a complete admission and the Board should accept it as such standing alone."[8] Blatt assured the commissioners that her statement did not have to stand alone. Was it possible to believe, Blatt asked the commissioners, that Aiko Reinecke had not read "What Must We Do?" at the time her husband wrote it? He pointed to a letter Aiko Reinecke had written in which she said that reading *New Masses*, a Marxist publication, had helped her thinking. He pointed out that she had belonged to a consumer group in New Haven that met in a room above Communist party headquarters. Blatt even offered, as evidence of her membership in the Communist party, that Aiko Reinecke had participated in the tour of the southeastern United States sponsored by the Yale University Department of Race Relations, saying: "Although Aiko Reinecke was not a student at Yale University, didn't she too take the trip through the Deep South to experience personally the race prejudice which all of us acknowledge and hope to see disappear? This playing up race prejudice, while all the time deploring it, is another aspect of the Communist Party plan to set group against group and to apply the ancient military concept of divide and rule."[9] The irony of Blatt's invocation of the "divide and rule" theory, in light of Hawaii's labor history, seems not to have occurred to him. His conclusion had no surprises: "Certainly the entire conduct of the Reineckes since their connection with the Department of Public Instruction has been far from exemplary. Their vicious bias in labor, political and sociological fields . . . is enough to show their utter lack of proper academic temperament and gross unfitness in the teaching field."[10]

Finally, pointing to the central issue of the Reinecke hearing, Blatt said: "We feel that the board will concede, as have the vast majority of Americans in the Gallup Poll . . . that the Communist Party does not bear undivided allegiance to the Government of the United States."[11]

Harriet Bouslog was first to speak for the defense. She concentrated on the Reineckes' constitutional right to silence on the question of their alleged membership in the Communist party. "I experienced a sense of shock," Bouslog protested, "when Mr. Blatt said that this Commission, from their refusal to testify should assume guilt—should assume that the answer . . . was tantamount to an admission."[12] Bouslog pointed out to the commissioners that even Jesus had "kept his peace" when he appeared before Pilate, an analogy of questionable value for commissioners who would not readily assume the symbolic role of Pontius Pilate. More aptly, Bouslog quoted Thomas Jefferson, from an 1803 letter to Benjamin Rush: "It behooves every man who values liberty of conscience for himself to resist invasions of it in the case of others or their case may, by change of circumstances, become his own. It behooves him, too, in his own case, to give no example of concession, betraying the common right of independent opinion."[13]

Myer Symonds opened his part of the summation with a quotation from Supreme Court Justice Frank Murphy. "The strength of this nation," Murphy had written in the 1945 decision reversing the deportation of Harry Bridges, "is weakened more by those who suppress the freedom of others than by those who are allowed freely to think and act as their conscience dictates."[14] Symonds continued:

> Governor Stainback, Attorney General Ackerman and Dr. Loper, in whose minds originated the sinister plot to remove the Reineckes from the school system—as Governor Stainback stated, for the reason and for the purpose of setting an example for the ILWU to clean up its own house. They are the persons who are not possessed of the ideals of democracy because it is they, contrary to the statement made by Justice Murphy, who are seeking to weaken this government by denying freedom of thought to others. . . .
>
> Thought control is growing in the United States. A form of mental regimentation is taking place. A person either subscribes to the present *status quo* of our political and economic life or else he is a subversive. If unchecked, this growing straight-jacketing of the minds of the American people can have only one final result—fascism, which is the real antithesis of democracy.[15]

Symonds them moved to a theme that was central to the defense of many accused of communist associations during the period examined in this book. He pointed out that the word "capitalism" is not synonymous with the word "democracy." One can, he argued, believe in socialism and remain true to the ideals of democracy at the same time. Symonds pointed out that even Louis Budenz and W. Harold Loper had admitted that a theoretical belief in socialism was not necessarily in conflict with the ideals of democracy. He also quoted Karl Mundt, conservative coauthor of the Mundt-Nixon bill, to the effect that even a theoretical belief in Marxism was not in and of itself un-American.

Symonds then turned to a review of the evidence for the commissioners. First, he talked about the book-burying incident. He pointed out that John Reinecke "had nothing to do with the burying of the books"; in fact, "he testified that he had disapproved of it." Further: "Mr. Blatt tried to make it appear that there was something sinister about burying the books. Yet the FBI, the military and naval authorities . . . did not consider it important enough to call Dr. Reinecke in to ask him any questions with reference to the incident."[16]

Symonds then dismissed Budenz' testimony: "His willingness to say anything which comes to his mind in an effort to destroy the Communist Party which he hates" certainly disqualified him as an "expert" witness.[17] Symonds went to some length to show that portions of Budenz' testimony were internally contradictory. Loper was cast aside with the comment that the superintendent of public instruction lacked the qualifications to bring these charges against the Reineckes. Loper, Symonds contended, had acted dishonorably and had himself been badly used by both the attorney general and the governor.

Finally, the fiery defense counsel turned his full powers of scorn and indignation on Ichiro Izuka, "famous author, lecturer and liar." Symonds said that he felt certain that "never in the history of the Territory of Hawaii has a witness taken the witness stand and told as many lies as did Mr. Izuka under oath in this proceeding." He continued: "A complete review of his testimony would consume several days. He admitted lying to his own union, to the Army, to the FBI, and in this very hearing."[18] Symonds went on to enumerate a list of discrepancies in Izuka's testimony, virtually all of which had been covered during cross-examination, concluding:

> Now, that's the sort of man—I've named fourteen or fifteen examples; I could go on and name many more—but that's the type of testimony that Mr. Izuka gave in this courtroom. They are examples of deliberate lies by Mr. Izuka. . . . The lies in this case were not the result of the failure of a human mind, not when you are dealing with a fanatical, mechanical robot like Izuka who went right into the Communist Party tendering his resignation [in a letter that] made it clear that he was not leaving the Party because Communism was wrong. . . . No, that isn't what Mr. Izuka said. He merely said that the Party is out of step with Mr. Izuka. Mr. Izuka knows what's best for all the workers in the Territory of Hawaii and the Communist Party does not; now, whenever they get around to agreeing with Mr. Izuka, he trusts he will come back into the Party. Mr. Izuka is an egotistical maniac; the same as Hitler—a person who believes he is the only one who knows what is the best for others and when others do not agree with him he's ready to do anything at hand to destroy them.[19]

In attacking Izuka, Symonds leaned heavily on the testimony of Tony Kunimura, who had portrayed Izuka and Ed Berman as aspirants to the positions held by ILWU leaders Jack Kawano and Jack Hall. Symonds called John and Aiko Reinecke the "innocent victims of Izuka's hatred for Hall and Kawano."[20]

Attorney Symonds challenged the commissioners to examine their own lives and search their own souls and ask themselves whether their lives, if examined with the same scrutiny as the Reineckes', would stand up so well. "I believe it can be safely said," Symonds responded to his own question, "that there is not a single member of this Board who could truthfully state to himself or herself, 'I am more possessed of the ideals of democracy than the Reineckes.' "[21]

Two days after the closing arguments had been heard in the Reinecke case, in a preemptive move, a young soil chemist from the University of Hawaii resigned his research position at the university to become the full-time chairman of the Communist Party of Hawaii. In his letter of resignation Charles Fujimoto gave the following reasons for his decision: "By this action I can make my greatest contribution to the general welfare of the people of Hawaii. The Communist Party of the United States is contributing immeasurably toward the welfare of the American people and the peoples of the world. It is courageously and consistently fighting against the drive of the monopolists toward fascism and a third world war." Fujimoto continued, discussing some of the repressive measures being taken against communists and suspected communists in the United States. Then he brought the issue home to Hawaii:

> In Hawaii the same policy is being followed. The Governor has caused to be removed, two school teachers after 20 years of faithful service. This is only the beginning of a campaign to remove progressives from government jobs. The drive against the labor movement by the Big Five is becoming increasingly bold and violent. The civil liberties of the people are being threatened. . . .
>
> My resignation does not mean that the right of any Communist to a position in any capacity has been relinquished. I am resigning because my new responsibilities will require my full time.[22]

Charles Fujimoto's public announcement produced no great rush of communists wishing to step forward. He was and continued to be Hawaii's only open member of the Communist party. The reaction of the press was restrained. Fujimoto was treated as a pathetic, rather than sinister, figure. The *Star-Bulletin* was first to comment editorially on his announcement:

> By the Constitution of the United States and in the lack of statutes to the contrary, the Communist Party is not illegal. Fujimoto is perfectly at liberty to join it and to promote it. Likewise, he is presumably at liberty to give details about the Communist Party in Hawaii. We can conceive of no reason for this apparently candid young man to be so reticent about his party here except that to give details would reveal its paucity in numbers and its lack of substantiality.[23]

The *Advertiser*'s response was more personal and sought to get at Fujimoto through his family, a strategic target in the family-oriented Japanese-American community of Hawaii:

> There is no more pathetic figure in Hawaii today than Charles K. Fujimoto, who has traded his Americanism for Moscow totalitarianism. His father traded the lot of a Japanese peasant for that of a workman in Hawaii, where his children were given the world's best educational opportunities.
>
> Now one of the children chooses a totalitarian oppression worse than

> that from which his father fled in preference to the American system that made his own success possible, to which he owes all that he has. Russians who flee their native land say conditions there are too horrible for belief.
>
> Perhaps Charles should go and see.
>
> Goodbye, Charles.[24]

The timing of Fujimoto's resignation was probably due as much to expediency as to idealism. It was clear that the Reineckes were going to be dismissed from their teaching positions, and it was not difficult for Fujimoto to assume that he would be the territory's next target. Like John Reinecke, Fujimoto had been closely identified with the Communist party in the Izuka pamphlet. Charles Fujimoto's wife, Eileen, had also been named as a Party member by Izuka. To further complicate matters, Eileen Fujimoto was a secretary at ILWU Longshore Local 136.

On 29 October 1948 the territorial commissioners of public instruction rendered their decision in the Reinecke case. In the "findings of fact," it was stated that the commissioners were satisfied that John Reinecke had been a member of the Communist Party of Hawaii from an undetermined date in 1938 until and including the date of his suspension as a teacher, and that the Communist party was not truly a political party, but "an underground organization . . . in blind subservience to the interests of the Communist Party of the Union of Soviet Socialist Republics."[25] The commissioners found that John E. Reinecke had faithfully followed the "party line" and that he had been not only an aggressive member of the Communist Party of Hawaii, but one of its principal officers.

Turning to John Reinecke's teaching, the commissioners observed that:

> The subjects in which John E. Reinecke had specialized, was best versed, and which he was teaching at the time of his suspension consisted in part of economics, labor affairs, and the social studies, in all of which said subjects the Communist Party and Marxists, so-called, had a definite bias and slant; and that in the employment of a teacher who is imbued with the principles of Communism and subject to the control and domination of the Communist Party, there is a potential danger of slanting in teaching in an attempt to advance the principles of Communism.[26]

Thus, although no single example of bias in John Reinecke's teaching had been offered by the territory of Hawaii in its case against the man, the "potential danger" was considered to be great enough, in the eyes of the commissioners of public instruction, to be included among the "statements of fact" in their decision.

The commissioners also stated that, prior to his suspension, John Reinecke's membership in the Communist party had been given wide publicity and had threatened to bring the Department of Public Instruction into disrepute. Thus, the same people who had brought Reinecke's membership in the Communist party into the public eye were using the publicity they had created as an excuse to suspend and, ultimately, dismiss its target.

The "statements of fact" continued with the assertion that "the Communist Party of the United States and its subsidiary units, including the Communist Party of Hawaii, did, at all times hereinabove set forth, advocate the overthrow of the government of the United States by force and violence."[27] In this statement, the commissioners must have relied on the testimony of Louis Budenz entirely, for Ichiro Izuka had specifically denied this allegation, and Celeste Strack had pointed out that the constitution of the Communist Party of the United States of America explicitly forbade the use of force and violence.

Finally, it was held that membership in the Communist party was in direct conflict with the possession of the ideals of democracy and that, therefore, John Reinecke did not possess them. The result was a foregone conclusion: John Reinecke's suspension had been necessary for the good of the Department of Public Instruction; suspension without pay had been warranted. Having justified their past actions, the commissioners then proceeded to rescind John Reinecke's teaching contract for the 1947–1948 academic year and to revoke his teaching certificate.

In Aiko Reinecke's case, the "findings of fact" were similar, except that her Communist party membership, for reasons not clear from the proceedings, was dated from 1945. Only at the end was there a significant difference in the two decisions. The commissioners stated: "We are not satisfied that Aiko Reinecke so completely accepted and adopted as her own a philosophy of beliefs as to preclude her possession of the ideals of democracy and, therefore, we are not satisfied that she does not possess the ideals of democracy."[28] Nevertheless, the commissioners upheld Aiko Reinecke's suspension without pay and rescinded her 1947–1948 teaching contract. In a magnanimous gesture, the commissioners allowed her to keep her teaching certificate—an empty gesture, indeed. In a 1973 interview, Mrs. Reinecke said she attempted to obtain a teaching position in one of several private schools. None would even reply to her request for an application.[29]

Thus, John and Aiko Reinecke, with collective teaching service to the territory of Hawaii of almost forty years, were teachers no more. The decision was a product of its time. The final verdict received little attention in the press. The issue of communism, however, would return soon enough.

Chapter 11

Hawaii's Politics in 1948

As the Reinecke case moved toward its inevitable conclusion, the territory of Hawaii found itself in the midst of another political season. The ILWU, sensitive to past criticism of its political action committee, had announced in December 1947 that the PAC was being reorganized to address "educational concerns." This announcement was greeted with skepticism. Kauai's newspaper *The Garden Island* headed its editorial on the subject "You Wouldn't Kid Us Would You PAC?" Editor C. J. Fern wasn't far from the mark when he commented that the real reason for the PAC decision might have been "that too many of the lads who had an active part in the PAC in the last election have been charged with being linked too close to Communism for comfort recently."[1]

The ILWU had a different idea of how to make its presence felt in territorial politics in 1948—through Democratic party precinct organizations. Quick to sense what was happening, Democratic party conservatives David K. Trask and Harold Rice sent a joint letter to the party's territorial central committee, asking them to address the problem of communism immediately. The result was a ringing denunciation of communism and a declaration: "Any member of the Democratic Party in Hawaii who shall affiliate with the Communist Party will, in accordance with our rules, be expelled from our party."[2]

When the Oahu County Democratic Central Committee met three days later, on 13 January 1948, a similar resolution was tabled on the motion of John A. Burns. A month later Burns introduced an alternative measure, condemning "the current witch-hunting and name calling by which persons are branded." The resolution, bitterly denounced by Ed Berman, passed by a vote of 34 to 3.[3] The battle lines within the Democratic party were clearly drawn, months before the election campaign was to begin.

Conflict intensified as the ILWU drive to encourage its members to join Democratic precinct clubs began to bear fruit. The new precinct club members prevailed upon county chairman Lau Ah Chew to exercise a little-used rule that would declare all precinct clubs disbanded at midnight on 31 March 1948, allowing them to reorganize on 1 April. The result was a very strong—but by no means majority—position of ILWU members in Oahu's precinct clubs and in the delegations they sent to the Democratic party's territorial convention on 2 May 1948.

In the midst of the furor over the reorganization of the precinct clubs, there was a move to establish a staunchly anticommunist Young Democratic Club. This movement was led by Ed Berman and Art Rutledge, stalwarts of the Stainback wing of the Democratic party. Rutledge defended his position vehemently: "Among the Red element here in Hawaii, the worst thing you can call a man is a Stainback Democrat. I call that a compliment and something far better than being a stooge of Stalin."[4]

Always seeking consensus, John Burns pointed out the obvious when he said that if the Democrats were going to grow, they must attract membership from within the ranks of labor. "We don't question the motives of those who join the Democratic Party," Burns intoned. "It is not up to us to judge whether they are communists or ILWU or anything else. If, after joining it, they fail to abide by the party rules and party policies, then the party itself has the power to act."[5] Charles M. Hite, acting territorial chairman owing to the ill health of David K. Trask, echoed Burns' remarks: "I have repeatedly said that we have no objection to labor taking over the Democratic Party if they do it as Democrats first." "I think your committee," Hite told Wilfred Oka, the ILWU Democrat who was responsible for organizing the precinct clubs, "has done a bang-up good job."[6]

Unresolved protests eventually found their way onto the floor of the Democratic territorial convention on 2 May 1948. Most were ultimately resolved in favor of the newly reorganized clubs. Eleven candidates for the territorial central committee, however, were rejected for lacking the requisite three years of party membership. They included five prominent members of the ILWU: Jack Kawano, Ernest Arena, Levi Kealoha, Hideo "Major" Okada, and Antonio Rania. Kawano, Arena, and Okada had been named as Communist party members in the Izuka pamphlet.

On the surface, the Democratic party came out of its 1948 convention unified. The convention was, however, a subdued gathering, and trouble was barely avoided. As Lawrence Fuchs observed, "Democrat fought Democrat in the 1948 campaign, enabling the Republicans to win another sweeping victory despite the fact that private Republican polls showed most voters now leaning to the Democratic party."[7]

After the convention, it became apparent that there was a serious possibility of a bolt by the right wing of the Democratic party. Ed Berman announced the formation of a group called the Independent Democrats of Hawaii. The organization went nowhere in 1948, but it proved a harbinger of 1950, when the Democratic party came unglued. In 1948 the right wing of the Democratic party did not break ranks openly, but Governor Stainback complained to Attorney General J. Howard McGrath in Washington, D.C., that the communists had taken over the Democratic party in Hawaii "lock, stock and barrel."[8]

When the Democratic Women's Organization of Hawaii met on 13 May 1948, the members declared themselves unalterably opposed to communism. As if to compensate for the failure of the Democratic party convention to do so, they voted their support of both the Truman and Stainback administrations. Shortly after the meeting of the Democratic Women's Organization, one of the organization's leading lights, Victoria K. Holt, announced that she was a candidate in the Democratic primary for delegate to Congress. Her 25 May announcement caught Democratic party leaders off guard; they had no comment for the press. Mrs. Holt ran her campaign on one issue and one issue alone—communism.

As summer went on and the campaign began to heat up, the Democrats suffered a significant setback when A. T. Longley resigned as president of the thirtieth precinct club of the fifth district on Oahu. Longley had been a member of the Democratic party for thirty-six years and was chairman of the Hawaii Statehood Commission. Longley wrote to Wilfred Oka, secretary of the Oahu County central committee: "Since the Democratic Territorial Convention, I have become convinced that the subversive and radical elements are in control of the Party with whom I, as an American and Democrat, do not agree. I now feel that I can be of more service to the Party and the Territory if I hold no office."[9]

On Kauai, George Aguiar had returned to the Democratic party in the spring. At the Kauai Democratic convention in August, he announced his intention to stand for reelection to the territorial House of Representatives. He offered a scathingly anticommunist resolution defining communism as "slavery and atheism" and labeled the Communist party a "secret organization devoted to the overthrow of the government of the United States by force and violence."[10] The Kauai Democrats tabled Aguiar's resolution, passing a more moderate statement calling on Democrats "to appreciate the significance of their heritage . . . and with cool and calculated courage face and deal with the avowed communists of Hawaii and any other subversive group that may seek to overthrow the free institutions of the Territory of Hawaii."[11]

Governor Stainback, still smarting from his repudiation in 1946, did not directly involve himself in the 1948 campaign. This posture did not stop him, however, from speaking out against communism. Stainback told the fifteenth annual Young Buddhists' Association convention at Hilo: "This Territory is, as the communists themselves boast, the most fertile field in the whole United States for communist infiltration; furthermore, I regret to say that the most numerous converts in the Territory are the Japanese-Americans." Stainback added: "The record of my friendship and respect for the Japanese of this Territory is beyond question."[12] The Young Buddhists, not to be outdone by the governor, passed a resolution declaring, "When one removes the various masks of liberalism behind which it hides, one sees the devil face of Communism—the syphilis of civil government."[13]

On 23 August 1948 Mrs. Alice Kamokila Campbell, a recent convert to the Republican party, announced that she would run for the territorial Senate. In statehood hearings before visiting United States senator Guy Cordon of Oregon, Mrs. Campbell had offered this tortured analysis of communism in Hawaii: "Why has all this Communism come into the country? From the Japanese, because they do not have enough land to live on. . . . They tell you the Chinese and the Japanese hate each other. Don't you believe it, senator. They are tied together. What is to prevent the Russians from saying to the Japanese and the Chinese: 'You come and fight for us and we'll give you the Territory of Hawaii.' "[14] Refusing to endorse the Republican party plank for statehood, Mrs. Campbell was denied participation in Republican rallies. She ended up running a rather odd campaign in tandem with Victoria K. Holt, a Democrat who shared a common Hawaiian ancestry and a passionate distaste for communism.

In a power play against Mrs. Holt, several members of the territorial Democratic Central Committee supported William Borthwick's 28 August 1948 announcement that he would run for delegate to Congress if Mrs. Holt would withdraw. In his statement Borthwick suggested the type of campaign he might be expected to conduct: "If I am defeated by Delegate Farrington, it will show conclusively that subversive elements are in control of Hawaii."[15] Victoria K. Holt was not bowing out, and Borthwick withdrew his offer to run. The following day he left for the mainland, where he sat out the campaign. One day later John A. Burns, always the team player, announced that he would run for the Democratic nomination for delegate to Congress.

As the primary elections approached, the anticommunist chorus was augmented by the appearance of a pamphlet by Tom O'Brien with the evocative title *The Plot to Sovietize Hawaii*. O'Brien, a Hilo radio announcer and *Honolulu Advertiser* correspondent, told his readers: "The enemies of democracy among us are gambling mightily on a rapid time-table built around the territory's 1948 elections."[16] The plot, according to O'Brien, was the ILWU's strategy to take over the Democratic party and to make a few secret alliances with key Republicans so the union could have some voice in the selection of a governor in the event of a Republican victory. It had been hatched in November 1947, when Harry Bridges was alleged to have sent J. R. Robertson to Hawaii to meet with "nine trusted friends here, two of whom significantly were not members of the union." O'Brien pressed on: "The task of overhauling the Democratic Party was assigned to plodding and faithful Jack Kawano. He picked two assistants: aging but still agile Marshall McEuen . . . and hustling, bustling Wilfred Oka. They tackled their job with almost fanatical enthusiasm."[17]

O'Brien analyzed the goals of this nefarious "plot." They included the control of the territorial legislature and the boards of supervisors of each island, the elimination of Governor Stainback, the preparation of CIO union members for prolonged labor strife, and, finally, the creation of a crisis justifying the intervention of the ILWU-controlled territorial legislature. How was the "plot" working? O'Brien explained:

> The ILWU made a clean sweep of the Territorial Democratic Convention [and] holds in a tight fist today not only the Democratic Party's Territorial Central Committee, but also the county committees on Oahu, Hawaii, Maui and Kauai, and looks confidently to the appointment of a new governor willing to submit to their advances.
>
> Simultaneously, the union has pushed the third objective, preparing the membership for a prolonged strike. . . . A letter to the international representatives, however, emphasized that the strike cannot be expected to materialize until after the elections, forestalling a repetition of the mistake of 1946.
>
> The timetable is on schedule. . . .
>
> Christmas, 1948, if the ILWU plans hold to schedule, will find Hawaii in the grip of the most widespread, paralyzing strike in its history.[18]

The sponsor of this extravagant polemic, according to the *Star-Bulletin*, was Big Island Republican senator William C. "Doc" Hill, one of the territory's leading opponents of statehood.[19]

Certain elements of the O'Brien story were true. Jack Hall admitted—and later regretted—the ILWU's venture into Democratic party politics in 1948. Hall told a *Star-Bulletin* reporter in 1956: "We made a grievous error in 1948 when we tied ourselves to the Democratic Party. . . . Some of our worst enemies have been Democrats, masking as liberals and friends of the workers."[20] John Burns, who was one of the principal architects of the postwar Democratic party, didn't see Hall as trying to "take over" the party in 1948 or any other year. "Jack [Hall] didn't want the ILWU even in the Democratic Party," Burns recalled in 1975, "because he figured that labor should run on its own and pick and choose . . . reward your friends and punish your enemies and don't give a damn what party they belong to."[21]

O'Brien was correct in observing that Jack Kawano was active in Democratic party politics, but Kawano had been involved with that effort since 1944. Wilfred Oka was the most visible ILWU leader in

1948 Democratic party politics. His efforts in behalf of precinct club reorganization could be interpreted as having some potential for conflict of interest. To interpret the ILWU's political interests as a part of a plot to sovietize Hawaii was a big leap, but it was one O'Brien did not hesitate to make.

Into this highly charged political atmosphere came the Republican candidates for the delegate's race. On 2 September 1948 Joseph R. Farrington announced that he would seek his fourth term. The following day, Walter H. Dillingham threw his hat into the ring, creating the first primary contest among Republicans for the delegateship in more than twenty years. Among the forty-three signatures on Dillingham's petition were those of Lorrin P. Thurston, publisher of the *Honolulu Advertiser*, and O'Brien's literary sponsor, "Doc" Hill.

Walter H. Dillingham was a nephew of kamaaina business leader Walter F. Dillingham and a cousin of Benjamin F. Dillingham, a Republican candidate for the territorial Senate. Walter H. Dillingham had served in the territorial House for two terms, one before the war and one after. During the war he had been a combat pilot, a fact Dillingham regularly called attention to by flying his own plane around the campaign circuit. O. P. Soares, territorial Republican Central Committee chairman, was not happy with Dillingham's entry into the race. Soares made it clear that there had been an understanding that Dillingham would remain in the territorial House. Dillingham declared that his reason for running was quite simple: "My decision to run is based entirely upon patriotic reasons," he explained. "I feel I can be of service to Hawaii and our country as delegate and I can be counted upon to make an all-out fight against communism."[22]

Dillingham reached the rhetorical peak of his campaign at a Republican rally on 18 September 1948, when he declared: "Today, America and our home islands are threatened by the Red menace! And I want each and every citizen in these islands to know that I abhor, I detest Communism, whether it be in the ranks of labor or in the ranks of capitalism." If his statement of 18 September was a bit silly, his declaration of 26 September was misleading and irresponsible: "Today we are beset with strikes on most every hand. Our waterfront is tied up. . . . Our mass transportation service of busses is tied up by strike. . . . The telephone system throughout the islands has been struck. These strikes are caused by the 'mother of the PAC,' the un-American, irresponsible, labor agitators who have brought their curse to these islands of ours."[23] By the "mother of the PAC" Dillingham could only be referring to the ILWU. However, only one of the three strikes mentioned involved the ILWU, and that was on the West Coast, not in Hawaii. The other two strikes were by AFL unions whose leaders were vigorously anticommunist.

Joe Farrington continued to face the *Advertiser's* demands that he retroactively repudiate the 1946 PAC endorsement, but editorials to that effect had been appearing in Thurston's paper since early spring. The delegate made it clear to anyone who would listen that communists would find no comfort in his presence. Former delegate to Congress Victor S. K. Houston brought some perspective to the charge when he correctly observed: "Joe is attacked in this election because two years ago he did not denounce the endorsement that the CIO-PAC had given to him before the last primary. . . . I can vividly recall how others were seeking the endorsement which is now being held up against Joe Farrington."[24] The "others" of whom Houston spoke included many Republicans.

In the meantime the Burns-Holt race continued, with Burns running a low-key campaign on "bread and butter" issues and Holt running against the "Red menace." She warned the voters:

> The Communist situation here is dangerous. As long as this Communist group controls the leadership of the ILWU, it controls sugar, pineapple and shipping—three of our principal industries. If it ever called a general strike, on orders from Moscow, it would ruin our economy. . . . I promise all of you that should I be elected delegate, my first step will be to have a congressional committee come to the Islands and investigate the Communist situation. That will be the best way to bring the traitors out into the open.[25]

More responsible Democratic party leaders, concerned about the damage Victoria Holt was creating within the party, demanded that she be specific if she had any new information about the issue of communism in Hawaii. Mrs. Holt promised that she would speak out at the proper time. She had "contacts in Washington and elsewhere," she pointed out. "I know what is going on and they know back there what is going on. . . . People have asked me, 'How can you tell a Communist?' [My response is] you don't have to see a skunk to know he's there."[26]

Pushed further to be specific, Holt finally responded by saying that at an April 1948 meeting of the county central committee, Art Rutledge had named "a half-dozen or so" members of the Communist party who were in attendance. Mrs. Holt indicated that the charges must have been true, because they had been made in front of 150 people and "nobody sued him."[27] In a later interview, Art Rutledge confirmed that he had, at the spring meeting of the county central committee, looked around the room and pointed his finger at those he identified as members of the Communist party, saying, "You, you, you, and you."[28]

Art Rutledge's comments about Victoria Holt during the 1948 election season were somewhat enigmatic. "Mrs. Holt is a fine lady and I have nothing against her," he told the *Advertiser.* "She has been a good

Democrat for many years, but it is my opinion that she has been taken in by a person who was once a Communist, and now states he doesn't want to be one but who privately wants to get back with them."[29] In 1974 Rutledge confirmed that this reference was to Ed Berman, the ubiquitous behind-the-scenes anticommunist.[30]

On the eve of the primary election, the *Honolulu Advertiser* published an eleventh-hour statement by Robert K. Mookini, Jr., former president of ILWU pineapple local 152. Featured in Mookini's statement was an old charge from a new source. He charged that, as an officer in both the ILWU and the PAC, he was privy to information that there had been a deal between the ILWU and Joseph R. Farrington in 1946. Here was the old Izuka-Berman charge, trotted out in an effort to make the delegate appear "Red," while giving him no time to respond. Mookini finished his statement, which was published in the *Advertiser*, with a flourish: "I broke with the ILWU because its policies were and still are Communistic. I have been asked to go back with the ILWU, but I absolutely refuse because I will have nothing to do with a bunch of Communists. For the same reason, I refused to speak for the Democrats."[31]

Taking advantage of the fact that his paper, the *Star-Bulletin*, was published in the afternoon, Farrington was able to respond before the voters went to the polls the following day. Farrington called Mookini's statement "a sneak attack by my opponent in exactly the character I predicted," and noted: "It exposes in full the shameful methods being employed in the effort at election of my Republican opponent. Mookini is not telling the truth. Knowing something of his past record, I strongly suspect that his statements are prompted by considerations that, to say the least, are improper."[32]

Mookini had been suspended from the ILWU in May 1947, six months before Governor Stainback's Armistice Day speech. When Mookini charged that his dismissal was part of a communist plot, his statement received little public attention. Mookini went to work for the AFL almost immediately, seeking to lure pineapple workers away from the ILWU and into the AFL. Whether he quit the ILWU or was asked to leave, it was clear that Robert Mookini had an axe to grind and was a willing participant in this eleventh-hour attack on Farrington. The ILWU's Robert McElrath dismissed Mookini's statement as "just another smear attack."[33]

The results of the primary races made it clear that the territory was not about to be stampeded into a single-issue, anticommunist vote. In the delegate races Farrington easily took the Republican nomination over Dillingham, 49,864 to 32,686; Burns took the Democratic nomination from Holt, 7,977 to 5,021. In other Oahu races where the communist issue had been raised extensively, Alice K. Campbell finished last in a five-way race for a Republican Senate nomination. She was beaten by a six-to-one margin by the leader, Benjamin F. Dillingham, who did not share his cousin Walter's obsession with the issue of communism. On the Democratic side, the most active anticommunist candidate, other than Victoria Holt, was James G. Needles, who insisted on having an American flag at his side whenever he spoke. Needles finished fifth in a six-way race for a Senate nomination. He trailed the leader, Arthur K. Trask, by a seven-to-one margin.[34]

In the neighbor islands, militant anticommunists did no better than on Oahu. Amos Ignacio, putative leader of the Union of Hawaiian Workers, failed in his bid for a Senate nomination on the Big Island, finishing seventh out of seven candidates in the Democratic primary. His fellow UHW officer Akoni Pule, seeking reelection to the territorial House of Representatives, finished fifth out of six candidates for his party's nomination. George Aguiar of Kauai, best known for his role in breaking the 1947 organizational deadlock in the territorial House of Representatives, was seeking reelection to the House. He finished eleventh out of eleven candidates for the Democratic party's nomination.[35]

After the primary elections, virtually nothing was said about the issue of communism. The general election provided no great surprises. Farrington was returned to Congress and the territorial legislature was safely in Republican hands. The Democratic party was still nominally intact, but not for long. Efforts to get Truman to dump Stainback were rebuffed in Washington. William H. Ewing of the *Star-Bulletin*'s Washington bureau reported that Truman was not happy with Stainback but was not inclined to give encouragement to his opponents.

On this note of quiet, the first year of a six-year crusade against communism in Hawaii had ended. It had begun on Armistice Day 1947 with Governor Stainback's speech, seen the Izuka pamphlet rock the Islands, felt the Ignacio revolt shake—but not shatter—the ILWU, witnessed the sad spectacle of John and Aiko Reinecke's suspension, hearing, and dismissal, and managed to end with a modicum of order restored to the democratic processes in the fall elections. It was the year the specter of communism in Hawaii first attracted wide notice. It was just the beginning.

Aiko and John Reinecke, dismissed as teachers by the territorial supervisors of public instruction in 1948. *(Honolulu Advertiser)*

Richard Gladstein *(right)*, ILWU attorney from San Francisco, questions former communist Ichiro Izuka *(left)* during the Reinecke hearing in 1948. *(Honolulu Advertiser)*

Mrs. Richard Cooke *(left)* and Mrs. Walter H. Dillingham *(right)* march as members of the "Broom Brigade" during the 1949 dock strike. *(Honolulu Star-Bulletin)*

Charles Fujimoto, chairman of the Communist Party of Hawaii, takes the oath before the House Un-American Activities Committee in 1950, with attorney Harriet Bouslog at his side. *(Honolulu Star-Bulletin)*

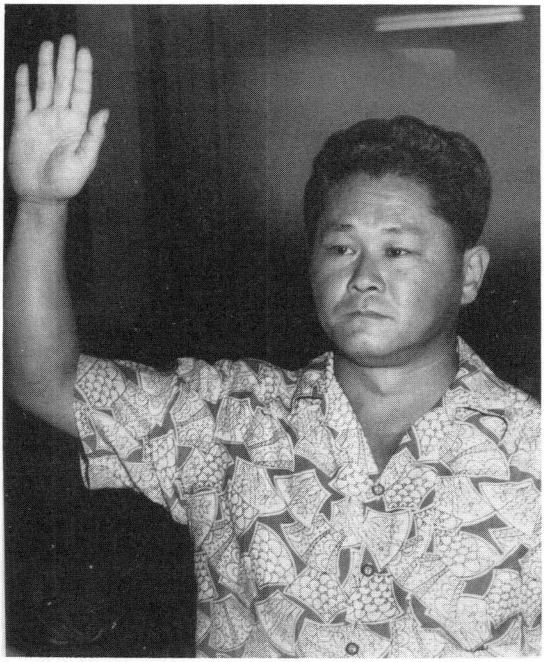

Jack Kawano, who would testify again before the House Un-American Activities Committee in Washington, D.C., takes the oath in Honolulu in 1950. *(Honolulu Star-Bulletin)*

Denichi "Jack" Kimoto *(left)*, onetime chairman of the Communist Party of Hawaii, and Koji Ariyoshi *(right)*, publisher of the *Honolulu Record*, at the time of their 1951 Smith Act arrest. *(Honolulu Star-Bulletin)*

John Reinecke *(left)* and noted civil liberties attorney, A. L. Wirin *(right)*, confer in 1953 during later stages of the Smith Act trial. *(Honolulu Advertiser)*

ILWU regional director Jack Hall *(left)* with Governor John A. Burns *(right)*, who refused to testify against Hall in the Smith Act trial. *(Honolulu Advertiser)*

John and Aiko Reinecke in 1976, at the time of their "rehabilitation" by the Hawaii State Board of Education. *(Honolulu Advertiser)*

Jack Kawano in 1979, a broken man living in "exile" in California. *(Honolulu Advertiser)*

PART THREE

THE SPECTER GROWS

Chapter 12

The 1949 Longshore Strike

Hoping to benefit from the West Coast longshore settlement of 1948, the ILWU opened negotiations in Hawaii in January 1949, months before their existing contract was due to expire. To the ILWU leadership the issue looked simple. They were dealing with many of the same employers as on the West Coast and discussing the same kind of jobs. Having slipped forty-two cents behind their West Coast brothers, Hawaii's longshoremen were simply seeking to close the gap. To make the proposal more palatable in Hawaii, where the local economy was soft, the ILWU was offering to settle for a pay raise of thirty-two cents an hour. The employers offered eight cents. They claimed that Hawaii's longshoremen should look to other industries in Hawaii for their wage comparisons, not to the West Coast. The union expressed its willingness to submit the dispute to arbitration. The owners refused, saying they did not want people with no stake in the decision calling the shots.

Although there has been some dispute over the matter, Jack Hall and Lou Goldblatt claim to have received an offer of fifteen cents from the employers just hours before the strike deadline. This was the amount the West Coast longshoremen had received in 1948. Hall and Goldblatt are reported to have told Alexander G. "Pinky" Budge, president of Castle & Cooke, that they would take a sixteen-cent offer to the membership "so we could begin to close the gap with the mainland." According to Goldblatt, "He just wouldn't make a deal for sixteen cents."[1] If this is true, for a penny's difference, Hawaii entered into the most divisive strike in its history.

At midnight on 1 May 1949 two thousand longshoremen went on strike. They would not return for 177 days. Research Associates of Honolulu estimated the cost of the strike at one hundred million dollars. Dozens of small business enterprises failed. When the strike finally ended, on 23 October 1949, both sides claimed victory. The employers based their claim on the fact that the dock workers were going back to work with a fourteen-cent pay increase. The ILWU based their claim on the fact that they would receive an additional seven cents in less than five months.

Although the strategy of the employers was clearly based on numbers, the tactics quickly turned to anticommunism. As John Burns pointed out in a 1964 interview: "The Big Five called it a political strike. They called it Communist. What else *could* they do? Their position was completely untenable."[2] Only three days after the strike began, the *Honolulu Advertiser* began a scurrilous series that came to be known as the "Dear Joe" letters. The unsigned articles were later attributed to Lorrin Thurston, publisher of the *Advertiser,* who boasted that he had written "every damn word."[3] The message was obvious:

What Are Your Next Orders, Joe?

Strike the ships. Two thousand men can and have tied up a community of 450,000 people. Every man who strikes is tying up the hopes, prospects, job security and welfare of 220 people. Good stuff! . . .

Give those strikers what they want. Then let those strikers kid every other worker—sugar, pineapple, office workers, clerks, saying, you're "suckers." Look at our union—We got ours. We should worry, you poor sap!

Let's have a sugar strike. A few plantations made money last year—others have some hopes of making some—so let's strike-em.

Why should ANY plantations make money? It ought to be ours. Worry about the stockholders?—Nuts—even if they are widows and orphans. The hell with them. . . .

Come on, Joe Stalin! We've got Hawaii all set for you. It's a pushover. Easy. We've brought business to a standstill—busted a lot of people, even some war heroes. We've caused untold hardship. Right down the alley!

What are your next orders, Joe? We're ready—your dope sure works![4]

This article was written when the 177-day strike was only in its third day!

The *Honolulu Record,* an avowedly radical labor weekly that had begun publication in the summer of 1948, responded to the "Dear Joe" letter:

In his front-page, four column editorial . . . Thurston implies that longshoremen are brutal, callous to the needs of others, and agents of Moscow. In contrast, he identifies Big Five stockholders only as "widows and orphans," and inconvenienced businessmen only as "war heroes." But the people of Hawaii have learned much since 1920—even if Thurston and the *Advertiser* still pipe the same tune.[5]

Two of the principals in the management and operation of the *Honolulu Record*—Koji Ariyoshi, editor, and Jack Kimoto, circulation manager—had been identified by Ichiro Izuka as members of the Communist Party of Hawaii. The link between the *Record,* the Communist party, and the ILWU would be exploited by the anticommunists throughout the paper's ten-year history.

The "Dear Joe" letters continued throughout the strike with regular, generally anonymous, letters of agreement appearing in the editorial pages. There was some confusion because the *Advertiser* had so regularly attacked rival publisher Delegate to Congress Joe Farrington. On at least two occasions the *Advertiser* felt it necessary to point out to its readers that the "Joe" in the "Dear Joe" letters was Stalin, not Farrington.

By mid-May the strike was commonly referred to by anti-ILWU forces as a blockade. Dwight C. Steele, president of the Hawaii Employers' Council, described it as a strike against the territory rather than the stevedoring firms. Three weeks into the strike, the *Advertiser* made this editorial assessment:

> Hawaii's crisis today is San Francisco's and the Pacific Coast's problem. And in a large sense it is the nation's problem. In a word, it is the crucial issue of how much longer this nation is going to allow its economic heritage and prosperity to be sabotaged deliberately by a small group of greedy, ruthless Moscow party line leaders. . . .
>
> Taken by itself, the present longshore wage demands might well be resolved were it not for the fact that the union demands are a part of the greater "ruin" Hawaii strategy.[6]

The *Star-Bulletin* was more restrained in its rhetoric, preferring to take a more pragmatic view of the ILWU's tactics: "If it is ILWU strategy that the waterfront employers are to be brought to terms by imposing food shortages on the people of Hawaii, then it is a strategy which the rank and file should repudiate—such tactics can't in the long run win the battle for recognition and respect which are the avowed goals of unionism over the nation."[7] The *Star-Bulletin*'s chief preoccupation with communism was related to the paper's concern about statehood. The newspaper was convinced that the *Advertiser*'s constant hammering away at the communist menace was hurting Hawaii's chances for statehood. The editors called for outside investigations of Hawaii and the strike that would, they contended, demonstrate that Hawaii was not at the center of a massive communist plot.

Women joined in the protest against the strike, forming antistrike clubs, writing letters to the editor, initiating a "Cables to Truman" program, and organizing one of the most colorful groups in Hawaii's labor history, the "Broom Brigade." Under the leadership of Mona Hind Holmes, the part-Hawaiian wife of a dairy industry executive, the women took their positions in front of the ILWU headquarters on 31 May 1949. They returned day after day until mid-August, when the Dock Seizure Act went into effect. They became a symbol of resistance to the 1949 longshore strike. They not only picketed ILWU headquarters, but for a time they targeted the *Honolulu Star-Bulletin*. Upset with the *Star-Bulletin*'s failure to see the strike as the communist plot that they perceived, the "Broom Brigade" marched and even led an unsuccessful advertising boycott against Joe Farrington's newspaper. Lou Goldblatt recalled the "Broom Brigade" years later:

> It became an hilarious thing in some situations to see some of *our* members in effect taking the red-baiting issue and turning it against the people who were attacking them. As when the women were picketing the union headquarters to clean out the union and so forth, the "broom brigade" they called it. You'd have Longshoremen there who'd find some Halloween masks, and one of them would be walking along with a sign saying: AREN'T WE DEVILS? and just having themselves nothing but fun with it.
>
> The main subject of discussion in the morning was whether everybody had gotten their checks from Moscow.[8]

The ILWU also had a good laugh over members of the "Broom Brigade" who paraded in front of union headquarters shouting, "Where are your leaders, where's Art Rutledge."[9] The irony was that Rutledge was a strong foe of the ILWU and had been publicly critical of the ILWU for its failure to rid itself of its "communist leadership." When Rutledge had run for the territorial House of Representatives in 1948, he was attacked from both sides regarding the communist issue. He was assumed to be procommunist by some because he was a labor leader. Others resented the divisive way in which he had used the communist issue within the Democratic party. When the votes were counted, Rutledge finished tenth out of eleven candidates for the Democratic party's nomination. He trailed the leader, Charles Kauhane, by a five-to-one margin.[10]

Within the ranks of the ILWU on the mainland, there was an abortive attempt to oust Harry Bridges. Joseph Maldonado, a member of ILWU Local 10 in San Francisco, organized a group calling itself the Maritime Democratic Committee. The group was alleged to have authorized Maldonado to go to his native Hawaii to set up a chapter. On his arrival in early June Maldonado explained to the press that he had come because "the strike must be concluded. He charged that the leading elements of the ILWU in Hawaii were not working for the interests of the workers, but to further the cause of socialism in the islands."[11]

Maldonado quickly became the toast of anticommunist civic groups. He spoke at meetings, picketed with the "Broom Brigade" at Pier 11, and made anti-Bridges statements on cue. Although he claimed to speak for 2,200 men in ILWU Local 10, Maldonado was repudiated by that local and expelled from the union. According to the *Honolulu Record*, W. Tip Davis, second vice-president of the Hawaii Residents' Association (IMUA), admitted having brought Maldonado to Hawaii "to bottle up subversive elements on the Territory's waterfront."[12]

While strike activity was commanding the attention of the public,

Governor Ingram M. Stainback was working behind the scene, lobbying for legislation to prevent dock shutdowns during labor disputes. Joseph Farrington submitted several bills to Congress, and many public officials called upon President Truman to take action under the Taft-Hartley Act. The Bar Association of Hawaii sent a resolution to New York representative Emanuel Celler, chairman of the House Judiciary Committee, asking for a federal investigation to determine whether the longshore strike was communist-inspired. Celler turned the investigation over to John S. Wood, chairman of the House Committee on Un-American Activities. Wood announced that he would investigate and make a preliminary report to the committee. All told, six separate entities of the federal government made at least a preliminary investigation of the strike. Stainback also announced on 15 June 1949 that he had appointed a fact-finding board, giving them seven days to conduct hearings and present their recommendations.

Lou Goldblatt, representing the ILWU, opened his presentation with a challenge for the employers. Goldblatt challenged them to present, "as a finding of fact," an assertion that the strike was communist-inspired. "The union will be most eager," Goldblatt said, "to hear testimony and consider evidence on this issue; to cross-examine witnesses and to present evidence and testimony on its own behalf." Board member Ernest De Silva, supervising principal of the public schools for the island of Hawaii, asked Jim Blaisdell if the employers were intending to allege that the strike was a communist plot. Blaisdell, who represented the Hawaii Employers' Council, replied: "Well, I could refer to our statement and you will find . . . it is conspicuous by its absence."[13] On 28 June the fact-finding board submitted to Governor Stainback a recommendation that the union receive a fourteen-cent pay raise. The employers accepted the recommendation; the longshoremen rejected it by a vote of 826 to 59.[14]

If the employers were reluctant to press the communist issue in their negotiations with the ILWU, there was no lack of community groups formed to press for an investigation of the strike as a communist plot and to draw national attention to the communist menace in the territory. The most vocal of these organizations, the Hawaii Residents' Association—better known as IMUA—was formed on 14 June 1949.[15] Their stated purpose was to call attention to "the creeping paralysis of Communism in Hawaii." On 25 June 1949 another group calling itself the Conference of Civic Organizations met for the first time, "to combat attacks of Communist agents against civic organizations."[16]

These groups were greatly aided by the publication, in June, of a report published by Senator Hugh Butler of the Senate Committee on Interior and Insular Affairs. Butler was a bitter foe of Hawaiian statehood. The title of the report by the Republican senator from Nebraska was *Statehood for Hawaii: Communist Penetration of the Hawaiian Islands*. It came to be known, simply, as the Butler Report. In the report, which Butler claimed to have "researched" in 1948, it was charged that communism had a firm grip on the economic, social, and political life of the Islands, that Harry Bridges was the unseen communist dictator of the territory of Hawaii, that the ILWU was responsible for directing the spread of communism in accordance with Moscow's orders, and that Moscow regarded Hawaii "as one of its principal operating bases in the campaign for a Communist United States of America." Butler gave as his source "official Communist documents . . . now in the hands of the Department of Justice in Washington." Then Butler pinpointed the "documents" in question:

> On February 24, 1948, Lieutenant Governor Arthur W. Coolidge of Massachusetts said in a public address before the American Veterans of World War II, at Quincy, Massachusetts: "I charge that Communism's key assault on the United States is starting in Hawaii. I accuse Moscow's secret agents of launching a new surprise attack on Pearl Harbor. If this attack is successful, it will be fully as harmful to our national security as was the sneak blow delivered by Japanese bombs." Lieutenant Governor Coolidge based his charges on a set of secret instructions issued by the Communist Party to its agents in Hawaii. These documents outlined a four-pronged Communist offensive in Hawaii, aimed simultaneously to undermine all religion, to penetrate and capture all labor unions, to discredit and undermine the free press, and to infiltrate all education.
>
> These documents were seized in the Hawaiian Islands by Federal authorities. They have become the basis of a determined further investigation of Communist penetration in the islands.[17]

Thus John Reinecke's paper of 1934–1935, "What Must We Do?" is referred to again. Butler had cited Lieutenant Governor Coolidge, who received the document from Governor Stainback, who received it from John Akau, who received it from John Reinecke—two or three years before the existence of a Communist party in Hawaii.

The *Honolulu Star-Bulletin* was thoroughly disgusted with Butler's accusations—and with his timing:

> The Senator's entire demeanor when he was in Hawaii last fall, as since, showed that he was against statehood legislation and the current statehood campaign. He apparently selected the period of the waterfront strike in Hawaii as the occasion most favorable to emphasize his theory that the strike is directly due to Communist influence, and manipulated by Communist leaders, and that Hawaii is in the political as well as economic grip of Commies taking their orders from Moscow. . . .
>
> He has charged that, under statehood, the Communists could elect the government, run the courts, boss the police, and rule Hawaii in the interests of Soviet Russia.
>
> This is in plain effect a charge that *the people* of Hawaii can and will be

> buncoed, bluffed and bamboozled into letting the Commies seize the islands.[18]

The cause of the anticommunists went national on 23 June 1949, when Lorrin Thurston took a two-page advertisement in the *New York Times* and subsequently the *Washington Post* and the *Washington Star.* Thurston's rhetoric was somewhat more restrained than in the pages of the *Advertiser,* but his message was the same:

> We are NOT in a position to prove this strike is Communist directed. But we do know that every move in the whole picture for fifteen years tallies exactly with the Communist manuals and their teachings—without any exceptions. We do know that every Communist list, as issued by the Un-American Activities Committee of the House of Representatives, contains as listed Communists the names of the men who are crucifying Hawaii.[19]

The advertisement's plea for help resulted in a flood of letters and telegrams urging President Truman to use the injunctive provisions of the Taft-Hartley Act to force the longshoremen back to work.

On 18 July 1949 a hearing was held in Washington, D.C., in the Senate caucus hearing room before the Senate Committee on Labor and Public Welfare. Jim Blaisdell represented the Hawaii Employers' Council; Harry Bridges represented the ILWU. Bridges complained of the employers: "Instead of treating it as a simple economic strike, they are blowing it up as a dangerous threat to the economy of the islands and they are trying to make it appear as a Communist plot. Neither charge is true." In an inevitable followup on the communist issue, Senator Wayne Morse of Oregon asked, "Mr. Bridges, do you deny the allegation that the motivation of the union and your leaders . . . is to communize the economic life of the islands?" Bridges shot back: "Oh, absolutely. . . . We are after a wage increase, nothing more and nothing less. If that is going to lead to communism, well, that is just too bad."[20] When Senator Robert A. Taft of Ohio asked Bridges, "Do you have any Communists as officers in your Union?" the response was not reassuring to those who feared the communist menace: "Offhand, I do not know," said Bridges. "We do not run around [looking for them], and I do not inquire."[21]

If Harry Bridges wasn't looking for communists among the union's leadership, others were. Speaking before a group of prominent Republicans in Honolulu, Edward Gibbons pushed the specter of communism beyond Hawaii and even beyond Moscow. Gibbons, publisher of a mainland anticommunist news service, charged that "Harry Bridges and his boys are forced to put their future in American labor on the block to help the cause of the Chinese Communists."[22] This was a sobering charge in the eyes of many anticommunists in 1949—the year America was alleged to have "lost" China to communism.

A New York magazine called *Plain Talk* printed a horror story about communism and Hawaii's dock strike under the title "How to Capture an Island: 5th Column Attacks Hawaii." The author, Steve Woods, described how "on May Day—the International Working Class Day in Moscow—the Communists launched their offensive to capture this strategic island group." Woods invited anyone who doubted him to consult with Ichiro Izuka.[23]

Perhaps the most elaborate mainland version of the conspiracy theory was the one developed by Edwin C. Heinke, assistant managing editor of the *Indianapolis Times*. Heinke wrote a four-part series describing "Moscow's operation in Hawaii." The series was syndicated by Scripps-Howard Newspapers and carried throughout the United States. The *Honolulu Advertiser* printed it in full. The series turned out to be almost entirely drawn from the Butler Report, the Izuka pamphlet, and "What Must We Do?" For four days in August 1949 the series was offered as "new evidence" of what the *Advertiser* had long been telling its readers.

By the end of July, Jack Hall was worried about federal intervention in the dock strike. He asked John Burns to go to Washington to see what he could do to educate people in the federal government about the true nature of the strike. Burns, the Democratic party's Oahu County chairman, went to the nation's capital—at union expense. Burns convinced Secretary of Labor Maurice Tobin that the strike was economic in nature and that the Big Five encompassed a nest of interlocking directorates that controlled the economy of the territory of Hawaii. The communist issue, Burns reported to Tobin, was a smokescreen. Through Tobin, Burns eventually made two key contacts that greatly aided the cause of the ILWU. First, he spoke with Alex Campbell, chief of the Department of Justice's Criminal Division, and convinced him to delay the federal government's prosecution of Harry Bridges, Bob Robertson, and Henry Schmidt for perjury in Bridges' 1945 naturalization hearing. Second, he convinced Frank Tavenner, chief counsel of HUAC, to delay hearings in Hawaii until after the strike was ended. For his efforts, Burns earned the undying appreciation of the ILWU—appreciation he would later convert into tangible political support.

On 6 August 1949 the territorial legislature, in special session, passed the Dock Seizure Act, which had been proposed by Governor Stainback. On 15 August the territory began operation of the Honolulu waterfront. The ILWU was enjoined against any further picketing. On 16 August there were two lonely pickets—Harry Bridges and Art Rutledge. Bridges had convinced Rutledge that, in spite of their differences, organized labor in Hawaii had to respond to the kind of strikebreaking activities into which the territorial government had entered.

For many the Dock Seizure Act was a measure sure to end the 1949 longshore strike. It did not. It was one thing to load ships in the territory of Hawaii. It was quite another to unload them in California. The real key for the Big Five was Matson. Four of the Big Five owned 40 percent of Matson's stock. Matson was losing $800,000 per month. Until Matson could unload sugar at the C & H refinery at Crockett, California, and the *Lurline* could once again sail between Hawaii and California, the union held the upper hand—and they knew it.

It was one of Matson's largest shareholders, Walter C. Buck of San Francisco, who started informal conversations with Harry Bridges that led to the end of the strike. Buck summoned Dwight Steele, president of the Hawaii Employers' Council, to San Francisco. By the time they headed back to Hawaii, on 2 October, the stage was set for the final negotiations. On 5 October the "fourteen plus seven" agreement was concluded. On 23 October, 177 days after it had begun, the 1949 longshore strike finally ended. The ILWU had reconfirmed itself as a major force in Hawaii's economy, but its victory came at a high price. The legacy of mistrust and bitterness would continue for years to come, often expressing itself in the fight against the perceived threat of communism.

Chapter 13

HUAC Comes to Hawaii

On 7 October 1949, two days after the longshore strike had been settled, the territorial legislature passed a concurrent resolution requesting the United States House Committee on Un-American Activities to come to Hawaii. The legislature wanted HUAC to investigate and report on the threat of internal subversion in the territory. The resolution stressed that HUAC's coming to Hawaii would provide an opportunity for any having been falsely accused of communist associations to clear their names. An example given at the time was Major Arthur B. Chun, whose name had appeared in one of the documents accumulated by the Roberts Commission while it was studying the attack on Pearl Harbor. Major Chun, with the aid of Senator Thelma Akana, was seeking to have his name cleared of any communist taint.

The resolution also made it clear that one of the reasons for inviting HUAC to Hawaii was to clear the last barrier standing between the territory and statehood. The resolution made no mention of the recent longshore strike. Copies were sent to President Harry S Truman, Speaker of the House of Representatives Sam Rayburn (D-Texas), Chairman of the House Committee on Un-American Activities John S. Wood (D-Georgia), and Delegate to Congress from the Territory of Hawaii Joseph R. Farrington.[1]

The *Honolulu Record* was skeptical about the resolution. The *Record* charged that the purpose was "not to provide the opportunity of proving one's 'innocence,' but to do a smear job on the Democratic Party and the ILWU."[2]

Senate president Wilfred Tsukiyama expressed his feelings about the resolution inviting HUAC to come to Hawaii at the regular monthly meeting of the board of directors of the Republican Club of Hawaii:

> The thing, in my opinion, that is dangerous about those tainted with Communism is that the very principle of the doctrine is one which not only advocates but encourages violence, disturbance, disorder, race clashes and, in the end, total revolution.
>
> I am very happy that the legislature has favorably entertained a resolu-

> tion to request the House subcommittee on Un-American activities of the Congress to come to Hawaii for the purpose of checking Communist activities in Hawaii. . . .
>
> If, however, the subcommittee should find it impossible to come to Hawaii to carry on investigations, the territory itself should undertake the same.[3]

It turned out not to be a question of one or the other. On 10 October 1949, by a vote of 25 to 4, the territorial House of Representatives passed a bill creating a territorial Subversive Activities Commission. Four days later the measure was approved by the territorial Senate. On 26 October 1949 Governor Stainback signed the measure into law. The idea was not a new one to the territorial legislature; two days before the beginning of the longshore strike, a similar measure was passed by the Senate, only to die in the House. The earlier bill, however, had called for a legislative committee rather than an independent commission. It was now felt that an independent commission would be less political in its approach to the problem. The Legislative Holdover Committee later created a Subcommittee on Un-American Activities, headed by Representative Charles E. Kauhane. A late entry into the anticommunist fray, the legislative committee was generally looked upon as superfluous and was never a significant force.

The territorial Subversive Activities Commission was to be composed of seven members, three of whom were to represent the islands of Kauai, Maui, and Hawaii. Members were to be appointed by the governor with the advice and consent of the Senate. At least three members, including the chairman, were required to be attorneys licensed to practice in all courts of the territory of Hawaii. The key functions of the commission were to investigate subversive activities and to file the results of their investigations with the territorial legislature. The commission was restricted from making any report public without prior approval of the governor or the legislature. The commission had subpoena power, and persons swearing falsely before it were subject to prosecution for perjury. Initial two-year funding was approved in the amount of $75,000.[4]

Governor Stainback announced the members of the territorial Subversive Activities Commission in December. The chairman was Edward N. Sylva, the man who had presided over the Reinecke hearing. Also included was William Borthwick, the political ally of Stainback and a vigorously anticommunist candidate for delegate to Congress in 1946. The history of the commission was not spectacular. They were constantly being upstaged: first by the coming of HUAC and then by Hawaii's Smith Act trial. There was pressure from many members of the territorial legislature to avoid anything that smacked of witch hunting. As the years passed, the legislature regularly lowered the appropriations for the commission. Careful scrutiny of the semiannual reports of the commission reveal that most of their information was derivative; the rest was of little consequence.

After the end of the 1949 longshore strike, there was an optimistic feeling among many in Hawaii that the issue of communism was being laid to rest. The *Honolulu Star-Bulletin*, in a four-part series on communism, summarized the results of three congressional statehood reports. The first, prepared in 1946 by Representative Henry D. Larcade, Jr., of Louisiana, made no mention of communism at all. The second, prepared in 1948 by Senator Guy Cordon of Oregon, observed: "The allegations of communist influences in Hawaii are no different than those directed against other places and the situation prevailing throughout the country." The third was the Butler Report, which recommended "without equivocation, that statehood for Hawaii be deferred indefinitely," saying that "international revolutionary Communism has, at present, a firm grip on the economic, political and social life of the Territory of Hawaii." The *Star-Bulletin* expressed hope that Senator Butler's allegations would be recognized as alarmist and untrue.[5]

With the national hysteria over communism growing rapidly, it was wishful thinking to believe that the communist scare in Hawaii would pass quickly. Scarcely a week after the resolution of the dock strike, the eleven Communist party leaders being tried in New York for violation of the Smith Act were found guilty. The story was given extensive coverage in the Honolulu press. The *Advertiser* editorialized: "Conviction of Communist leaders in America of plotting to overthrow the government may not outlaw their party, but it does remove the mask of innocence from Americans who remain in that party or who join it henceforth."[6]

The *Honolulu Record*, not surprisingly, saw the convictions in a different light:

> At Foley Square [in New York City] the freedom of thought and the freedom to express beliefs were put on trial, and not criminal acts committed by the Communists.
>
> In our country it is generally accepted that ideas are not subject to trial in court. We place confidence in individuals who are free to examine ideas, and to decide on the merits or lack of merits in them.
>
> During the trial—which was underlined heavily with thought control—the prosecution introduced as evidence Marxist books which are found in public libraries throughout the country and testimonies to show what these books mean. But defense efforts to present the defendants' understanding of the books were drastically curtailed.
>
> Political dissent thus became a crime.[7]

Koji Ariyoshi, editor of the *Record* and author of the editorial cited above, would be under indictment for violation of the Smith Act in less than two years.

Charles K. Fujimoto, chairman of the Communist Party of Hawaii, was even more vehement in his denunciation of the Foley Square decision:

> This blow against the Communist Party is not directed against the Communists alone, but against all those who uphold and fight for the best ideals of freedom and democracy. Just as Hitler, Mussolini and the Japanese militarists failed to destroy the Communist Parties in their respective countries, so will fascist minded monopolists and their stooges fail to smash the Communist movement in America.[8]

Fujimoto would also find himself under indictment for violation of the Smith Act in less than two years.

As the anticommunist movement gained momentum, in November 1949 the National Association for the Advancement of Colored People (NAACP) revoked the charter of the Honolulu chapter. The reason was an unresolved leadership struggle involving charges of communist infiltration. The national board of the NAACP, like the ACLU, did not want to risk appearing friendly to communism.

The Hawaii Residents' Association kept the anticommunists vigilant with a monthly newspaper called *IMUA'S Spotlight* and five radio broadcasts each week. IMUA often spoke of the burden of competing with the well-financed efforts of the Communist party. When IMUA produced figures on public relations dollars spent by Hawaii's Communist party, they always included in that figure an amount equal to the public relations budget for the ILWU.

IMUA was not without its critics in government. W. K. Bassett, administrative assistant to Mayor Wilson, looked upon this self-appointed group of superpatriots with distaste. "IMUA may mean 'forward' in Hawaiian," Bassett said, "but to me it means forward with a sheet over its head and carrying a flaming cross." With the arrival of HUAC expected, Bassett suggested: "This IMUA is something for the un-American committee members to investigate when they come to Hawaii. This IMUA, I charge, is a subversive organization, trying by force and threats of violence to overthrow reason and common sense in Hawaii."[9]

One of the reasons for Bassett's outburst was the role of IMUA in the coming constitutional convention, slated to begin in Honolulu on 4 April 1950—just six days before HUAC was scheduled to begin its hearings in Honolulu. The constitutional convention was funded by the territorial legislature for the purpose of drafting a constitution that would demonstrate Hawaii's fitness for statehood. IMUA had no official role in the constitutional convention but had taken upon itself to send a questionnaire to each of the candidates seeking to become a delegate. IMUA's questions included "Do you favor a state government patterned upon the individual, free enterprise system, or patterned to provide a welfare or social type of government?" and "To what extent do you believe in the rights of collective bargaining and the right to strike?"[10]

Bassett, as it turned out, had more to worry about than IMUA. While the territory of Hawaii was electing a very safe slate of candidates to the constitutional convention, Bassett found himself being denounced as a communist in the nationally syndicated column of labor writer Victor Riesel. Mayor John Wilson was most curious about Riesel's source of information. He had good cause to be curious, in light of Riesel's earlier association with Governor Stainback. Wilson wrote to four friends in Washington, D.C., to determine whether Stainback was involved. The mayor was concerned about more than Bassett's reputation, since Riesel had referred to Wilson as a "fatigued elderly fellow" who was totally under the domination of the "Red-tinged" Bassett. Riesel called Stainback, by contrast, "an intelligent and sophisticated opponent of Communists and Communism." Bassett wrote a three-page letter to Secretary of the Interior Oscar Chapman explaining that he was not nor had he ever been a member of the Communist party. He also denied Riesel's charge that the *Pacific Weekly*, a newspaper he had published in Carmel, California, in 1935, followed the Communist party line.[11]

Passage of a Hawaiian statehood bill on 7 March 1950 by the United States House of Representatives by the impressive margin of 212 to 110[12] gave fresh impetus to the coming constitutional convention. When the final selection of delegates was voted upon on 23 March 1950, almost 80 percent of Hawaii's eligible voters turned out. The constitutional convention opened on 4 April 1950, with Kauai businessman Randolph Crossley acting as temporary chairman. Crossley passed the gavel to Samuel W. King, who served as permanent chairman. Governor Stainback delivered an opening speech filled with hope and confidence to the assembled delegates. All delegates swore an oath declaring that they were not now nor had they been in the last five years members of the Communist party. It was an oath that one delegate would personally repudiate, with his surprise testimony before HUAC, less than a week after the convention began.

The subcommittee sent to Hawaii by HUAC was chaired by Francis E. Walter, a Democrat from Pennsylvania. HUAC, as it operated in 1950, advertised itself as the "new look" committee. It lacked the flamboyance it had known during the heyday of chairmen Martin Dies, John Rankin, and the recently disgraced J. Parnell Thomas. In addition to Walter, subcommittee members included Burr P. Harrison of Virginia, John McSweeny of Ohio, Morgan Moulder of Missouri, and Harold H. Velde, a former FBI agent, of Illinois. HUAC members not participating in the Hawaii hearings included chairman John S. Wood of Georgia and Richard M. Nixon of California. Nixon, the real star of the committee in its banner year of 1948, was in California preparing to take on Helen Gahagan Douglas for a seat in the United States Senate.

There was much speculation in Hawaii about the predisposition of the visiting HUAC members regarding statehood for Hawaii. According to "reliable sources" quoted in the *Honolulu Star-Bulletin*, HUAC members favored statehood for Hawaii by a six-to-two margin. This figure was based on a straw vote taken in Washington, D.C., after the members previewed the evidence that had been gathered by the committee's investigators.[13] On the day the HUAC hearings began, chairman Walter made it clear that he was aware of the Butler Report but that he disagreed with the senator from Nebraska on Hawaiian statehood.

In his opening remarks, Walter made his purpose clear: "The citizens of Hawaii have written a noble page in American history during the last war against totalitarian fascism. They have faced death with unflinching heroism and self-sacrifice. Today we are confronted with a new menace—the menace of totalitarian communism, which would destroy our democracy and lead us all down the road to slavery. This menace must be pitilessly exposed for what it is."[14]

The first of sixty-six witnesses came as a great surprise to the people of the territory of Hawaii. It was Richard Kageyama, an elected member of the board of supervisors of the City and County of Honolulu and a delegate to the constitutional convention. Only six days before, Kageyama had taken an oath that he was not and had not for the last five years been a member of the Communist party. Now, on 10 April 1950, Richard Kageyama revealed to HUAC that he had been a member of the Communist party for nine months in 1947. A former student of John Reinecke on the Big Island, Kageyama told how he had contacted his former teacher when he first came to Oahu in 1946. He told of having joined a Marxist study group and of having been invited to join the Communist party by Charles Fujimoto. Kageyama indicated that he had received his Party card from John Reinecke in February 1947. Disillusion was not long in coming, according to Kageyama. "I found that the Communist party was not meant for the people who live in a democratic nation," he explained. "I was disillusioned by the belief that they were for the common people, which, in later years, has proven to be otherwise."[15]

Kageyama's testimony about the Communist party itself provided no new revelations until he told of the Party's instructions to those who received subpoenas to appear before HUAC. He described a conversation with Charles Fujimoto in which he was told to contact Harriet Bouslog should he be served. Fujimoto was unaware that Kageyama had already agreed to appear before HUAC as a friendly witness. When Kageyama did appear, it was with his own counsel, Yasutaka Fukushima.

The most troubling aspect of Kageyama's appearance was that, although he had agreed to appear as a friendly witness as early as November 1949, he had gone ahead and run as a delegate to the constitutional convention. Kageyama explained that when he was contacted by HUAC, on 7 November 1949, investigator William A. Wheeler "told me that I would be called as an important witness when hearings would be held here in Hawaii and "impressed upon me the importance of disclosing this information to no one, no matter what the cost."[16] Kageyama's point was that his failure to seek a delegate's slot would have tipped people off that something unusual was afoot.

Within the hearings there was no opportunity for cross-examination. Outside, there were a number of assertions that Kageyama was acting in concert with the Stainback wing of the Democratic party. Gorman Noland, a member of the Democratic territorial central committee, was quoted in the *Honolulu Record* as having said that Kageyama had been advised to run as a delegate to the constitutional convention by people in "high places." Dr. Ernest Murai, another member of the Democratic Central Committee, indicated that he felt sorry for Kageyama, who was, in his estimation, "being used."[17]

Lau Ah Chew, chairman of the Democratic Central Committee, was less charitable, asserting, "Kageyama has struck a foul blow not only at the Democratic Party but primarily at our hopes for statehood."[18] Lau asserted that Kageyama was no longer a member of the Democratic party, having automatically relinquished his membership when he joined the Communist party in violation of the Democratic party's rule that no member could belong to another political party. Francis Walter, in contrast, praised Kageyama for his courage and asked that he not be punished for his actions. Walter went on, "In my judgment my party in Hawaii might better think of a thorough spring house-cleaning instead of discrediting courageous, real Americans."[19] Lau Ah Chew was furious with Walter, going so far as to wire President Truman to protest this intrusion into Hawaii's internal politics. The *Advertiser* quoted Walter's parting volley in their editorial pages: "Congressman Walter said with disdain, 'Lau Ah Chew is not my kind of Democrat.' "[20]

Another who felt that Kageyama had acted honorably was Governor Ingram Stainback:

> Richard Kageyama is to be commended for his courageous statement to the subcommittee of the House Committee on Un-American Activities Monday at Iolani Palace. Mr. Kageyama's determination to tell the truth, regardless of personal consequences, should serve as an example to others in the Territory. . . . Mr. Kageyama is probably a victim rather than a culprit, having fallen under the influence of his former teacher John Reinecke.[21]

At the constitutional convention, there were mixed feelings about how to handle Richard Kageyama as a delegate. He had clearly perjured himself when he took the loyalty oath, but there were those, like Randolph Crossley of Kauai, who felt Kageyama should be commended rather than expelled. A letter of commendation introduced by Crossley to the convention was rejected. Kageyama made it easy for the delegates by resigning, saying, "Further attendance at the Constitutional Convention as a delegate would embarrass my fellow delegates and prejudice the cause of statehood for Hawaii."[22]

Kageyama served out his term as a member of the board of supervisors in spite of efforts to force his resignation. He did not run for reelection in 1950 but did make a comeback in 1954 and 1956, when he served two more terms on the board of supervisors. In an interview in 1974, Richard Kageyama indicated that he had not, in 1950, acted on the basis of instructions from Governor Stainback; he had acted on his own. He expressed no bitterness over the events that had interrupted his promising political career.[23]

If Richard Kageyama's testimony had come as a surprise, the testimony of the second witness before HUAC was highly predictable—with one major exception. The witness was Ichiro Izuka. The bulk of his testimony repeated assertions made in his 1947 pamphlet *The Truth about Communism in Hawaii* and his testimony in the Reinecke hearing. But if it was an old story, it was not a short one. Izuka's testimony filled sixty-seven pages of the 455-page transcript of HUAC's hearings in Hawaii. Seventy-two of those pages contain the testimony of HUAC investigators William A. Wheeler and Courtney E. Owens. Thus, Izuka's testimony represents 17.5 percent of all testimony given by local witnesses. The testimony of the other sixty-five local witnesses averaged fewer than five pages each.

The one surprise in Izuka's testimony raised a furor at least equal to that unleashed by Richard Kageyama's testimony. Izuka named Frank G. Silva, ILWU business agent from Kauai, as a member of the Communist Party of Hawaii. As Izuka spoke, Silva sat as a delegate to the constitutional convention. It was not a case of a witness placing a man at a meeting of the Communist party and drawing possibly incorrect inferences. That sort of testimony was common in such hearings, but Izuka was not ambiguous:

> Frank Silva, I knew Frank Silva for a long, long time in the plantation, and many efforts was made to recruit Frank Silva in the Communist Party, but the only one who can contact him was Jack Hall, and Jack Hall did, or was instructed many, many times to recruit Frank Silva, but I think that no contact was made for a long time, officially, but after Frank Silva volunteered for the Army and after discharge from the Army, I had many,

> many talks with him in the restaurant, and finally one day at pier 11, he told me, "Well, Ichi, are you a Communist? Did you join the Communist Party?" And I said, "Yes, I joined way back in 1938." And he told me that he joined the party, and he showed me his card. That is the only incident that I know that Frank Silva told me that; he showed me the card. He said, "See my card, this is my card."[24]

The veracity of Izuka's statement was subject to serious question. HUAC counsel Frank Tavenner asked Izuka when the alleged meeting with Silva had taken place. "Oh, that was, I believe it was after the sugar strike," Izuka responded, "sometime early in 1947." That date would square with the end of the sugar strike, which came on 19 November 1946, but it seemed a doubtful conversation for Izuka to be having in early 1947, since he had testified that he had resigned from the Communist Party of Hawaii on 20 October 1946. Although Izuka did not have to fear cross-examination, Tavenner realized that Izuka's testimony was erroneous and that it would be exposed as such. Tavenner recalled Izuka, presumably after a conference, and asked him if he would like to correct any errors in his earlier testimony. Izuka replied: "Yes, by reading the papers, I found out that I would like to make a correction on the part when I said that Frank Silva showed me his party card in 1947. I am sure it is all of the members who joined the Communist Party, including Frank Silva, that was during the time before I resigned from the party in 1946, and that actually took part during the same time, instead of 1947."[25] This quotation is shown exactly as it appears in the transcript of the hearings. It was not uncharacteristic of Izuka when he was flustered. During the Reinecke hearing such statements were subjected to the withering cross-examination of Richard Gladstein. At the HUAC hearing there was no cross-examination, and HUAC counsel Frank Tavenner allowed Izuka's testimony to stand without so much as a question about what the witness was attempting to say.

After Izuka's initial statement, Frank Silva was immediately issued a subpoena to appear before HUAC to respond to the charge that he had been a member of the Communist party. On 13 April 1950 Silva appeared before the committee, taking his Fifth Amendment privilege against self-incrimination. Silva subsequently declared that he was not and had never been a member of the Communist party. He later explained that his unwillingness to testify before HUAC was based on the fact that he could have been subject to indictment for perjury had a grand jury believed Izuka rather than him. The freshness of the conviction of Alger Hiss for having perjured himself before HUAC gave weight to Silva's argument. In the eyes of his colleagues at the constitutional convention, however, it was not persuasive. The delegates argued that an innocent person should have nothing to fear from telling the truth to a committee of Congress. Frank Silva was expelled by a vote of 53 to 7.[26]

In all, thirty-nine witnesses took shelter behind the Fifth Amendment during the HUAC hearings in Hawaii. All were subsequently cited for contempt of Congress. They came to be known as the Reluctant Thirty-nine. They could have been known as the Reluctant Forty-seven were it not that seven individuals were released from their subpoenas and one could not be served. Those released were Mrs. Charles Fujimoto, Mr. and Mrs. Robert Wenkam, Mrs. Robert McElrath, Mrs. Jack Hall, Mrs. Ralph Vossbrink, and Mrs. John Reinecke—there was clearly some chivalry at work here. The witness who could not be served was David Thompson, educational director of the ILWU. In a 1975 interview, Thompson declined to comment on his avoidance of the subpoena, preferring to allow his absence to speak for itself.[27]

The Reluctant Thirty-nine were all represented by the law firm of Bouslog and Symonds. All submitted an identical motion to quash their subpoenas commanding them to appear before HUAC on the grounds that the subpoenas violated their constitutional rights under the First, Fourth, Fifth, Ninth, and Tenth amendments. The composition of the Reluctant Thirty-nine reveals the most notable element of the HUAC hearings in Hawaii—the apparent involvement of a significant portion of the leadership of the ILWU in the Communist Party of Hawaii. Of the thirty-nine, twenty-six stated under oath that they were either officers or employees of the ILWU. The list included not only the ILWU's regional director, Jack Hall, but such notable leaders of the union as Ernest Arena, president of ILWU Local 150; Marshall McEuen, who had been codirector of the ILWU's political action committee; Robert McElrath, the ILWU's director of public relations; and Jack Kawano, former president of ILWU Local 136.

Although Jack Kawano was included as one of the Reluctant Thirty-nine, his testimony was significantly different from that of the others so labeled. Nominally represented by Bouslog and Symonds, Kawano strayed from their instructions. After stating his name and employer, Kawano stated emphatically that he was not a member of the Communist party. Beyond that he would not go, taking the Fifth Amendment on all other questions. It was not a dramatic moment in the hearings. No mention was made of Kawano's unique testimony in the press. The moment assumed greater significance when Kawano later split with the ILWU.

Others among the Reluctant Thirty-nine who had close relationships with the ILWU included Ralph Vossbrink, president of the Oahu CIO Council; Jack Kimoto, number two man at the *Honolulu Record;* Rachel Saiki, an employee of the *Record;* and Jeanette Nakama Rohrbough, wife of a staff writer for the *Record.* Three of the Reluctant

Thirty-nine told the committee that they were unemployed: John Reinecke, the dismissed school teacher, and Mr. and Mrs. Dwight James Freeman. Mr. Freeman was frequently mentioned as an organizer for the Communist party. He was alleged to have been sent to Hawaii by district thirteen of the Communist Party of the United States (California and Hawaii) shortly after the end of World War II, to assist Jack Kimoto. Evidence was also offered that sought to demonstrate that Pearl Freeman, James Freeman's wife, had been an openly registered member of the Communist Party of California before coming to Hawaii with her husband.

One of the thirty-nine who attracted considerable attention was Wilfred Oka, secretary of the Oahu County Democratic Central Committee. Oka had led the charge in 1948, when the ILWU turned away from its political action committee, considering the Democratic party a better vehicle for the achievement of its political goals. Oka had played a critical role in the organization of voter precincts for the benefit of the ILWU. Now he was a suspected member of the Communist party.

The frequent charge, as that made by Robert McElrath on an ILWU radio show, that the primary purpose of the HUAC hearings was to "bust" the ILWU was not without foundation. Ralph Tokunaga, former president of ILWU Local 150 and one of the Reluctant Thirty-nine, used the radio to explain the reason he had not testified before the committee:

> I first began to think about it back in November 1949.
>
> At that time, agents of the [House] Un-American Activities Committee called at my home. They promised me all kinds of protection if I would cooperate with them. "You don't have to worry," they said, "We're out to get the big boys like Jack Hall and the rest." They said when Jack Hall and Robert McElrath and other union leaders are brought up on charges, nothing would happen to me. They even put pressure on my brother in an attempt to force me to give them a statement.
>
> Actually, I made up my mind to take the course I took after reading yesterday's newspapers about what happened to Richard Kageyama. . . . No doubt Mr. Kageyama was told, as I was told, that nothing would happen to him. Well, he took a chance. Look what happened.[28]

Ralph Tokunaga's desire not to appear as a witness before HUAC was not realized. William A. Wheeler, a HUAC investigator who had interviewed Tokunaga on 22 November 1949, took the stand and played a recording of his interview with the former ILWU officer. Tokunaga's conversation with Wheeler was filled with names of union members who were associated with the Communist Party of Hawaii. It was from such interviews that HUAC's counsel prepared themselves for the hearing.

In his taped interview with Wheeler, Tokunaga had freely admitted having been a member of the Communist party. He described his reasons for leaving the Party:

> Ichiro Izuka put out a pamphlet about Communism in Hawaii and that thing made such a big splash in the newspapers that I was scared. I didn't know what it was all about and just from what I saw at the meetings and Ichiro Izuka said did not jibe and I started thinking and told myself that there might be more than what's on the surface. This idea about Communists being the vanguard of the working people sounded all right but the ideas about communism taking over the world and making this a people's world, etc., had me scared. I didn't like the idea of any revolutionary overthrow of the American government. I like this government. It's done all right by me.[29]

Tokunaga's recorded testimony was typical of the experience of many union members who became involved with the Communist Party of Hawaii. They joined as an adjunct to their union membership, with the understanding that their membership would add to union solidarity and benefit the movement. The success of the union was their key concern and motivation. When they were confronted with communist theory, they became uninterested, confused, or frightened. When communism became a burning public issue, particularly with the publication of the Izuka pamphlet, there was a good deal of scurrying to get out of the Communist party.

The final witness to appear before the committee was Edward Berman, the controversial, outspoken Honolulu labor lawyer. Berman had offered himself as a witness after Emil Muller, a friendly HUAC witness, placed him at what Muller thought was a Communist party meeting in 1938. When Tavenner pushed Muller a bit, he indicated that he was not sure the meeting in question was actually a Communist party meeting, and he had no personal knowledge that Berman was a member of the Communist party. He added that he had seen Berman at no other meeting of the Communist party he had attended while he had been a member. Although Muller's testimony was hardly incriminating, Berman insisted on responding to it. He dismissed it, saying that Muller must have mistaken a trade union meeting for a Communist party meeting. With that rebuttal out of the way, Berman spent the remainder of his time outlining his anticommunist credentials. Berman was particularly proud that he had helped kill two local organizations rather than let them fall into the hands of the communist infiltrators. The first was the Hawaiian Association of Civic Unity (HACU); the second was the NAACP.

With Berman's testimony, the HUAC hearings in Hawaii came to a close. Those who had hoped that the hearings would bring peace to Hawaii's political scene were greatly disappointed, as the upcoming territorial Democratic convention would demonstrate. For those who had sought to display their militant anticommunism, the HUAC hearings had been a rousing success. "Now what do you think about Communism in Hawaii?" IMUA asked. "The recent congressional unAmerican committee investigation certainly verified what 'IMUA' has been preaching for many months: there is a well organized, well financed group of Communists operating in Hawaii. . . . Now is the time to do something about this foreign menace."[30]

Chapter 14

The Crest

The year 1950 proved to be the high tide of anticommunist activity in Hawaii. Like a wave that crests and breaks on the shore, creating a new shoreline with its constant pounding, the anticommunist surge sought to shape Hawaii's political and social future.

In the wake of the bitterness created by the 1949 longshore strike, it was clear that 1950 would not be an ordinary political year. A rift in the ranks of the Democratic party seemed inevitable. In December 1949 the party had established a five-man "harmony" committee. It consisted of two pro-Stainback men, Harold Rice of Maui and Foreman Thompson of the Big Island; two anti-Stainback men, Chuck Mau of Oahu and Takaichi Miyamoto of Maui; and one uncommitted "peacemaker," Ernest Heen of Oahu.

Harmony, however, was not to last—even among the members of the harmony committee. By the end of February the group had made three basic decisions: first, Harold Rice, former Maui senator and Princeton classmate of Governor Stainback, would run as the Democratic party's candidate for delegate to Congress; second, Governor Stainback would be induced to accept a position on the territorial supreme court; and third, a "native son" would be endorsed by the party for governor. These recommendations of the harmony committee were by no means unanimous. Foreman Thompson was in vigorous opposition. When the "deal" was leaked to the press, there was anger within the group over the leak and outside the group over the proposed deal.

The arrangement was probably doomed from the start. The vagueness of the third proposition, that a "native son" be endorsed for governor, posed a serious problem. To many, the natural way of fulfilling this proposition would be the endorsement of the venerable mayor of Honolulu, Johnny Wilson. Wilson was a political institution in his own right, but he was anathema to Governor Stainback. Although Wilson was personally impregnable, his enemies adopted the strategy of attacking the mayor through his controversial administrative assistant W. K. Bassett.

During the 1949 longshore strike, Bassett had been openly critical of

Stainback and the Dock Seizure Act. He was also an open critic of the U.S. government prosecution of the Smith Act case at Foley Square in New York City in October 1949. On 27 October 1949 the right-wing Democrats in the tenth precinct club of the fourth representative district of Oahu ousted Bassett as the club's president and voted resolutions supporting Judge Medina in the Smith Act case and Governor Stainback in the Dock Seizure Act. To compound the situation, Bassett emerged as a critic of the House Committee on Un-American Activities during its hearings in the spring of 1950.

While the Democratic party was making futile efforts to achieve harmony, the territory of Hawaii turned to the task of writing a constitution that, it was hoped, would serve the people of the nation's forty-ninth state. The election of delegates to the constitutional convention, nominally a nonpartisan contest, did not create significant tensions within the Democratic party; it was primarily a celebration of the Republican party's continuing control of the territory. The Democratic party's precinct club elections, however, were a different matter. Picking up where they had been so successful in 1948, the anti-Stainback forces' work at the grass-roots level assured that they would control the coming territorial Democratic convention.

Surveying the magnitude of the left-wing victory, the *Honolulu Record* reported that one Big Island delegate claimed, "There are only two delegates to the convention from the whole island we think might vote for the governor." The *Record* reported that, on Kauai, "some have said the anti-Stainback representation . . . may be as high as 90 percent." Maui reported a substantial anti-Stainback majority, as did Oahu's fourth and fifth districts. The governor's own precinct club, the twenty-first precinct of the fourth district, passed a resolution demanding that Stainback not be reappointed by President Truman.[1]

Hawaii's two pro-Stainback Democratic National Committee members, Charles Kauhane and Victoria Holt, made an effort to get permission from the Democratic National Committee to reorganize Hawaii's Democratic party. Governor Stainback called a meeting of twenty friendly party leaders at the governor's mansion to discuss the postponement of the territorial Democratic convention. The meeting, which took place on 24 April 1950, four days after the conclusion of the HUAC hearings, reflected the way in which the HUAC hearings had exacerbated the rift in the Democratic party. When the territorial Democratic convention convened on 30 April 1950, fourteen delegates and two alternates were members of the so-called Reluctant Thirty-nine, providing the issue that would tear the Democratic party apart.

On the eve of the territorial Democratic convention, the *Honolulu Advertiser* and the *Honolulu Record* demonstrated the polarity of views about the Democratic party that existed in the territory. They both spoke in tones of cautious optimism, but they did so in vastly different ways. The *Advertiser* opined,

> Hawaii's Democrats meeting in Territorial Convention today face a dual responsibility: an obligation to the political party whose principles they profess and an equal duty to the people of Hawaii to preserve the two-party system of government. If the delegates allow themselves to be subjugated to the Left Wing elements who took over their party machinery in 1946 and have been striving to establish rule or ruin of Hawaii's Democracy ever since, they will fail on both counts. . . .
>
> There is more hope that reason and party loyalty will prevail in this convention than was shown four years ago. Then the schemers were able to pose as "labor leaders" who had the confidence of a large section of Hawaii's wage earners. That pose carries no conviction today. Rank and file members of the ILWU have seen these self-elevated leaders exposed as political manipulators, defiant of the American people and their principles, and under a cloud with their own national CIO parent organization.
>
> They have seen these "leaders" working their own interests, employing the tactics of the Communist Party Line, defending convicted Communists and devoting their energies to gaining political power rather than to the welfare of labor.[2]

The *Record*, not surprisingly, took a different tack:

> During the past few years the Democratic Party has taken on a semblance of a real political party, based on active precinct clubs. . . . A great deal of planning, organizing and leg work were required. . . . Some of those who gave unstintingly of their time and effort to build the party are today under attack. The Big Five employers, their associates and the Republicans want nothing more than to see the Democratic Party split many ways. It is said that the Red Issue will be brought up Sunday at the convention as a move to oust those labeled "Communists." The last convention in 1948 weathered the same storm, and this convention evidently will too, with liberals holding the party together.[3]

As the convention began, Maurice Sapienza, a right-wing delegate, introduced a motion to deny seats to fifteen of the sixteen delegates and alternates who were among the Reluctant Thirty-nine. The sixteenth, Jack Kawano, was not asked to leave, because he had denied being a member of the Communist party before HUAC. (Kawano was cited for contempt of Congress for having refused to answer any of the other questions put to him by HUAC.) When Sapienza's motion failed, Ernest Heen and Harold Rice led ninety-one delegates, controlling 118 of the 510 floor votes including proxies, out of the auditorium at Kalakaua Intermediate School. They reconvened at the American Legion hall. To Frank Marshall Davis, a black writer for the *Honolulu Record*, "the Sunday walkout was a replica of the 1948 National Democratic Convention when a number of Southern delegates got tired of democracy."[4]

After the right-wing delegates had walked out, John A. Burns was unanimously elected chairman of the convention. O. Vincent Esposito, a rising young figure among the liberals, declared: "This is the new Democratic Party."[5] Esposito's rhetoric proved to be prophetic, for it was out of the left-wing coalition that remained at the Kalakaua Intermediate School in 1950 that the "political revolution" of 1954 was fashioned.

Although the Walkout Democrats, as they were called, saw themselves as the enemies of communism within the party, it did not follow that the Standpat Democrats saw themselves as friends of communism. The Standpat convention passed six resolutions, the last three of which proved their orthodoxy: first, they endorsed Johnny Wilson for governor of the territory of Hawaii; second, they condemned the administration of Governor Stainback; third, they declared the seats held by Walkout Democrats Charles Kauhane and Victoria Holt on the Democratic National Committee vacant; fourth, they passed a resolution supporting the Truman administration; fifth, they declared their support of the Marshall Plan; and sixth, they passed a resolution condemning communism.

Governor Stainback gave his stamp of approval to the Walkout Democrats by phone from the mainland. Approval also came from representatives Francis Walter and Morgan Moulder of HUAC. Acting Governor Oren E. Long spoke to the Walkout Democrats at the American Legion hall in the role of peacemaker: "A development of this kind sometimes is essential and such developments have the possibility of building a much stronger Democratic Party. . . . But let us be careful of labels and name calling. Let us be certain that we keep in our ideal of democracy that which will make Americans of great diversity of opinion feel at home".[6] The Walkout Democrats, however, were more interested in the reorganization of the Democratic party along conservative lines than in making peace. After Ernest Heen and Harold Rice were elected cochairmen by acclamation, a committee was appointed to draft a statement enumerating the reasons for their action. This committee consisted of Hyman Greenstein, Maurice Sapienza, Arthur K. Trask, Foreman Thompson, and William Miles.

The formal statement only repeated what had already been said. More subtle factional struggles within the party would be articulated only in back-room discussions. The public reason for the walkout was repeated in a letter from Harry Kronick, right-wing advisor to the Young Democrats. Kronick wrote to William Boyle, chairman of the Democratic National Committee: "There can be no flag of peace flying the hammer and sickle. We can make peace and reorganize the party with fellow Democrats, not fellow travelers."[7]

The Standpat Democrats named Chuck Mau chairman of the territorial central committee, replacing the controversial Lau Ah Chew, and proceeded to go to work to establish itself as visibly anticommunist. John Burns was retained as chairman of the Oahu County central committee, but Wilfred Oka was replaced as secretary. His place was taken by a young war veteran just out of law school, Daniel Inouye.

Addressing themselves to the specific issue that had split the convention, the Standpat Democrats announced on 9 May 1950 that the fifteen delegates whose seats had been contested would be required to sign the following affidavit:

> A request has been made of me by Takaichi Miyamoto, a member of your committee, that I again inform the Democratic Party that I am not a member of the Communist Party.
>
> Obviously, this request is prompted by my refusal to testify before the House Un-American Activities Committee, on the advice of my attorneys, as to whether or not I am now, or ever have been, a member of the Communist Party.
>
> While I believe that my application for membership in the Democratic Party should be sufficient proof that I hold membership in no political party other than the Democratic Party, and while I believe that the Democratic Party should be fighting more vigorously in defense of our Bill of Rights, I am compelled to recognize that a refusal to comply with your request might damage the public position of the Democrats in these trying times.
>
> Therefore, I repeat, although reluctantly, that the only political party to which I belong is the Democratic Party and that I support and will continue to support its platform and principles. I am not a member of the Communist Party.[8]

Takaichi Miyamoto, who was given the responsibility of obtaining the signed affidavits from the fifteen Democrats in question, had been an active Democrat since 1918. He had been a member of the territorial Democratic central committee for thirty years. Miyamoto was selected for this task as a symbol of the Democratic party's long history in Hawaii. The letter, a carefully worded compromise document, had been approved unanimously by a committee that included four of those required to sign it. The committee made it clear that failure to sign the letter would be interpreted as an admission of membership in the Communist party. Those found guilty of such membership would be expelled from the Democratic party.

The Walkout Democrats' reaction to the affidavit was predictable. The most common criticism was that the affidavit failed to address the question of whether the affiant had *ever* been a member of the Communist party. Charles Kauhane challenged Miyamoto's right to obtain the affidavits. Kauhane suggested that, as chairman of the territorial legislature's holdover Un-American Activities Committee, he "would welcome anyone who was willing to come in and purge himself of Communist taint." Leon K. Sterling, Sr., echoed Kauhane's statement, adding that he was offended by the word "reluctantly" in the affidavit. "Why should anyone be reluctant about signifying his political affiliation?" Sterling asked. "If you take out the 'although reluctantly' and put in 'emphatically' I might believe them." Victoria Holt was more blunt, saying that the affidavit was "not worth the paper it's written on."[9]

Faced by the Standpat Democrats' appointment of Johnny Wilson and Harriet Magoon to the Democratic National Committee (DNC), Charles Kauhane and Victoria Holt took their case to the DNC meeting in Chicago in mid-May. The DNC refused to become involved in a factional dispute in the territory of Hawaii. Kauhane and Holt were seated at the meeting, without consideration of the merits of the Walkout-Standpat dispute, on the basis that only death or resignation would create a midterm vacancy. The DNC requested that Hawaii's two members return to the territory and build a unified Democratic party. The DNC's plea for harmony was interpreted by Kauhane and Holt as a mandate for the reorganization of the party. In the eyes of the *Honolulu Advertiser*, it was "a warning to all Democrats in Hawaii that they are expected to clean house in their local organization."[10]

When confronted with the Kauhane-Holt interpretation of the DNC's statement, Johnny Wilson bristled: "They are going to have one hell of a time reorganizing the party when they get back. . . . Our precinct clubs are already organized and they are not going to reorganize."[11]

Although the language being bandied about was highly charged, the general public was notably disinterested. On 19 May 1950 the Honolulu Elks Club held what was billed as a "giant" rally in Ala Moana Park to cap its "Wake Up America Week." The speakers included Samuel Wilder King, president of the constitutional convention, the Reverend Henry P. Judd, and spokesmen from the army and the navy. When the speakers almost outnumbered the audience, the rally was scrapped.

IMUA, the most vocal anticommunist organization in the territory of Hawaii, chose the same moment to launch a fundraising campaign "to finance our educational program against Communism, socialism and all other un-American, subversive activities in Hawaii."[12] IMUA's campaign was approved by the Honolulu Chamber of Commerce, the Honolulu Better Business Bureau, and J. Edgar Hoover, among others. In a letter to IMUA, the FBI director wrote: "It is heartening to note that the Communist conspiracy is daily being subjected to the pitiless glare of publicity. As I have said many times, Communism cannot thrive out in the open where it can be seen and measured by the American public. The work which your Hawaii Residents' Association (IMUA) is doing will undoubtedly help expose the true menace of Communism."[13]It is significant that IMUA never reported the results of this fundraising campaign. In a 1975 interview, Tony Todaro, a leading writer for *IMUA Spotlight* during the early 1950s, confirmed the organization's frustration over its failure to gain a broad public following. Although initially well financed, IMUA represented only a small segment of Honolulu's business community.[14]

Without public support for their virulent brand of anticommunism, the efforts of the Walkout Democrats to reorganize the Democratic party were destined to fail. On 5 June 1950 the Walkout Democrats called on all true Democratic party members to reregister during the period from 10 June through 10 July. Applications were made available through Leon K. Sterling, Sr., who was both chairman of the Walkout territorial Democratic central committee and Honolulu's city clerk. Sterling further proclaimed: "No one is authorized to solicit or accept funds, or to incur any indebtedness in the name of the Democratic Party unless authorized by me." John Burns called Sterling's move "an attempt to rule by minority."[15] The ploy did not work. By the end of the monthlong campaign, Sterling's office was able to report only 1,181 membership cards processed—far short of the goal of ten thousand that had been sought.[16]

By mid-July both wings of the Democratic party were in a state of disarray. The Walkout Democrats were arguing over whether their walkout had committed them to support Governor Stainback for reappointment. William E. Miles, president of the thirty-third precinct club of the fifth district of Oahu declared, "It was understood beforehand that the walkout was not to cover endorsement of the governor or any other action except to protest the seating of the fifteen challenged delegates."[17] Miles announced not only that he was leaving the Walkout faction of the Democratic party, but that he was taking his 130-member precinct club with him. Miles and his followers were among the many Democrats who, in essence, sat out the 1950 elections. Arthur K. Trask, another of the original Walkout group, complained that, when he asked the thirty-member organizing group to work in the interest of party unity, he had been shouted down. Trask took another walk and returned to the Democratic party's mainstream.

In the meantime, the Standpat Democrats had expelled five of the fifteen challenged delegates to the territorial Democratic convention for failure to sign the required affidavit. The five were Rachel Saiki, John Akana, Tadashi Ogawa, Ben Kaahawinui, and Levi Kealoha. A sixth, Adele Kensinger, had resigned from the party. The nine who signed were Yasuki Arakaki, Thomas Yagi, Kameo Ichimura, Robert K. Murasaki, Shigeo Takemoto, Robert Kunimura, Wilfred Oka, Yukio Abe, and Fred Kamahoahoa. In mid-July there was a move to obtain a less equivocal loyalty statement. This time they intended it to be signed by all thirty Democrats among the Reluctant Thirty-nine, not just the fifteen delegates to the territorial Democratic convention. The new affidavit was short and to the point: "To Whom It May Concern: I am NOT a Communist. I am a member of the Democratic Party of Hawaii. I endorse the principles of the Democratic Party and pledge my undivided support of its rules and platforms."[18]

What was left of the Walkout Democrats in early August unanimously pledged themselves to submit any plan for party reconciliation to Francis Walter, chairman of HUAC, for his approval. A small group of Walkout Democrats who called themselves the "young Turks" met with Governor Stainback on 14 August 1950 and reported with pleasure that the governor had assured them that he would have nothing to do with any Democratic party that had not purged itself of the Reluctant Thirty-nine.

The national Democratic party did not intervene in the Hawaii situation. When President Truman had to select two circuit court judges for the territory of Hawaii, he did so with great care. The president appointed Chuck Mau, one of the leaders of the Standpat Democrats, and Maurice Sapienza, one of the leaders of the Walkout Democrats. While the Truman administration sought to be evenhanded, others on the national scene were less so. Whereas Maurice Sapienza's nomination was quickly approved by the U.S. Senate, Chuck Mau's nomination was bottled up in the Senate Judiciary Committee by Senator Pat McCarran, the author of the Internal Security Act of 1950 and a fervent anticommunist. McCarran, a longtime supporter of Governor Stainback, delayed Mau's confirmation into 1951. Mau, of course, was strongly opposed to Stainback's reappointment. There is little doubt that McCarran's actions were directly related to his efforts in behalf of Stainback. In a letter to Secretary of the Interior Oscar Chapman, McCarran made the following observations:

> About the most complete Communist organization I have yet encountered, I found to exist in the Hawaiian Islands. It was not at all strange that this group was working actively to embarrass and, if possible, to defeat the reappointment of Governor Stainback. They are undoubtedly still at it from all that I can learn, and the fact Governor Stainback has not been reappointed is water on the Communist wheel. . . .
>
> To be very frank with you, Mr. Secretary, I am sick and tired of this placating and appeasing Communist organizations and Communist fronts, and I don't think it behooves your department or the administration to indulge in it.[19]

In 1951 Chuck Mau accompanied Jack Kawano to Washington, D.C., where Kawano told the full story of his involvement with the Communist party to HUAC. Part of Mau's purpose in encouraging Kawano to go and in accompanying him on the trip was to overcome any feeling in Washington, D.C., that he was soft on communism.

As the 1950 election campaign got under way in Hawaii, there were efforts to achieve at least some surface unity. The Walkout Democrats endorsed Standpat Democrat Chuck Mau's nomination to the federal bench. The two Oahu County central committees merged into one, although the territorial central committees did not. Tommy Wong, a legislative candidate from the fifth district of Oahu, expressed the frustration of many Democrats when he announced that he would run an independent campaign, not wanting "to be associated with the party, split the way it is now."[20]

There was no candidate with any "taint of communism" running for office in 1950. Thus, in a column titled "Political Notes," a *Star-Bulletin* reporter observed: "The anti-Communist theme is down but not out in the Republican campaign strategy. Chairman Randolph Crossley has put the slogan, 'Sell the Republican Record of Achievement,' in the number one spot. But in almost every speech recently he also has reminded the voters that the Republican Party is the only one that's free of any suspicious taints."[21]

The only race among the Democratic primary contests of 7 October 1950 that had dramatic overtones related to the territorial Democratic convention of the previous May was the mayor's race. In that contest, Walkout Democrat Ernest Heen was challenging the Standpat incumbent, Johnny Wilson. Wilson's victory over Heen by a vote of 15,608 to 10,058 reflected Wilson's immense personal popularity.[22] In spite of his victory, Johnny Wilson was in a surly mood. Commenting on the poor Democratic voter turnout, Wilson blamed the Walkout Democrats. "The price we have had to pay for this foolishness," Wilson said, "is too high."[23] Wilson went on to win the general election over Republican attorney James Gilliland by more than 12,000 votes. Joseph R. Farrington was returned to Congress by a wide margin, and the Republicans retained comfortable majorities in the territorial House and Senate.

The most significant event of 1950 was the beginning of the Korean War on 25 June. Beyond the obvious impact the Korean emergency would have on Hawaii as a center of military activity in the Pacific, it also raised the question of loyalty for the ILWU.

In April 1950 Harry Bridges had been convicted of perjury for having lied about his alleged membership in the Communist party at the time he became a citizen in 1945. That conviction was under appeal when, on 16 June 1950—just nine days before the invasion of South Korea began—Bridges' citizenship was revoked. The implementation of the order revoking Bridges' citizenship was set aside by the courts pending the outcome of his appeal, and Bridges was free on bail.

Shortly after the Korean War began, Harry Bridges became an outspoken critic of American intervention and of the internationalization of the conflict through the United Nations. On 28 June, three days after the outbreak of the Korean War, at a regularly scheduled meeting of San Francisco's ILWU Local 10, a group of officers of the union offered a motion giving full support to President Truman and pledging no interruption of shipping during the conflict. Bridges' efforts to block the motion resulted only in delaying it for one week.

Bridges' opposition to the Korean War caused wheels to turn in Washington, D.C., among those who wanted to get rid of the ILWU leader. On 2 August 1950 Harry Bridges was back in the courtroom of Judge George B. Harris, the man who had presided over his perjury trial. Bridges was asked to show cause for not having his bail revoked. Speaking in his own defense on 4 August, Harry Bridges said: "I am against the war. If I cannot speak my opinion on war, I might as well go to jail now." Judge Harris was happy to comply. In his ruling, Harris wrote:

> Mr. Bridges is an agent dedicated to the execution of the Communist program nationally and internationally. I am led to believe from the proceedings before me that he probably is one of the most important figures in the Communist Party in America today.
>
> Mr. Bridges' conduct since the inception of hostilities in Korea has been such as to justify this Court in concluding that when the welfare of his country is at stake, his loyalty is and must be with the Communists.
>
> He has spearheaded, since his release on bail, a serious opposition to security measures designed to protect the people of San Francisco, this port and the welfare of our armed forces. This opposition was taken to protect the Communist Party and his Communist cohorts within his union —not for the benefit of the union. . . .
>
> The Army and Navy and Marine Corps will hold the beachheads in Korea. Our duty at home is to protect the beachheads that involve internal security. Mr. Bridges instituted a delaying action regarding certain vital resolutions before his union.
>
> I say he will continue this delaying action as long as this country is engaged in conflict with the Communists on the other side.
>
> Accordingly, and for good cause, I revoke and vacate the order admitting Harry Bridges to bail.[24]

With Bridges in jail, the union rallied around their leader. At the Pacific coast ILWU convention at North Bend, Oregon, in mid-August, the delegates gave Harry Bridges a resounding vote of confidence as their president and voted to deny CIO representatives, including Phil Murray, the right to address the convention. Two weeks later, on 29 August 1950, the ILWU was officially expelled from the CIO. Although the delegates had supported Bridges the man, they went on to repudiate his views on the Korean War. The convention condemned the North Korean aggression and went on record declaring that the union would tolerate no work stoppages or demonstrations that would hamper the war effort. When asked about the seeming contradiction between the union's support of Bridges and the repudiation of his views, Richard Gladstein responded that not giving Bridges a vote of confidence "would have been like the Israelites repudiating Moses after he had led them out of Egypt just because it wasn't all they had expected."[25]

In Hawaii, Bridges' jailing ignited a series of protest strikes that the ILWU called spontaneous and the employers branded as illegal. Regional director Jack Hall protested:

> This jailing is a gross violation of the fundamental right to bail guaranteed in the Bill of Rights except for capital crimes. Bridges is certainly less of a threat to the "security" of our nation than the Wall Street and Missouri crowd surrounding President Truman. . . .
>
> War cargoes are moving to the Korean front and no member of the ILWU, including Bridges, is making any effort to impede that movement. The war situation is being used simply as a phony excuse to carry out the illegal detention of Bridges.
>
> You can't blame the thousands of workers who left their jobs this morning on the Big Island in protest against the jailing of Bridges. . . . They respect and support him. They know he could have taken the easy way out for himself—at their expense. . . .
>
> What the working people of Hawaii have gained in the last decade has been achieved in spite of those who are out to get Bridges and in the face of their determined opposition.[26]

In all, seventeen twenty-four-hour work stoppages, involving some eight thousand workers, were reported in the territory of Hawaii. In most cases the workers were hit with twenty-four-hour suspensions in retaliation for their action. The *Honolulu Advertiser* was agitated enough to initiate another series of "Dear Joe" letters, the first of which began as follows:

> Dear Joe:
>
> Just thought you might like to be brought up to date, Joe, on what's going on in Hawaii. You'll remember that this is the year of labor peace—1950.
>
> Yes, sir! Joe! Peace by negotiated legal contracts—signed, sealed and delivered just like they was legal, honest and to be lived up to by both sides (What a laugh!).
>
> Think you'll be pleased to know that we've had 39 (or is it 29) strikes, though, since the first of the year. Been able to keep things stirred up. All the time. Just like you teach. . . .
>
> The boys have been able to make hay over 'Arry's being put in the clink! Gave a swell excuse to pull "indignation" stop work jobs everywhere.
>
> Just spontaneous, you know! No planning—no schedule—just Island by Island, business by business, plantation by plantation. Remarkable!
>
> Distressing as hell to the Union leaders! They all say nothing—just act-

ing surprised each day (like you when Korea was attacked). But they has to work like the devil to keep from laughing out loud.

We'll keep it up, Joe, as long as we can. As loyal Americans helping the boys over in Korea, that's our job ain't it?

What we don't like, tho, is the fact that Congress is getting tough. 39 guys that wouldn't talk before the un-American Committee (as we call it) ain't beginning to sleep so well. . . .

Well, Joe, you got problems too. Plenty of 'em. Just remember one thing. These dumb Americans get sore after you kid 'em too long—and when they get sore, they get tough.[27]

There were those in Hawaii who saw the expulsion of the ILWU from the ranks of the CIO as an opportunity to break the power of the union in the territory. A week before the decision to expel the ILWU was announced, Timothy Flynn came to Hawaii. Flynn was Harry Bridges' replacement as the CIO's regional director for northern California and Hawaii. His mission was to explore the possibilities for separating Hawaii from the west coast, keeping the territory's workers in the CIO. Commenting on such efforts, Robert McElrath snapped, "We expect the termites to crawl out of the wood very shortly. I think we'll be able to use a flit gun on them."[28]

By Labor Day 1950 the ILWU had reason to feel better about matters. The U.S. Court of Appeals in San Francisco had overturned Judge Harris' order to revoke bail in a two-to-one split. Harry Bridges had been released from jail on 24 August. On Labor Day in Honolulu the AFL and the ILWU held separate parades and rallies. At the conclusion of the AFL parade, a crowd estimated at 250 heard Governor Stainback say: "The time has come when we should face the facts and no longer pussyfoot for fear of offending the so-called labor leaders who are Communist organizers behind the mask of labor leadership." At the same time, a crowd estimated at 2,500 heard W. K. Bassett, Mayor Wilson's much maligned administrative assistant, praise the leader of the ILWU: "I have known Harry Bridges for 40 years," Bassett told the gathering, "and I have never known anything about him except that he has worked every waking minute for the little man."[29]

Hopes for statehood also began to rise in September 1950. In March 1950 the U.S. House of Representatives had passed HR49 by a two-to-one margin. In June the Senate Interior and Insular Affairs Committee had approved sending the bill to the the floor of the Senate by a nine-to-one vote, the sole dissenting vote having come from Hugh Butler. The Korean War had given an imperative quality to the statehood bill for many. In September Democratic Senator Frank P. Graham of North Carolina told his Senate colleagues: "Statehood would strengthen the Hawaiian and Alaskan position against Communism. Now is a most strategic time for the admission of both as timely expressions of self-determination of people."[30] Graham, a liberal southern senator and a highly respected former president of the University of North Carolina, was defeated in his 1950 bid for reelection. One of the principal reasons given for his defeat was Graham's support of President Truman's civil rights program, of which Hawaiian statehood was a part. After the communist issue had become largely neutralized as an antistatehood issue, the real power behind the move to block Hawaiian statehood revealed itself: A coalition of southern Democratic senators, led by Richard B. Russell of Georgia, made it abundantly clear that they fully intended to filibuster any Hawaiian statehood measure that reached the floor of the Senate. As another member of the coalition, Senator Allen J. Ellender of Louisiana, put it, "When there is a snake in the grass, I believe in hitting it on the head."[31] The snake Ellender and Russell saw probably had more to do with race than with political persuasion.

On 11 August 1950, as the political season was beginning in earnest, the Reluctant Thirty-nine were cited by the U.S. House of Representatives for contempt of Congress. The citations were turned over to the United States attorney in Hawaii, Ray J. O'Brien, for legal action. O'Brien's next step was to put the citations before a federal grand jury for indictment. That action was delayed, however, when Francis Walter announced on 14 August that HUAC's hearings in Hawaii might be reopened. The Reluctant Thirty-nine would have an opportunity to purge themselves of their contempt. "They now realize," Walter said, "that we weren't putting on a show when we staged our hearing."[32] HUAC reported that eight of the thirty-nine had indicated their willingness to cooperate. No one was named, however, and the newspapers were unable to identify any of the prospective members of what was now being referred to as the Repentant Eight.

The newspapers were fed regular stories about HUAC's imminent return. On 8 September it was reported that the committee would reopen hearings in Honolulu on 23 September, with Chairman Wood and Representative Nixon slated to be among those participating. On 18 September HUAC investigator William A. Wheeler arrived in Honolulu "to conduct a supplemental investigation."[33] On 20 September Wheeler announced that "if" HUAC came back to Hawaii, there would be some "new faces" among those called as witnesses. On 26 September Wheeler told reporters that HUAC was not coming back to Hawaii because the committee had political commitments elsewhere and because they had been unable to obtain sufficient supplemental material to warrant a new hearing. Nothing was said of the Repentant Eight.

With the return of HUAC now out of the picture, U.S. Attorney Ray J. O'Brien presented the contempt charges against the Reluctant Thirty-nine before the federal grand jury in Honolulu. On 13 October 1950 the defendants were arraigned on the basis of indictments handed down by the grand jury. Thirty-eight were represented at the indictment by the law firm of Bouslog and Symonds; Jack Kawano was represented by his own attorney, Norman K. Chung.

Delay followed delay, as attention turned to Washington, D.C., where the U.S. Supreme Court was hearing a Fifth Amendment case involving Mrs. Patricia Blau of Denver, Colorado. Mrs. Blau had been cited for contempt for failing to answer, before a federal grand jury in Denver, questions concerning her employment by the Communist party and about her understanding of the inner workings of the Party organization. Mrs. Blau's right to silence was upheld in a unanimous Supreme Court decision. In a two-page opinion, Justice Hugo Black declared that in light of the recent conviction of eleven top Communist party leaders in New York for violating the Smith Act, Mrs. Blau's fear of prosecution was more than "a mere imaginary possibility; she could reasonably fear that criminal charges might be brought against her if she admitted employment by the Communist Party or intimate knowledge of its workings."[34]

Since the Blau decision did not deal directly with testimony before congressional committees, the U.S. Attorney's Office proceeded with its plans to prosecute the Reluctant Thirty-nine. Howard K. Hoddick, who had replaced O'Brien, selected five test cases. On 15 and 16 January 1951 Judge Delbert Metzger heard the cases, finding for the defendant in each instance. Hoddick had attempted to overcome the Blau decision with a three-part argument: first, he contended that there was a significant difference between a grand jury and a congressional hearing, the former being involved with criminal proceedings whereas the latter was not; second, he asserted that the thirty-nine were immune from criminal prosecution for any testimony they might have given before a congressional committee; and third, he pointed out that the admission of membership in the Communist party was not a crime, and, therefore, the defendants had nothing to worry about anyway. Judge Metzger ruled for the defendants, observing: "I can't see any actual difference in the procedure, whether before a grand jury, a congressional committee or any inquisitorial body. The Constitution stands like a rock of Gibraltar with the same force and effect whether the questioning is before a grand jury or any other body."[35]

After the first five judgments of acquittal, Hoddick sought to have the remaining thirty-four cases dismissed. Defense counsel Myer Symonds objected: "It would be a gross injustice for them not to know what is going to happen in the next couple of years." Judge Metzger agreed, saying, "If the defendants want a trial, they are entitled to it."[36] On 19 January 1951 the remaining thirty-four were granted a joint verdict of acquittal. Perhaps to demonstrate that his decision should not be interpreted as one friendly to communism, Judge Metzger expressed his hope that members of the local community would not become "contaminated . . . by association with the Communist Party."[37]

At the conclusion of the trial of the Reluctant Thirty-nine, Harriet Bouslog and Myer Symonds issued a statement:

> Vindication of the 39 witnesses in Hawaii who refused to be coerced and intimidated into violating their conscience and surrendering their constitutional rights is good news to all liberty loving people. . . . This decision emphasizes and makes more shocking the [injustices done to] those courageous men and woman who have served and are serving jail sentences for refusing to surrender to the committee and give up their rights. . . .
>
> Hawaii's 39 reluctant witnesses stood on the ancient right to silence guaranteed by the Fifth Amendment to the Constitution of the United States. The Hollywood 10 stood on the right to freedom of speech and of conscience guaranteed by the First Amendment.
>
> Our constitutional history makes it abundantly clear that the Bill of Rights was intended to protect and guarantee the right to speech, conscience and silence.
>
> Time and time again during the hearings of the un-American Committee in Hawaii, Chairman Francis Walter and the other members of the committee and the counsel for the committee sought to intimidate witnesses by telling them flatly that they faced jail for contempt and that their lawyers were giving them bad advice in advising them to refuse to answer on the grounds that their answers might tend to incriminate them.
>
> No more un-American conduct can be conceived than coercion by elected representatives of government to force persons against their will to surrender their constitutional rights.[38]

The year 1950 was, indeed, the year in which the wave of anticommunism in Hawaii crested and broke. It was not over—the force and backwash of this powerful wave would be felt by many—but the ILWU and the Democratic party had been hit with everything the opposition could throw at them, and both were still intact. No single year produced a greater volume of anticommunist activity than 1950: the HUAC hearings, the Reluctant Thirty-nine, the constitutional convention, the walkout at the territorial Democratic convention and the subsequent elections, the onset of the Korean War, the statehood bill, and the expulsion of the ILWU from the CIO. There was more to come, but by the end of 1950 those with exceptionally good vision could see the light at the end of the tunnel.

Chapter 15

Kawano Goes to Washington

After the fireworks of 1950 Hawaii looked forward to a more peaceful year in 1951. It started quietly enough. The acquittal of the Reluctant Thirty-nine attracted little attention, except among the superpatriots of IMUA. In March, however, the issue of communism came to life on the campus of the University of Hawaii.

Controversy arose when university president Greg Sinclair canceled an invitation that had been extended to the noted scientist Linus Pauling. Pauling, a member of the faculty at California Institute of Technology (Caltech), had been asked to speak at the dedication of the university's new chemistry building. Sinclair explained, "After learning that Dr. Pauling has affiliations with organizations that have been referred to as subversive, and also that he has refused to testify under oath that he is not a Communist, I felt that it was not in the best interest of the university to invite him to be the speaker."[1] There was a touch of irony in Sinclair's explanation, as he was a member of the Institute of Pacific Relations, an organization labeled subversive by the U.S. attorney general.

Pauling, who would receive the Nobel prize in chemistry in 1954 and the Nobel peace prize in 1962, protested Sinclair's action, which apparently had been dictated by the university's board of regents. In a letter to Sinclair and the regents, Pauling stated that the decision to rescind the invitation had caused him great embarrassment. He went on to say that he was not nor had he ever been a member of the Communist party. He defended his right not to testify publicly on the question, however, as a matter of conscience. Sinclair and the regents were unyielding.

Student protest was immediate, led by two students who would later achieve substantial reputations in the fields of politics and journalism. Shunichi Kimura, a future Big Island mayor and judge, was then president of the student body at the University of Hawaii. Kimura headed a movement to bring Pauling to the campus as a student-sponsored speaker. John Griffin, later a distinguished writer for the *Honolulu*

Advertiser, spoke out in *Ka Leo O Hawaii*, the student newspaper: "In light of recent events, it should start to become obvious to the average man that the crusade against 'creeping Communism' could, and may, be a thinly veiled cover-up for creeping Fascism. . . . The sad part of it is that most of these men who would preserve democracy by limiting it are sincere."[2]

Soon after the Pauling controversy, the territorial legislature passed a series of loyalty measures, one of which required university faculty members to sign a loyalty oath. Petitions were circulated on the campus, signed by 250 faculty members and an almost equal number of students, asking the territory's newly appointed governor, Oren Long, to veto the measures. Koji Ariyoshi commented on the matter in a *Honolulu Record* editorial:

> The dangers to our institutions as well as to individual liberties inherent in these bills are all too clear in light of recent developments in world history and in the attitude and conduct of the type of man who would administer the loyalty oath program.
>
> For example, Edward N. Sylva, chairman of the Territorial un-American commission, in trembling emotion and illogical argument, this week tried to dismiss the flood of protests from the Manoa campus by calling deans, professors and instructors, "sincere but misguided intellectuals," whose opposition to the loyalty bills "contrasted with the devotion of our brave boys who are clinging to the blood soaked peninsula of Korea."
>
> The faculty at the university is aware of the historical parallel of what is happening today with what has happened in the past.
>
> Max Ascoli, a professor in Italian universities until the year of the loyalty oath, 1931, wrote in 1938 a brief description of how the oath in Italy proved to be a preliminary to something else:
>
> "The fall of 1931, when all professors [in Italy] but twelve took the oath marked the turning point. . . . From that time on, the pressure upon the university teachers went on with increased impetus. The oath had meaning only if supplemented by more positive acts of loyalty . . . more and more exacting and detailed."[3]

The territory of Hawaii was simply seeking to stay in line with the loyalty procedures being developed in Washington, D.C., by the Truman administration. One month before the passage of the new Hawaii statutes, the standard for dismissal of federal employees had been amended. A 1969 report by the American Friends Service Committee discussed the significance of the change:

> As originally established, the program reflected a concern to insure against the abuse of loyalty charges and provided that dismissal should be based on hard evidence that "reasonable *grounds* exist for the belief that the person involved is *disloyal* to the government of the United States." The revised loyalty standard (April 1951) stipulated that "reasonable *doubt*

> exists as to the *loyalty* of the individual involved to the government of the United States." The changes from grounds to doubt and from disloyalty to loyalty were not semantic; rather they reflected a different set of priorities and expedited dismissal of suspect individuals.[4]

Protests notwithstanding, Governor Long signed the new loyalty measures on 22 May 1951.[5] One week later the *Honolulu Record* printed a statement that had been written by Oren Long while he was the territory's superintendent of public instruction in 1936. Long protested a measure passed by the territorial legislature that required all school teachers to submit to a loyalty oath. "It is those who would make of a teacher a cloistered monk," Long wrote, "something less than a citizen, who suggest that the teacher be required to take a loyalty oath." Long concluded that he "should not wish to sign one."[6]

The territory's loyalty measures seem to have been borne lightly by the university's faculty. Professor Alan Saunders, one of the leading liberals on the faculty during the late 1940s and early 1950s, later indicated that there was no further campus unrest over the issue. He explained that individual problems were handled quietly and privately with great tact.[7] Professor John Stalker, a spokesman for the faculty group protesting the loyalty oaths, confirmed Saunders' recollection. Stalker added that much of the credit for campus calm belonged to Paul Bachman, dean of the faculty.[8]

Soon after the passage of the loyalty measures, on 6 July 1951, Jack Kawano went to Washington, D.C., to tell the House Committee on Un-American Activities the story he would not tell in Honolulu in April 1950. Kawano was accompanied by Judge Chuck Mau. What would cause Kawano to turn against his old friends in the ILWU? There is no doubt that Jack Kawano had become upset when Matt Meehan recommended Jack Hall to become the regional director of the ILWU in 1944. When Hall took command, the ILWU was on the brink of its greatest growth. This growth would have been impossible without the Little Wagner Act, which was passed in 1945. In turn, the Little Wagner Act would have been impossible without the success of the CIO's political action committee in the 1944 elections. Jack Kawano played a great role in getting Hawaii's workers registered to vote. If Jack Hall had written Hawaii's Little Wagner Act, Jack Kawano had provided the votes to pass it.

Kawano's political skills were probably valued more highly outside the union than within the ILWU. In 1945 a small Democratic strategy group came into existence. Originally composed of five members, it was to become the nucleus of what later came to be known as the Burns group. The five were Chuck Mau, John Burns, Mitsuyuki Kido, Dr. Ernest Murai, and Jack Kawano. Chuck Mau, generally considered the leader of the original group, gives much of the credit for its existence to Jack Kawano. In a 1975 interview, Mau said: "It was through his auspices that the five of us got together. He was the sparkplug. . . . He was the one who held us together. He was a moving spirit of this 'New Deal,' if you'd like to call it that, that was in the making. And he was powerful enough because he had an organization behind him. None of [the rest of] us had any organization behind us."[9]

When asked whether Kawano was more important than John Burns in forming this Democratic strategy group, Mau responded, "Oh, absolutely." Mau recalled that the group thought of Burns more as a worker than as a serious political figure, finding a "lack of charisma" on Burns' part. He said that the group watched with amazement as Burns developed as a political figure in his own right. From 1944 to 1946, however, Kawano was more important to the growth of the Democratic party than was Burns. Mau was not the only person who thought so. Dr. Ernest Murai, active in Democratic party politics since the 1920s, said in 1975, "I think if it weren't for the help that Jack Kawano gave us on the plantations, among the ILWU members . . . it would have taken us maybe several years longer to organize the Democratic party."[10] Mitsuyuki Kido, longtime member of John Burns' inner circle, echoed Mau's and Murai's feelings in 1975, saying, "[Kawano] did a terrific job of getting the ILWU, lock, stock, and barrel, to come into the Democratic party."[11]

From 1947 to 1950 this informal strategy group continued to meet, with the inclusion of some new members: Dan Aoki, Dan Inouye, Sakae Takehashi, and Matsuo Takabuki. The newcomers were the nucleus of the veterans group that would eventually become the backbone of John Burns' political support. As Jack Kawano lost influence in the ILWU, he sought validation from his Democratic party associates.

Between the time he left the Communist party in 1949 and the arrival of HUAC in 1950, Kawano began to talk with his political associates about the issue of communism. He did not, however, reveal that he had been a Communist party member until the night before the hearings opened at Iolani Palace. When he did, it was to Chuck Mau that he turned. In 1975 Mau recalled that Kawano had come to his house on the eve of the HUAC hearings and informed him that he had been issued a subpoena to appear. Mau remembered their conversation this way:

> "Well Jack, there's nothing to worry about, they're trying to ferret out the Communists. All you have to tell them is that you're not a Communist."
>
> And he said, "But I am."
>
> I said, "You what?" I said, "You've been leading us astray? Do you remember the talks we had about American history and the Constitution of the United States and about Russian philosophy? And in the end I said

> which of the two systems do you think is best, and you said, 'Of course, the capitalistic, free enterprise system.' And Jack, how could this be?"
>
> He said, "But I am."
>
> And I said, "Well, do you still want to be a Communist?
>
> He said, "No, as a matter of fact, I've broken with them." He said, "I can't testify because I want to stay in the union and fight the Communists." He said, "If I testify, I will have no influence in the union."
>
> I said, "That's right. But," I said, "you have friends who have relied on you, who've believed in you. . . . These people have spoken about you very highly as a very honest labor leader who really wanted to fight for the working man. It's a great let-down to them."
>
> And we talked until four o'clock in the morning. Finally, he consented to do this—he would say that he was no longer a Communist and stop at that. And that's exactly what he did.[12]

That is not "exactly" what Kawano did. What Kawano did before HUAC in April 1950 was to state that he was not a member of the Communist party. There was no explicit or implicit admission that he had ever been a member.

Mitsuyuki Kido and Daniel Inouye had somewhat different recollections of Kawano's moment of decision. Kido recalled that Kawano had brought the matter to the attention of the whole Democratic strategy group and just "threw the question open, 'What do you think I should do?' Kido continued: "I think it was the unanimous opinion of the group at that time that he should talk; he shouldn't invoke the Fifth Amendment. He should say what he knew about the movement, his part of it. Make a clean breast of it."[13] Kido said that he never regretted having given Kawano that advice, although he did acknowledge that stepping forth probably ruined Kawano's life.

In 1975 Senator Daniel Inouye offered a version of Kawano's actions dramatically different from Mau's or Kido's. Inouye recalled that Kawano had contacted him about a month before the HUAC hearings, asking for a meeting. Inouye remembered picking up Kawano in his car and driving around Ala Moana Park, "just circling, nothing being said, for about half an hour. . . . And then finally he said, 'You know, you fellows have been good to me and I think you should know this. I've been a member of the Communist Party. . . . You know I've been subpoenaed. All of us have met with the ILWU lawyers and we were told to plead the Fifth Amendment. I just want your views—what should I do?' "[14] Inouye recalled having told Kawano that if he did testify he would lose all of his old friends from the ILWU. "But there are certain times when you've got to be able to risk all of that, and I think this is one of those times. There are a lot of us who will help you."[15] Inouye's memory of Kawano's testimony before HUAC in April 1950 was that Kawano had answered all of the questions put to him, "all of them," and that he had created "pandemonium" at the Iolani Palace: "People were screaming and shouting and booing. And the lawyers are trying to grab the mike. Finally, he got through. . . . And I was standing on the side and I think a couple of people spat on him. Then he came to me and hugged me and then we left and went to lunch. A lot of politicians have wondered why I have never been endorsed by the ILWU. . . . Well, it could be those days."[16]

This, of course, never happened. Inouye's recollection of events twenty-five years after the fact, was obviously faulty. It stands as a warning to readers and writers of history alike that oral history interviews must be verified. But while Inouye's, Kido's, and Mau's recollections of events may differ in fact, they are totally consistent with the direction they were urging upon Jack Kawano.

Kawano's first public admission that he had been a member of the Communist party came on 10 February 1951. It came in the form of an open letter to the territorial Subversive Activities Commission:

> I joined the Communist Party because some individual Communists were willing to assist me in organizing the Waterfront Union. The waterfront employers were totally intolerant of labor unions. They did all they could to smash all attempts to organize the waterfront. No civic or community organizations showed any signs of willingness to assist in our organizing efforts. I did not think it was harmful to the union as long as the Communists were willing to assist me in bringing up the living standards of the workingman because they led me to believe that the basic existence of the Communist Party was primarily to promote the best interests of the workingman.
>
> I decided to quit the Communist Party because I found that the primary purpose of the Communist Party was not for the best interests of the workingman but to dupe the members of the union for purposes other than strictly trade-union matters. . . .
>
> Today I am more than ever convinced that I did right by quitting the Communist Party, for in view of the international situation, when our boys are giving their lives to their country which is at war with Communist Korea and China, I cannot help but believe that anyone who is a Communist and is willing to help Communist Korea, China, or any other Communist nation is dangerously flirting with treason against his own country.
>
> For the sake of the union, I call on you to check on what I have said. It is your duty to investigate, to ask pointed questions, to get information. When you have done so, you will find the destructive effects of Communism within the union. I strongly urge the rank-and-file members of the ILWU, every one of them, to fight to keep the control and the management of their union and union activities in the hands of rank-and-file members. To accomplish this important task, all Communists and those who follow the Communist line should be rejected by the rank-and-file membership.[17]

The full force of Jack Kawano's statement did not hit the community right away. Just three weeks before it was made, the last of the Reluctant Thirty-nine had been found "not guilty" on charges of contempt of Congress. Furthermore, the statement was very general and did not include the names of any fellow communists from the ILWU, and, with the territorial Subversive Activities Commission still in its organizational stages, there was no ready forum from which Kawano's charges could be voiced. He sought to have his letter read before the ninth biennial convention of the ILWU, a request denied to no one's surprise.

A full year after HUAC had visited Hawaii, Chuck Mau asked Jack Kawano to complete his unfinished business with HUAC. "Jack," Mau recalls saying to Kawano, "I think it's time . . . to have you go to Washington and testify, and since these people in the ILWU are treating you like dirt anyway, you might as well come out and tell the whole truth about the Communist apparatus in Hawaii."[18] Kawano agreed, on one condition—that Mau accompany him to the nation's capital.

Thus, on 6 July 1951 Jack Kawano found a larger forum for his story. Accompanied by Chuck Mau, he went to Washington, D.C., to reveal everything he knew about communism in Hawaii to HUAC. In more than fifty pages of testimony, Kawano cited chapter and verse, giving names, dates, and places. His testimony, which had a strong ring of authenticity, was aided by a friendly committee and no cross-examination.

Kawano described how he had been brought into the Communist party in 1937 by Bill Bailey, a recent arrival from the west coast. Bailey had given Kawano his Travelers Club card, "otherwise known as a Communist card." Then "he told us that as long as we carried that card we would be respected by all good union men from the mainland, and we could count on Harry Bridges to help us out."[19]

When asked what had transpired at his first Communist party meeting, Kawano replied, "The general trend of thought was like this—that the bosses are no good; that workers can live without the bosses, and we should try to get rid of the bosses by forming an organization and fighting the bosses, first through the union and later through the revolution."[20]

The preliminaries out of the way, HUAC counsel Frank Tavenner began feeding Kawano names, asking him to comment on whether, to his knowledge, each was a member of the Communist party. Of the first twenty-two names read to him, Kawano identified seven as members of the Communist party: Levi Kealoha, Jack Hall, Ben Kaahawinui, William Piilani (who, Kawano pointed out, was also known as William Kamaka, a friendly witness before HUAC in April 1950), Ed Berman, Jack Kimoto, and George Goto.[21]

Kawano was then asked about the early organization of the Communist Party of Hawaii and about how the Party was used to control the union movement. He began by describing how he was sent to the "Communist party school" in San Francisco during the months of September and October 1938. There has been much debate over whether the California Labor School, as it was properly called, was a Communist party school. Those who deny that it was point to the fact that the San Francisco school openly advertised in a number of California newspapers and that instruction at the school was available to veterans at the end of World War II under the subsidy of the G.I. Bill of Rights. Those who contend that it was a Communist party school point to specific members of the Communist party who studied and taught there as well as the unquestionable Marxist slant evident in the lesson plans and books used by the school. Each side can defend its position on narrow technical grounds. Still, there was, in the 1930s, a close working relationship between the radical labor movement in the United States and the Communist party. It is safe to say that Kawano went to San Francisco both as a labor organizer and as a member of the Communist party. At the school, there is no doubt that he was given a heavy dose of Marxist propaganda along with instruction in the techniques of labor organization.

Kawano's testimony then turned to the condition of the longshore union on his return from California. Having just lost a National Labor Relations Board election, union members were demoralized and ready to "throw in the towel." Kawano described how he pulled the union back together and led the ILWU to its first NLRB certification in 1941. Chairman Francis Walter, leading Kawano now, asked, "How did Hall muscle his way into the union then?" In an obvious effort to downgrade Jack Hall's contributions to the union movement during the prewar years, Kawano's response was "He was not in the union then."[22]

Jack Kawano continued to weave the thread of Communist party control of the ILWU into his testimony. At one point, he described how Robert McElrath had brought his drydock union into the CIO at the end of World War II. The following exchange is indicative of the manner in which Kawano's testimony was led by counsel for HUAC:

TAVENNER: Was McElrath known to you to be a member of the Communist Party at that time?
KAWANO: He was.
TAVENNER: And it was the Communist Party that brought McElrath's union into the CIO?
KAWANO: That is correct.[23]

Kawano then described the reorganization of the Communist Party of Hawaii at the conclusion of World War II, giving particular emphasis to the importation of a mainland Communist party organizer, Dwight James Freeman:

> We ran into a lot of problems because we signed up a lot of people in the Communist Party who had no idea what the Communist Party meant, and we needed to educate them and to recruit new people into the party. We needed a good live-wire person to do that particular work for the party in Hawaii. We requested the party in San Francisco to send such a person, and the party sent Freeman. After Freeman's arrival the party stepped up its activities even more. . . . Charles and Eileen Fujimoto were assigned to work under the direction of Jim Freeman.[24]

The line of inquiry then turned to the structure of Communist party leadership, party conventions, and the functions of the Party's executive board. Kawano also related the manner in which the Party decided to create the *Honolulu Record* as a Communist party front and how Koji Ariyoshi was selected to become the paper's editor:

> KAWANO: We heard the news he was already a Communist, and he was a local boy, so we felt he would be a logical guy to head up a newspaper that the Communist Party was interested in formulating. That is how we got him to come to Hawaii. . . .
> TAVENNER: "We" means who?
> KAWANO: Jack Hall, John Reinecke, Jack Kimoto, people like that.
> TAVENNER: In other words, Communists?
> KAWANO: That is right.[25]

Turning to politics, Kawano discussed the intimate relationship between the Communist party and the CIO-PAC. He then moved on to the "Communist party decision" to infiltrate the Democratic party in 1948. Kawano's description of the meeting at which the decision was made is most revealing:

> In 1948 there was a tremendous amount of discussion among the Communists regarding the failure of PAC in Territorial politics, and in early 1948, at Jack Hall's Manoa home, the executive board called an enlarged committee meeting to discuss the question of politics.
>
> This is not a regular executive board meeting, so there would be many people attending, and there might even be a few non-Communists attending. Party members felt pretty safe in having non-Communists come in because the subject we were going to talk about was only on politics.

Kawano then listed the decisions made at that "enlarged committee meeting," as follows:

> 1. The Communist Party, through the ILWU organizations will join the Democratic Party.
> 2. Take over leadership of it by getting the majority of convention delegates elected who were Communists, Communist sympathizers, or at least union men.
> 3. Elect a majority of this type people.

When Tavenner asked him to name some of the people who were present at the meeting, Kawano obliged by reeling off no fewer than thirty-three names, followed by the comment that there were "a flock of others I cannot now remember."[26]

Sensing that something had gone awry with his witness, Tavenner asked Kawano to run through the list once again to signify those who were and those who were not members of the Communist party. "As I understand," Tavenner probed, "this was not a meeting of the Communist Party?"

"Yes," Kawano insisted, "this was a meeting of the Communist Party . . . but there could have been someone attending who did not suspect it to be a meeting of the Communist Party."[27]

If the statement of Kawano concerning the three specific decisions made at the meeting is to be taken seriously, the conclusion that somebody could have been there without suspecting that it was a Communist party meeting makes little sense.

Kawano's testimony then turned to the Communist party's deliberations over whether or not the Party should come out into the open. He described a meeting of the executive committee of the Communist party at Foster Gardens in 1948. Among those present, according to Kawano, were attorney Harriet Bouslog and J. R. Robertson, first vice-president of the ILWU from San Francisco. Kawano recalled that he, Jack Hall, Robert McElrath, and J. R. Robertson opposed the idea of going public. Jack Kimoto, Jim Freeman, Koji Ariyoshi, Charles Fujimoto, Eileen Fujimoto, and Harriet Bouslog were said to favor doing so. The split was clearly along union, nonunion lines. In the end, the Communist Party of Hawaii did not go public, although its president, Charles Fujimoto, did. Kawano testified before HUAC that the fight over the issue was so vehement that it led, indirectly, to Robert McElrath's expulsion from the Party and to his own threatened resignation.

The end of Kawano's testimony was directed to the relationship between the Communist party and the ILWU during the 1949 longshore strike. Kawano told HUAC that he attended his last Communist party meeting in June 1949. He said that he was the only one present who opposed having the sugar workers go on strike while the dock workers were out. He concluded by saying, "Among the sugar workers I agitated against a strike and the strike did not materialize."[28] This statement appears to be more undeserved self-congratulation than reality. As labor historian Edward Beechert wrote:

> Preliminary negotiations and preparations for the 1950 sugar contract were not encouraging. The possibility of a sugar strike was a serious threat to the ability of the ILWU to support the longshoremen. There were too many signs of weakness in the sugar units. The organization had not yet recovered from the Ignacio affair, and unit leadership was still weak and often ineffective. Moreover, business agents reported little enthusiasm and frequently downright opposition to the notion of a strike.[29]

In his closing remarks before HUAC, Kawano thanked Democratic party stalwarts Chuck Mau, John Burns, Mits Kido, Ernest Murai, Sakae Takehashi, Dave Benz, Dan Aoki, and Dan Inouye, who had helped to make him "a good American." In turn, chairman Francis Walter offered words of thanks to Kawano: "Mr. Kawano," Walter said, "the committee is indebted to you for coming this great distance in order to give us the benefit of your deep knowledge of the machinations of this group of international conspirators."[30]

The executive board of ILWU Local 136, the local Kawano had led for so long, passed a formal resolution denouncing Kawano's testimony before HUAC. They charged that although he had been one of the original organizers, it had become clear that "Kawano had lost all interest in the union and was more concerned with making political deals." They pointed out that although he had stopped working months earlier, "the union and its officials continued to carry Kawano." Now "he has expressed his thanks by a betrayal of the Union." During the 1949 strike, the executive board charged, "Kawano declined to be Chairman of the Strike Committee, his logical responsibility as President of the Local." "The only time Kawano showed any interest in the strike," the resolution continued, "was when he tried to work out a political deal to settle the strike for fourteen cents." It was pointed out that Kawano had not stood for reelection in 1949 and could not have won if he had. Officially, Kawano was dropped from the ILWU roles for nonpayment of dues. Finally, the executive board revealed that several members had been approached by Kawano, who said that he was working for the CIO's national organization and was seeking to have the International Longshoremen's Association replace the ILWU after the ILWU was expelled from the CIO.[31]

The gloves were off. It is clear that the ILWU had refrained from attacking Kawano personally earlier in the hope that he would not speak out as he had before HUAC. In 1975 Kawano asserted that Jack Hall, as an "assignment from the Communist Party of Hawaii," had tried to talk him out of going to Washington to testify before HUAC. Kawano said that Hall promised him that Lau Ah Chew would set him up in a "promotional business." When asked whether this meant that Lau Ah Chew was a communist, Kawano replied that he was not. "He was just—I hate to say this—nothing but an opportunist, trying to make a go out of whatever he can bring together." Kawano concluded by saying, after he refused to accept the deal Hall was alleged to have offered, "We ended up calling each other traitors. He called me a traitor to the cause, I called him a traitor to his country. We shook hands and separated. We had that much respect for each other."[32]

After Kawano had completed his testimony before HUAC in the summer of 1951, Chuck Mau took him to see the attorney general of the

United States, J. Howard McGrath. When Mau asked McGrath when there was going to be a Smith Act trial in Hawaii, McGrath is reported to have said: "Why, you have nothing but buck privates in the Communist Party in Hawaii. The big ones, the big fish are on the Mainland." When Mau continued to press, he was referred to a "special deputy who had charge of communist prosecutions." Mau recalled pointing out to the deputy that in the event of war, "Russia would very much like to control the Hawaiian Islands; they would gain control of the whole Pacific." Whatever was said, the Justice Department seems to have been impressed. According to Mau, Hawaii leapfrogged "Los Angeles, Chicago, Seattle, Denver, and one or two other places" to become the target for the next Smith Act trial.[33] In Jack Kawano, they had found a star witness.

Chapter 16

The Hawaii Seven

On 28 August 1951 at 6:30 A.M., twenty-one FBI agents moved simultaneously to arrest seven alleged leaders of the Communist Party of Hawaii. These early morning raids occurred less than two months after Jack Kawano's testimony before HUAC in Washington, D.C. Those arrested were Jack Hall, regional director of the ILWU; John Reinecke, former teacher; Jack Kimoto, an employee of the *Honolulu Record;* Koji Ariyoshi, editor of the *Honolulu Record;* Jim Freeman, mechanic; Charles Fujimoto, announced chairman of the Communist Party of Hawaii; and Eileen Fujimoto, wife of Charles Fujimoto and secretary at the ILWU Longshore Local 136. Those arrested were quickly dubbed the Hawaii Seven.

The indictment of the Hawaii Seven charged that they had violated section 2 of the Smith Act by conspiring "(1) unlawfully, willfully, and knowingly to advocate and teach the duty and necessity of overthrowing the Government of the United States by force and violence, and (2) unlawfully, willfully, and knowingly to organize and help organize as the Communist Party of the United States of America a society, group and assembly of persons who teach and advocate the overthrow and destruction of the Government of the United States by force and violence."[1]

The Hawaii Seven were not necessarily considered the seven most dangerous communists in Hawaii. They were, however, the seven whose activities between 1 April 1945 and 28 August 1951, the chronological limits of the alleged conspiracy, were in violation of the Smith Act as construed by the U.S. Supreme Court in the *Dennis* decision.[2]

The indictment included eleven "overt acts" that were alleged to have been committed by as few as one and as many as seven of the defendants. The "acts" included everything from attending Communist party conventions and serving on the executive board of the Communist Party of Hawaii, to Charles Fujimoto's announcement that he was the chairman of the Communist Party of Hawaii, Koji Ariyoshi's publication of the *Honolulu Record,* and Jack Hall's having instructed a person who believed he would be subpoenaed by "a Committee of the Congress of the United States." One "overt act" read in full as follows: "On or about January 12th, 1949, Jack Wayne Hall did travel from the City and County of Honolulu, Territory of Hawaii, to the City of San Francisco."[3]

Conspiracy law has the special quality that all members of a conspiracy are held responsible for the acts and words of other members of the conspiracy. An interesting aspect of the indictment of the Hawaii Seven is that they were all made a part of a larger conspiracy by the technique of listing coconspirators "not defendants herein." These unindicted coconspirators included all eleven of the Communist party leaders who had been convicted in the *Dennis* case. It also included William Z. Foster, chairman of the Communist Party of the United States, who had been dropped from the *Dennis* case owing to ill health, and William Schneiderman, who had just been indicted on Smith Act violations in California. The indictment also charged that the conspiracy included "diverse other persons to the grand jury unknown."[4]

As soon as the Hawaii Seven had been rounded up, there arose a cry from within the ranks of the ILWU that the whole proceeding was nothing less than a Big Five effort to "get Jack Hall" and to "bust the union." The ILWU was in the final stages of sugar negotiations. To prevent charges of interference, the government went so far as to allow Jack Hall to hold a union meeting in the U.S. marshal's office. The sugar contract was successfully completed on 2 September 1951. The ILWU was pleased with the results of the negotiations, which were described by Edward Beechert in *Working in Hawaii:*

> In 1951 the wage level was raised to one dollar an hour and a pattern of seniority in the work force was written into the contract. This was the first step in protecting the workers from the erosion of mechanization. Paid vacations were introduced, three paid holidays were established, and, importantly, a forty-hour work week was guaranteed for at least twenty-six weeks of the year. . . . This 1951 contract marked the most significant change in working conditions since the appearance of the first modern union in 1939.[5]

More than a Big Five plot, the Hawaii Smith Act trial was part of a concerted governmental action to confront the perceived threat of communist subversion in the United States. Hawaii was fifth in a series of federal actions against alleged Communist party leaders throughout the country since the *Dennis* decision of 4 June 1951. Similar arrests had been made in New York City (20 June), San Francisco (26 July), Baltimore (7 August), and Pittsburgh (17 August). In all, the Justice Department would pursue sixteen separate Smith Act cases between 1951 and 1957. The reason for Hawaii's early involvement appears to have been

Chuck Mau's efforts with the Justice Department during his visit to Washington, D.C., with Jack Kawano. Mau sought to clear the Democratic party of any taint of communism by exposing and rooting out tainted elements within the party. In doing so, he also hoped to prove his own fitness for the federal bench.

The Justice Department had been preparing to move against the so-called second string communists from the conclusion of the Foley Square case in 1949. Howard K. Hoddick, acting U.S. attorney at the time of the Smith Act arrests in Hawaii, confirmed these plans in a 1975 interview. Hoddick recalled that he had attended a meeting in Washington, D.C., shortly after the original lower court decision in the *Dennis* case, at which Attorney General J. Howard McGrath revealed the Justice Department's plans to prosecute regional leaders of the CPUSA. He told the assembled U.S. attorneys that the FBI was, at that very time, preparing for such trials. Hoddick took issue with the charge that the Smith Act trial had been arranged by the Big Five. "I cannot assume," Hoddick said, "that the FBI's decision was influenced by any calls from the sugar factors or business interests in Hawaii."[6]

Reactions to the arrest of the Hawaii Seven were predictable. The ILWU's public reaction, that the arrests were part of a Big Five plot to bust the union, was echoed in the *Honolulu Record*. The *Record*, in its original response to the arrests, quoted extensively from the dissenting opinions in the *Dennis* decision, written by justices Black and Douglas. Both Standpat and Walkout Democrats were quoted with hopeful comments to the effect that the Smith Act trial might clear the air. The *Honolulu Advertiser* saw the arrests as "part of a national battle against treason."[7] The *Honolulu Star-Bulletin* saw the arrests as a "clear warning to individuals or unions which accept, as leaders, men who follow the Moscow instead of the American line."[8]

The Hawaii Residents' Association—IMUA—greeted the news of the arrests with an announcement that they would expand their Pier 7 headquarters and increase their hours of operation. An open house was announced for 6 to 8 September. It was during the period of the Smith Act arrests and trial that IMUA reached the peak of its influence in the community.

The popularity of *IMUA Spotlight*, the newspaper for the Hawaii Residents' Association, jumped dramatically with the addition of Tony Todaro as its featured columnist. Todaro's columns, which began on 26 September 1951, added a songwriter's touch to IMUA's anticommunist efforts. Todaro's two featured friends, "Minnie Stroni" and "Andy Pasta," were always "feeding" him information about the communist conspiracy. In a 1975 interview, Todaro, who had long since repudiated his IMUA days, revealed that "Minnie" and "Andy" were actually the local FBI agents. According to Todaro, the FBI allowed him to read their teletype dispatches from Washington, D.C., as they came off the wire. Looking back, Todaro said: "I made a complete turnabout on the question of whether Jack Hall was guilty. There was absolutely no proof that these people were enemies of the country."[9]

In an ironic turn of events, Todaro was involved in a lawsuit in 1972 over the fact that David Watumull, owner of the now defunct radio station KTGR, said over the air, "Someone told me that Tony Todaro is under the surveillance of the FBI." Watumull's announcer, Jeff Burnside, told the station's listeners that Todaro got his orders "direct from Moscow."[10] Todaro won his 1972 case and received $8,000 and a public retraction from Watumull. Twenty-one years earlier, it had been Todaro slinging the mud. No court in the territory of Hawaii would have found him guilty of libel at that time.

Todaro's enemies were introduced in his columns without the benefit of disguise—so willingly provided for his FBI informants. One of his favorite characters was "Rattletrap McElrath," alias "Robert McElmouse." Charles Fujimoto was given such names as "Charlie the Commie" and "Water Boy Charlie." Jack Hall was known as "Angel Hall." Another of Todaro's favorites was Koji Ariyoshi, who was always referred to as "My Boy Koji." Harriet Bouslog was the "Proletarian Pinup." The Hawaii Seven became the "Seven Mules of Moscow."

Todaro could be funny, as when the government's special prosecutor, John C. Walsh, tipped over backward in his chair during the Smith Act trial. "Minnie got scared silly the day Walsh . . . did a flip-flop to the floor," Todaro reported. "She thought the Commie revolution had started. As Walsh went down, she swore she heard 'Charlie the Commie' Fujimoto remark: 'Down with the Government.' "[11] Todaro could also be brutally vicious. The piece below was written concerning a story Koji Ariyoshi told about a kindness done by John Reinecke:

> During a time when canned cream was scarce, Reinecke overheard a stranger on a bus wail that he couldn't get any canned cream. Later on that evening, the stranger answered a rap on his front door and, lo and behold, there was Reinecke with an armful of canned cream.
>
> When Koji thought he had melted the hearts of his audience with his touching story, he remarked: "I ask you, could such a man be dangerous to his country?"
>
> I'm reminded of the gangster Al Capone, who threw lavish banquets for his enemies before he beat them to death with a baseball bat. I'm reminded of the child murderers who buy their victims ice cream and candy before they hack them to pieces.
>
> I'm not saying that John Reinecke is a sadist or a gangster, but giving canned cream to a stranger does not prove that Reinecke cannot or is not selling his country to its enemies, thereby rendering more physical violence than a thousand gangsters and sadists.[12]

Todaro's columns continued through February 1953. In March the editors explained the absence of Todaro's column by saying that his space had been needed for letters from readers. In May it was announced that the column had been received too late for inclusion in that issue. It was never mentioned again. In fact, Todaro had become disgusted with his role in portraying the "communist menace" in Hawaii. Although he did not publicly repudiate the position he had defended so staunchly for two years, he was through with IMUA.

During the fourteen-month period between the arrests and trial of the Hawaii Seven, there were a number of public exchanges that ventilated the issues surrounding the case. The ILWU and IMUA provided a constant radio dialogue as well as some major "literary" efforts. Two of these exchanges in print are worthy of note: first, an ILWU pamphlet called *Fear* and IMUA's response, *The Answer to "Fear"*; second, a special edition of *IMUA Spotlight* titled "The American Way of Life" and the ILWU response, *Americanism, as Defined by Great Americans*.

Fear was a reprint, in pamphlet form, of a speech by Harriet Bouslog. The speech was given at a Labor Day rally held by the ILWU just days after the arrest of the Hawaii Seven. Bouslog told the union men: "The reason for the prosecution of Jack Hall is the same as that for the prosecution of Harry Bridges. [It will continue] until the government silences all who dare to challenge the right of government to freeze wages, while profits soar; who demand peace when the government is bent on war."[13]

After a stinging indictment of the FBI, President Truman, Joe McCarthy, and the Supreme Court, Bouslog turned to the Smith Act prosecutions being undertaken by the Justice Department:

> How does the government . . . prove its point? Here is where the stoolpigeon, the professional witness, the political opportunist, the renegade, the Izukas, the Kawanos, come in. They announce that they were once Communists, and that when they were Communists, they were terrible people who engaged in all sorts of illegal activity, but now that they have seen the light, they would like to help the government put behind bars all their former associates whom they now hate. They are paid with publicity, with witness fees, with royalties from their books and pamphlets. One of these stoolpigeon-informers, Mr. Izuka, once testified that he directed a slow-down at Port Allen to hold up lend-lease ships. No lend-lease ship ever docked on Kauai, but no lie is too big for these stoolpigeons or the government prosecutors.[14]

Bouslog then pointed out the incongruity of the fact that the *Honolulu Record* had been granted the privilege of using the U.S. postal service by the same government that had charged that the production and distribution of that newspaper constituted an "overt act" in support of a conspiracy to teach and advocate the overthrow of the U.S. government by force and violence. Discussing Charles Fujimoto's avowed commitment to communism, Bouslog repeated the truism frequently cited by socialists or communists under attack: "Now there is nothing in the United States Constitution that says capitalism and democracy are the same thing."[15] *Fear* ended with this warning:

> Do not feel safe because your name is not among the seven, because if this conspiracy of the govenment against the seven succeeds, you and your children will have lost your liberties, and we will go again into the dark ages of thought-control against which we fought in Germany, in Japan, in Italy, and to which our government has now turned to maintain itself in power.[16]

On 26 November 1951 Honolulu attorney Urban E. Wild delivered a speech to the membership of IMUA that was a response to Bouslog. It was published with the title *The Answer to "Fear."* The pamphlet began with a recitation of the "pertinent" parts of the Smith Act, followed by a review of the *Dennis* decision. Wild asserted that the prosecution in the *Dennis* case had proved four key points to be basic to the program of the Communist Party of the United States of America:

1. To teach those subject to their influence secretly to prepare for the coming of some crisis such as a deep depression or war with the Soviet Union.
2. To spring into action when the word of command was given upon the coming of such a crisis.
3. To paralyze power houses, transportation systems, vast industrial machinery in the heart of our economic organization.
4. In the resultant chaos and confusion, to bring about by violence and unlawful means the overthrow or destruction of the government and the setting up of a "dictatorship of the proletariat."[17]

The defendants in the *Dennis* case were neither charged with nor convicted of anything so specific as Wild asserted. Where Wild came up with these four charges is difficult to say, but they were not contained in the indictment of the eleven Communist party leaders who were convicted in the Foley Square trial in New York.[18]

Wild then turned to the contempt convictions that were sustained by all five defense attorneys in the *Dennis* case and by Eugene Dennis, who had defended himself at the original trial. Wild quoted Judge Jerome Frank of the U.S. Court of Appeals, who had concurred in upholding the six contempt convictions. "We affirm," Judge Frank wrote, "for the plain reason that the crude antics of these lawyers, if copied in other cases, would almost surely disrupt trials." Wild commended Judge Frank's decision, saying, "These words of a learned judge certainly answer more eloquently than I could the propaganda that is the main theme of Bouslog's *Fear*.[19]

Wild criticized Bouslog for emphasizing the historic role of the ILWU in Hawaii's labor history. He asserted that her remarks were "merely brought in to bring quick sympathy on generalities, and to provide a reason for the reproduction and distribution of her Labor Day address, which of course was not on labor as such but was devoted to an attack on the Smith Act."[20]

IMUA was concerned that Bouslog's *Fear* was being distributed in such a way as to do "great harm" in the community. Thus, with the approval of the territorial Department of Public Instruction, IMUA produced a special edition of *IMUA Spotlight.* This special edition was intended primarily for use in the public schools; it was also available for sale to the general public. Called "The American Way of Life," the publication contained a combination of patriotic slogans and conservative social philosophy. One article, purporting to deal with the Bill of Rights, offered the following message: "We *say* we want personal freedom, but we *demand* government housing, government price controls, government guaranteed jobs and wages. We *boast* that we are responsible persons, but we *vote* for candidates who promise us special privileges, government pensions, government subsidies, and government electricity. Such schemes are contrary to the spirit of the Bill of Rights."[21]

The special edition's treatment of labor emphasized that labor-management cooperation was the way to prosperity. It was highly critical of those who assume labor and management to exist in an adversarial relationship. In a section that sought to describe what the term "sweet land of liberty" meant, it was stated that one of its meanings was "the right to organize . . . competitive labor unions."[22]

Tony Todaro wrote the feature piece for the special edition, an apocalyptic description of the struggle of "Communism vs. the American Way of Life," which he called "the climatic [*sic*] struggle of human rights." Todaro first addressed religion: "Communism destroys religion. Can you imagine what this means to hundreds of thousands of religious institutions in America which are benefitting the spiritual and economic welfare of millions of God fearing Americans? This is the kind of life that William Z. Foster, Charles Fujimoto and the rest of America's Stalinists are preparing for we 'unhappy' Americans." Todaro dismissed the possibility that there could be such a thing as a uniquely American variant of communism. "The answer is simple," Todaro asserted. "Communists are liquidated if they fail to blow their noses whenever Joe Stalin sneezes. It must be remembered that actually there is no 'American' party or movement." Todaro ended his column with the pronouncement "Communism without a violent revolution is like Christianity without Christ."[23]

The ILWU, angered by IMUA's version of "The American Way of

Life," published its own view of America for Hawaii's school children. It was called, *Americanism, as Defined by Great Americans.* In the foreword the ILWU writers commented on what they conceived to be unequal treatment from the territorial Department of Public Instruction:

> In our judgment, IMUA presented only the reactionary businessman's concept. We felt that students had the right to know that Americanism is not narrow and rigid—that Americanism, as defined by great Americans, is a strong, living, growing, beautiful expression of ever increasing freedom for *all* people.
>
> The Department of Public Instruction has called the writings of the people quoted in this booklet—Franklin D. Roosevelt, Henry David Thoreau, Frederick Douglass, Thomas Jefferson, Abraham Lincoln, Oliver Wendell Holmes, Jr., Wendell Wilkie and others—"cleverly woven propaganda." They have censored these great Americans, and have declared that they will not allow distribution of this booklet through the public schools as they allowed the partisan IMUA publication to be distributed.[24]

A look at some of the quotations used in *Americanism, as Defined by Great Americans* provides an idea of the flavor of the ILWU offering. Thoreau was quoted on the law: "The law will never make men free; it is men who have got to make the law free." Justice Holmes' plea for "freedom for the thought we hate" was there. Wilkie was similarly quoted: "Whenever we take away the liberties of those we hate, we are opening the way to loss of liberty for those we love." Lincoln was quoted as saying "Labor is the superior to capital, and deserves much the higher consideration." Franklin D. Roosevelt was called upon many times. His speech about the "economic royalists" was cited, as was his statement "The test of our progress . . . is whether we provide enough for those who have too little." And so it went, concluding with selections from important international documents such as the Atlantic Charter, the Preamble to the Charter of the United Nations, and the United Nations Universal Declaration of Rights.

More was happening during the period between the arrest and trial of the Hawaii Seven than the running ideological battle between IMUA and the ILWU. One of the most dramatic events took place in late December 1951 and early January 1952. Two FBI agents, Richard Burress and James Condon, met with the ILWU's education director, David Thompson, in an effort to get Jack Hall to repudiate communism in exchange for dropping his indictment. Thompson had three meetings with Burress and Condon, the first on 15 December, the second on 18 December, and the third on 9 January. The latter two were at David Thompson's home and were recorded by Robert McElrath, who, with Thompson's knowledge, had concealed himself in Thompson's basement with recording equipment.

The tapes do not reveal exactly what would have been required of Hall to make a deal, but Thompson indicated on many occasions that one of the key points the FBI agents made was that Hall was to pull the Hawaiian units of the ILWU out of Harry Bridges' international union. Although the two sides may not have seen the arrangement in the same light, there was an attempt to make a deal. In the 18 December meeting, one of the agents put it this way: "We couldn't say, 'Jack, if you say so-and-so we'll get the indictment dismissed,' or 'You won't have to go to trial, we'll back you to the hilt.' What we could do would be to explain his position to the guy who regulates these indictments, who's going to press the thing and see if it couldn't be straightened out whereby it would be six instead of seven."[25]

In the interview on 9 January 1952, David Thompson reported to the FBI agents that Jack Hall had not been receptive to the suggestion that he cooperate with the FBI:

> THOMPSON: I told him that . . . when those guys were up to see me that they mentioned the fact that if you weren't a Communist they wished you weren't in this deal and they wished there were six instead of seven. And Jack says you guys know darn well he's not a Communist, and that you're trying to get him to break the union.[26]

A few moments later, the following exchange took place:

> AGENT: Well . . . if Jack . . . were really out of it and got out a while back, and has been fighting them and isn't an undercover for them. . . . You see, that's the thing we have to watch out for. Just kinda telling you our business a little bit, but you can see the person in fact that's undercover is possibly a greater danger to the country than the one who is more open about it, and easier to keep tabs on. But we can't be naive about it, and not fully protect the security of the country and do the job that they give us to do. But I don't know. Did you have a chance to read the paper tonight?
>
> THOMPSON: No. I just read the thing on Churchill.
>
> AGENT: Check page 14, first column. [The article in question, which Thompson apparently checked as he sat there with the agents, concerned a possible defect in the original indictment, a situation that might make it necessary to bring a new indictment against the Hawaii Seven[27]—or Six.]
>
> THOMPSON: Yeah, well I kind of figured this might happen.
>
> AGENT: If what he says is true, then that's when we'd like to make it six instead of seven.
>
> THOMPSON: Um hmmm.
>
> AGENT: We're coming to a logical place here that if it slips on beyond there'll be no turning back for anyone.[28]

There would be no turning back. Hall never seriously considered abandoning his codefendants. On 24 January 1952 Robert McElrath went on the air with the recordings of the FBI interviews. McElrath's revelation was met by friends of the Hawaii Seven with great enthusiasm, but it was not mentioned in the *Advertiser* or the *Star-Bulletin*. Neither Burress nor Condon could be reached. When the *Record* asked for an official reaction, the FBI agent on duty replied, "We don't comment on those things."[29]

During the trial of the Hawaii Seven Attorney Richard Gladstein attempted to bring Richard Burress to the stand to be interrogated about the interviews he and Condon had with David Thompson. The government's counsel objected, saying: "He is only called here to bring a red herring into this case. It is an old trick, one often employed, trying the agent, trying the policeman . . . trying the State, rather than meeting the issues of the case."[30]

After much debate, Judge Jon Wiig ruled for the prosecution. Testimony from Burress was not relevant to the case. "If these things were done in excess of their authority," Wiig added, "it would not be binding on the Government in any way."[31] Thus, posterity was denied an FBI explanation of the incident. However, the revelation of the Thompson-FBI interviews provided the ILWU leadership with a welcome and unexpected weapon in its continuing effort to demonstrate that the Smith Act trial was another episode in the government's unending effort to "bust" the union.

Two more sections of the Thompson-FBI interviews are worth noting. The first comes from the 18 December 1951 interview. The FBI agents had been telling Thompson that Hall's cooperation would be in the best interest of the ILWU:

> AGENT: For every point of issue between the union and the employers, they've thrown up the issue of Communism. If they disagree with Jack Hall in anything, they can say, "Goddamn red," and "Get out of here with your Communist union."
>
> SECOND AGENT: It's a strike, it's a Communist effort to paralyze the community.
>
> AGENT: If he'd get rid of that he thereby gets rid of 90 percent of the things they've been trying to get on him, the wedge they've had on him all the time. Public opinion goes up, much better bargaining position.
>
> SECOND AGENT: Union members' morale would go up, I'm sure of that.[32]

The second excerpt is even more revealing. It took place during the 9 January 1952 interview. Thompson and the agents were discussing the possible danger the Hawaii Seven posed to national security. David Thompson indicated that he did not see how anybody could "lose a lot of sleep" over the threat they represented. One of the agents responded: "You can't put these guys out here on any basis at all with the Communist Party leaders on the mainland who've been picked up and are under process of being tried under the Smith Act. They just don't rate. These would make poor Communists in the lowest cell in California, but they're the guys who are the leaders of the Communist Party here and so we're stuck with them."[33]

In the spring of 1952 a good deal of excitement was created when John Wayne came to Hawaii to make what was undoubtedly one of his worst films, *Big Jim McLain*. It was a story about a communist effort to seize control of the labor movement in Hawaii. In the film Art Rutledge played the part of an anticommunist labor leader. People clamored for bit parts in the film and for the chance to meet John Wayne, who played the part of a two-fisted FBI agent. When Wayne left Hawaii, it was rumored that he had left IMUA two hundred dollars richer.

Territorial politics produced no real surprises in 1952. While Dwight D. Eisenhower was being elected president of the United States, Joseph R. Farrington was being returned to Congress. The Republicans, as usual, returned majorities to both houses of the territorial legislature. It would prove to be their last hurrah.

In the Democratic primary, to determine who would have the honor of losing to Joe Farrington, Judge Delbert Metzger defeated Superintendent of Public Instruction W. Harold Loper. The race was of interest because of Metzger's immense popularity in the ILWU and Loper's association with the Stainback wing of the Democratic party. Metzger was remembered for his decision in the contempt case against the Reluctant Thirty-nine and for his reduction of bail for the Hawaii Seven from $75,000 to $5,000. Loper was remembered, primarily, for his role in the Reinecke case.

Another old fixture in Hawaiian politics was returned to office, as Mayor Johnny Wilson easily defeated his Republican opponent, Neal Blaisdell. Wilson had more difficulty in the Democratic primary, defeating maverick Democrat Frank Fasi. While the *Honolulu Record* noted that the 1952 campaign had been "practically devoid of 'red-baiting,' it charged that Frank Fasi "stood out among the few who labor-baited."[34] Still, it was a far cry from 1950—and the political revolution of 1954 was just around the corner. But first, there was the business of the Smith Act trial.

Chapter 17

The Trial

It was a calm community that greeted the opening of the Smith Act trial in Hawaii on 5 November 1952, the day after the general election. In Hawaii, as elsewhere, the Smith Act trial was largely a literary exercise. The manner in which the conspiracy was construed only required a prosecution witness to mention the title of a book, pamphlet, periodical, or any other written document and connect it—however remotely—with one or more of the defendants. If the prosecution was unable to make that connection directly, it could achieve the same result by linking the material with an "unindicted coconspirator." Once a connection was made, all of the defendants became responsible for whatever piece of "evidence" had been introduced. When defense counsel sought to introduce documents that would support the contention that their clients had not conspired to teach and advocate the overthrow of the American government by force and violence, the court was reluctant to admit such material as evidence.

In all, the prosecution presented twelve witnesses to make its case against the Hawaii Seven. There were an additional twenty-one prosecution witnesses during the rebuttal phase, but they did not participate in the building of the government's case. Of the twelve witnesses who were central to the prosecution's case, nine were residents of the territory of Hawaii. One prosecution witness, A. A. Smyser of the *Star-Bulletin*, was on the stand only briefly to describe the news conference at which Charles Fujimoto announced that he was the chairman of the Communist Party of Hawaii.

Another local witness was Florence Tam, a young lady from Maui. Miss Tam had met John and Aiko Reinecke during their tour of the neighbor islands in 1948. She testified that John Reinecke had given her a copy of the constitution of the Communist party, with instructions that she should read it "with discrimination." The prosecution also sought to introduce a portion of a letter John Reinecke had written to Miss Tam, suggesting that she read certain pieces of communist literature. Counsel for the defense insisted that the whole letter be read.

When this was done, it revealed that Reinecke's suggested reading for Miss Tam included books that were critical of communism as well as some that were favorable.

The last seven local witnesses for the prosecution were all former communists. The first was Ernest L. Golden. He testified that he had been a member of the Communist party, briefly, in 1946. He named the members of his cell, none of whom was a defendant in the case. This testimony brought an objection from defense attorney A. L. Wirin. In a phrase that was to become quite common, government counsel Rex McKittrick explained, "We are attempting to show a pattern, and . . . certain individuals named by the witness will appear later as unnamed co-conspirators."[1] The objection was overruled.

The second local former communist witness was Ichiro Izuka, whose story was well known from his pamphlet, the Reinecke case, and the HUAC hearings. His testimony in the Smith Act trial added nothing significant. The third and fourth local former communist witnesses were Emil Muller and Henry Johnson, Jr. Muller and Johnson had been friendly witnesses before HUAC, and their Smith Act testimony provided no new information. Golden, Izuka, Muller, and Johnson appeared between 24 November 1952 and 12 December 1953, opening the government's case.

The last three local former communist witnesses appeared between 22 January 1953 and 25 February 1953, at the conclusion of the government's case. First was Robert M. Kempa, whose position as "literary director" of the Communist Party of Hawaii gave the prosecution a splendid opportunity to read a considerable amount of communist literature into the record, including extensive passages on the Russian revolution. The only surprise in Kempa's direct examination was that his name had never come up before. He had been, by his own admission, active in the Communist party from 1946 to 1952.

Much of Kempa's cross-examination involved testimony about the pressure that had been put on him by FBI agents Burress and Condon. Kempa indicated that he had initially resisted testifying. After losing his Navy Yard pass—and thus the right to work—in August 1952, Kempa said that he had reconsidered. He finally agreed to appear as a witness, "about two weeks" before his appearance.[2] After he agreed to testify, Kempa's navy yard pass was reinstated.

Near the end of his cross-examination, defense counsel Richard Gladstein discussed with Kempa the tightening of security measures by the Communist Party of Hawaii in 1950. The following exchange took place:

> Gladstein: Now, the purpose of that was to enable the Party to continue to do the kind of work and activity that it had been in the past . . . isn't that true?

KEMPA: Yes, to continue the operation of the Party at all costs, to work for the Party's ultimate aims that were to overthrow the government and establish socialism.

GLADSTEIN: Who suggested that you say that?

KEMPA: No one, it just came to my mind.[3]

After Kempa came Henry Toyama, who testified that he had been in contact with a significant number of the defendants as a member of the Party. He offered no new information, only variations on what had been said before. It was brought out in cross-examination that Toyama, like Kempa, had been under considerable pressure from the FBI to testify. After establishing that Toyama had signed at least two loyalty oaths in which he had perjured himself, Richard Gladstein questioned him:

GLADSTEIN: Isn't it true, Mr. Toyama, that by testifying here you expect that you will not be prosecuted for those false oaths that you gave back in 1950, am I right about that?

TOYAMA: Well, that is a reasonable assumption, but I am not banking on it.[4]

The last of the local former communist witnesses for the prosecution was Jack Kawano. Kawano's testimony in the Smith Act trial was particularly significant because it was the first time the former ILWU leader had been subjected to cross-examination. Kawano's cross-examination, alone, lasted for the better part of eight days and accounted for 861 pages of the trial transcript.

Kawano's direct testimony was a composite of his July 1951 statement to HUAC and a February 1952 article that had appeared in the *Saturday Evening Post* with some augmentations. The article had been written by Richard English and was titled "We Almost Lost Hawaii to the Reds." It opened by depicting a conversation at a cocktail party on the windward side of the island of Oahu. English set the scene: "Tradewinds sighed through the palms, and clouds scudded across a flawless sky." The hostess was talking with a "crew-cut Navy officer" about the communist menace: "It's awful," she said, "this gradually finding out how they had moved in everywhere. It's like living on a volcano and feeling the lava surging beneath you, ready to erupt at any moment."[5] The *Saturday Evening Post* article concluded:

> The first Americans to be subject to a communist invasion are still stunned at finding it can happen here. And where, in the past, Hawaii's boosters hoped that by minimizing communism it would, like yesterday's tropical rain, just go away, they know better now. They realize that the strong red roots of the ILWU beanstalk on which the communists climbed to almost terrifying power are much too malignant for that.[6]

One Kawano story from the English article concerned a trip to the Communist party headquarters in New York in 1947. It had not been mentioned in Kawano's HUAC testimony. It added considerable spice to the *Saturday Evening Post* article:

> "While I am at the Boston [CIO] convention," Kawano said, "it is suggested by someone that I drop in the national offices of the Communist Party on my way home. And at the party office I talk with Betty Gannett and Eugene Dennis, the secretary of the party, and then Gannett brings in an old guy. His job, she says, is getting information. This old guy is kind of a father type, not too clean shave, and he talks very slow. He wants to know all about Pearl Harbor, Schofield Barracks, and how much military activity goes on. He wants to know how much war materials are sent to Far East and what contact system we have with communists in Japan and China. Most of all he wants to know about defense operations. I tell him I don't know about such things. Then I wonder do they want me to be a spy or something, and I don't feel so good about it.[7]

When Kawano told the same story at the Smith Act trial, he went considerably beyond its brief mention in the *Saturday Evening Post* article. The "old guy" was identified as Emmanuel Levine, a security officer with the Communist party's national office. "Pop," as Kawano indicated Levine was known, had asked about one of his old friends, Jack Kimoto. Kawano explained that Levine and Kimoto had been friends in the Communist party in Los Angeles before World War II. Kawano testified that he had told Kimoto of the meeting in a rather vague way:

> I told him that I met one of his old friends and he said, well, who was he. And I told him that I do not recollect his name. And he said, well, what kind of a guy was he? So I told him that he was kind of old, that he stated that he worked with you in Los Angeles and that he also asked me whether we have established liaison between the Communist Party in Japan, China and the Philippines with Hawaii. And I told him that he told me to say hello to you, and he thought for a while about it and he said, well, maybe I know who you mean. But he did not tell me exactly whether he knew that guy or he did not try to repeat his name or anything like that.[8]

When asked directly by counsel for the prosecution whether this was the full extent of his conversation with Jack Kimoto about "Pop" Levine, Kawano responded affirmatively. In his cross-examination, Richard Gladstein pressed Kawano as to whether he had told Kimoto or any of the defendants about Levine's interest in "munitions, the shipments, the installations, the military personnel," and the other dramatic aspects of the *Saturday Evening Post* article. Kawano said that he had not, offering no explanation as to why he might have ignored such important matters.[9]

In 1977 Jack Kimoto, the former head of the Communist Party of Hawaii wrote, "I never heard of a person called 'Pop' Emmanuel

Levine. . . . That story was pure fabrication calculated to create an impression of international conspiracy on the part of the Smith Act defendants."[10] I have found no evidence to suggest the kind of espionage activities Kawano was seeking to attribute to the Communist Party of Hawaii. Nor is there any evidence that a link existed between the Communist Party of Hawaii and any Communist party units in Japan, China, or the Philippines.

Kawano was also questioned, during cross-examination, about those who had encouraged him to go to Washington, D.C., to testify before HUAC. Kawano listed Chuck Mau, Mitsuyuki Kido, Dr. Ernest Murai, and Daniel Inouye as having been principally responsible. He also mentioned that Sakae Takehashi and Ernest Heen had taken a lesser role in his decision. John Burns and David Benz, whom Kawano had mentioned in earlier testimony as having been influential in his decision to go to Washington, D.C., were not mentioned at the Smith Act trial. Having established the people who were involved, Gladstein moved on to his point:

GLADSTEIN: Isn't it a fact that during the time these people were constantly working on you to clear yourself, Mr. Kawano, they offered you money to set yourself up in business?

KAWANO: Absolutely not.

GLADSTEIN: Isn't it a fact that you did receive loans from them to set you up in business?

KAWANO: Correct. . . . I will read off to you the individuals whom I borrowed the money from: first, [from] Mr. Kido I borrowed $2,750; from Mr. Murai I borrowed $1,700; from Mr. Doo I borrowed $2,000; from my brother I borrowed $1,000; and from the Capital Investment Company I borrowed $1,000. . . .

GLADSTEIN: Did you give notes for this money?

KAWANO: Yes.

GLADSTEIN: Were any of them secured?

KAWANO: Yes . . . by Mr. Mau. . . .

GLADSTEIN: All the notes?

KAWANO: All the notes except the thousand dollars I borrowed from my brother. . . .

GLADSTEIN: Were they gifts or loans?

KAWANO: They were loans, as you can well see, as you can see for yourself.

GLADSTEIN: Did you pay any part of them back?

KAWANO: Not yet.

GLADSTEIN: When did you make them?

KAWANO: Sometime in the latter part of 1951.

GLADSTEIN: About a year and one half ago?

KAWANO: Approximately, yes.

GLADSTEIN: As a matter of fact, some of these notes have a little trick clause in there that says that you wouldn't ever have to pay them at all unless you are able to and willing to do it, isn't that right? . . .

KAWANO: The understanding was that, as I made profits by operating that store, I was to pay back any portion of the loan that I have borrowed from time to time. However, while operating the business, if I happened to go broke and became penniless again, then those few individuals who loaned me the money, particularly Mr. Kido, Mr. Doo and Mr. Murai, they stated that in the event that I go broke and go penniless, forget about it. But if I make the money, if I prosper, they expect me to pay back.[11]

The defense was trying to establish that Jack Kawano had been bought off by those who were using him to help purge the Democratic party of any taint of communism. Although the motivation of those who helped Jack Kawano get started in his liquor business cannot be established with absolute certainty, it is clear that the business had been financed in a highly irregular manner.

Not only was the financing of Jack Kawano's liquor store unusual, but the manner in which he obtained his liquor license raises questions as well. Richard Gladstein brought evidence into court from the liquor commission to show that (1) Kawano's liquor store was in an area that was designated as zone seventeen; (2) between 1 July 1945 and 28 September 1951, five applications for a liquor license had been made and rejected in zone seventeen by responsible individuals in the grocery and meat business; and (3) Kawano was granted his liquor license after a closed hearing, although such hearings were normally open. Gladstein offered the following conclusion: "We submit that the jury would be entitled to draw the inference that Mr. Kawano was the recipient of a very special and unusual—I will not say illegal—unusual and favorable benefit and advantage and that that, too, was a part of the entire consideration that was exchanged for his testimony."[12]

In his cross-examination Richard Gladstein made a strong effort to show that Jack Kawano had become derelict in his union duties during the last two years of his membership in the ILWU:

GLADSTEIN: Isn't it a fact that ever since 1947, your own local union had to beg you to come to union meetings and take care of their grievances for them, isn't that right?

KAWANO: If that was true, how come I was elected as an officer the following year?

GLADSTEIN: From 1947 on, didn't Mr. Kimoto talk with you again and again, begging you to pay attention to your union duties?

KAWANO: I believe Mr. Kimoto talked to me about two or three times. . . .

GLADSTEIN: In 1947, didn't the executive board of your union have to write to you and ask you to come and attend meetings?

KAWANO: Correct. . . . That was because I had other duties. At that time

I was also president of the Territorial Council of the ILWU and I had been working on assignments sometimes on this island and sometimes on the outside islands. The assignments on this island sometimes included the legislature. In 1949, I was the legislative representative for the Territorial group in the legislature.

GLADSTEIN: Did you ever tell that to the longshore local?

KAWANO: I did. They knew where I was.

GLADSTEIN: They knew you were shooting pool?

KAWANO: I shot pool once in a while.

GLADSTEIN: They knew you were playing golf instead of taking care of their grievances?

KAWANO: I played golf once in a while. I shot pool once in a while, and once in a while I played poker, just like Jack Hall.[13]

Jack Hall, in fact, was known by friend and enemy alike as a worker of monumental proportions. Both David Thompson and Robert McElrath, in 1975 interviews, had stories to tell about Kawano's progressive negligence in the performance of his union duties. McElrath gave, as one example, a situation in which Kawano had allowed a union contract to renew itself automatically at a time when it could and should have been reopened. Kawano was also reported to have put a slot machine in his office.[14]

Under relentless pressure from Richard Gladstein, Jack Kawano admitted that, on several occasions, he had said that he hated Jack Hall. Kawano was quick to explain that this hatred stemmed entirely from Hall's membership in the Communist party. More likely, Kawano's hatred of Hall dated back to 1944, when he was passed over as regional director of the ILWU in favor of Hall. Kawano's hatred increased as he saw the regional office being increasingly dominated by mainland haoles such as Hall, McElrath, and Thompson.

The net effect of Kawano's testimony was mixed. There was a basis of truth for much of what he said, but the way in which he colored his testimony gave the impression of a bitter and vindictive man. Those who shared Kawano's prejudices vis-à-vis communism and the ILWU believed that he had been a powerful government witness; those who did not share his prejudices did not. Few were on the fence.

Three prosecution witnesses from the mainland deserve attention: Paul Crouch, Daisy Van Dorn, and John Lautner, all professional ex-communists. Paul Crouch was a minister's son from North Carolina. He had drifted away from home at the age of twenty-one, coming to Hawaii in 1924 with the U.S. Army. Having been converted from the Baptist faith to communism, Crouch got into trouble at Schofield Barracks for preaching Marxism within the ranks. For these political activities Crouch was courtmartialed and served a three-year term at Alcatraz. Freed in 1928, Crouch went to work for the Communist party. He remained on the Party's payroll until 1942. When the cold war commenced after World War II, Crouch was recruited by the FBI as an expert witness.

As an expert witness, Crouch was allowed to go on at great length about his own personal experiences in the Communist party, even though he had been out of the Party for three years before the alleged conspiracy of the Hawaii Seven had begun. The most colorful part of Crouch's testimony was his description of a visit he had made to the Soviet Union shortly after his release from Alcatraz:

> I participated in meetings of the Executive Committees of the Communist and Young Communist Internationals, the World Congress of the Red International Trade Unions. I met with members of the general staff of the Red Army, reported to them and received directives from them. I received a commission as an honorary regimental commander in the Red Army. I met with leaders of the Soviet Government and the Communist International including Lenin's widow, Krupskaya, V. M. Molotov, Sen Katayama of Japan, Harry Pollitt of Great Britain, and many other leaders. I spoke over the Comintern radio station. I received a commission . . . to draw up a documentary program for infiltration of capitalist armies and methods for Communist activities during a future war.[15]

Such "evidence" was objected to again and again by defense counsel throughout Crouch's testimony. Judge Jon Wiig invariably held that such testimony gave insight into the workings of the Communist party and was, therefore, relevant and binding upon the defendants.

Crouch's testimony also provided the opportunity for the prosecution to read any piece of communist literature into the record. Crouch, as an "expert witness," had every opportunity to demonstrate his knowledge of communist literature. After he had introduced a work that had, for example, been used in one of the Communist party schools in which he had taught, the prosecution would read copious amounts of the volume in question into the record. This was done so often that the mere announcement that the prosecutor was going to read would have the immediate effect of emptying the courtroom of spectators. A joke was making the rounds:

> PROSECUTOR: Have you ever seen a coconut tree?
> WITNESS: Yes
> PROSECUTOR: Where?
> WITNESS: In front of the public library.
> PROSECUTOR: Good, I shall now read to the jury the history of the Russian Revolution.[16]

No effort was made to show that Paul Crouch's brief adventure in Hawaii in 1924 had put him into contact with any of the defendants. There was testimony, however, to the effect that he had taught Jim Freeman in a Communist party school in Alameda County, California, just before World War II. This was the only testimony he gave that was directly related to the Hawaii Seven.

Daisy Van Dorn's testimony can only be called outrageous. Describing her own Communist party training in San Francisco, "Bloody Daisy," as she came to be called, grew very excited. The erratic grandmother offered the following scenario for the coming communist revolution:

> We were instructed that we were to go as far as cutting the telephone lines of our neighbors. . . . Also we were taught that we were immediately broken down to smaller classes, clubs, groups, as it were, and we were to have, each club, eight guards. . . . We were to take all our orders from them when the revolution broke, which would not be long, and they promised us in this class that they had food stored up for us for the time of the revolution. . . . I was supposed to be the nurse in one of the houses and I was to assist and take care and bandage up only members of the Party.

When Howard K. Hoddick tried to interrupt Daisy's testimony, she became angry, telling Hoddick, "I'm not through yet." And indeed she wasn't. Speaking of her instructor, Ann Polanchek, Daisy uttered the words that were the source of her well-earned nickname: "She [Polanchek] said, 'Now there will be lots of blood running in the streets. It will be bloodthirsty, but we will gain our victory of socialistic government.' "[17]

Defense counsel sought to have a mistrial declared, owing to the inflammatory nature of Daisy Van Dorn's testimony. Howard Hoddick swallowed hard and said:

> We will submit now . . . that so far as the evidence of Ann Polanchek, it is material and relevant only as it goes to the nature and purpose of the Communist Party. . . . In this connection, upon showing that these defendants in this court knew the aims . . . and nature of the conspiracy, we submit that this evidence of Ann Polanchek's teachings and instructions would properly be binding against these defendants.[18]

Judge Wiig found Hoddick's argument reasonable and denied the motion without comment.

If Crouch and Van Dorn were flamboyant, the last of the government's professional ex-communists was not. John Lautner was one of the government's principal witnesses in every Smith Act trial after the *Dennis* case in 1949. Lautner was a Communist party wheelhorse from 1932 to 1950, when he was unceremoniously expelled from the party. Herbert L. Packer, in his volume, *Ex-Communist Witnesses*, chose Lautner as one of his four representative subjects. In his conclusion, Packer wrote the following:

> John Lautner's workmanlike role in the Communist movement was echoed in his stolid, pedantic, relatively unshakable testimony. To be sure,

> he has been tripped up on more than one occasion. He has also been evasive, militantly self-justifying, and all the other things one might expect of a man who, late in life, finds himself in the unenviable position of repudiating his life's work. Yet he gives the overall impression of close familiarity with the Party's ideology and, more important, with the day-to-day details of its operation.
>
> Strongly in Lautner's favor as a witness is the fact that . . . he has not carved out an extra-testimonial career as an ex-Communist. He has been paid, and paid well, for his testimony. But he has not had the additional impetus to fabricate that comes from the creation of a public image that must constantly be refurbished by yet another round of revelations.[19]

Howard Hoddick stated in 1975 that John Lautner was the government's most satisfactory witness.[20] He was surely their most heavily used witness. His testimony covers 2,239 pages of the trial transcript. Lautner was the "expert" on the aims and purposes of the Communist party. His testimony epitomizes what was earlier referred to as the "literary aspect" of the Smith Act trial. For a full month Lautner sat on the witness stand competently working at his job as a professional ex-communist. His employers were pleased, defense counsel was exasperated, and the public was generally bored.

When the government's case had ended, the defense responded by ignoring the prosecution's case and presenting a string of fifty character witnesses in behalf of the defendants. It might have been fifty-one, but John A. Burns was excused by Jack Hall. In Burns' own words, in 1975:

> I offered to Jack Hall that I would testify for him if he wanted me. . . . [The FBI] tried to call me in and use me on the other side of the picture. I told the counsel for the FBI . . . I've never lied on the witness stand yet, I'm not going to start now. . . . Jack Hall is one hell of an American. [After that] they were not very much interested in having me as a witness. So I offered to Jack [Hall] and Koji [Ariyoshi], I'd be happy to testify if they called me as a witness for the defense. But they decided that they didn't want to throw me to the wolves. It was Jack's decision.[21]

The prosecution, not to be outdone, produced its own parade of twenty-one rebuttal witnesses, who testified that the character of the defendants was bad. None of the testimony of the character witnesses, good or bad, contained any revelations. The whole exercise was irrelevant.

The nub of the case, as established in the *Dennis* decision, was whether or not the defendants had been members of the Communist party during the period of the alleged conspiracy—between 1 April 1945 and 28 August 1951. It is clear that all were guilty as charged. After sixteen hours, on 19 June 1953, the jury returned that verdict. The six men were sentenced to five years in prison and fined $5,000 each. Eileen Fujimoto was sentenced to three years in prison and fined $2,000. At the request of the government, bail was raised to $15,000 while the appeal of the decision worked its way through the courts. The ILWU Defense Fund was able to get Jack Hall released immediately, but the other six languished in jail for a week before bail could be raised. None of them would ever return to jail.

On 17 June 1957, almost exactly four years after the verdict in the Hawaii Smith Act trial, the U.S. Supreme Court made the decision that would lead to the reversal of the conviction of the Hawaii Seven. In *Yates v. United States* the conviction of fourteen leaders of the Communist Party of California was overturned. Justice John Marshall Harlan looked at the *Yates* case from several viewpoints. His first ruling was procedural, rather than substantive, having to do with the term "organize." The government had argued that the term "organize" connoted a continuing process and was not, therefore, subject to a three-year statute of limitations. Justice Harlan and the majority of the court held that the statute of limitations did apply, thereby overturning the convictions.

On the substantive question, Harlan, despite his own protestations to the contrary, led the Supreme Court back to a position more closely in tune with Justice Holmes' "clear and present danger" doctrine: "We are faced with the question of whether the Smith Act prohibits advocacy and teaching of forcible overthrow as an abstract principle, divorced from any effort to instigate action to that end, so long as such advocacy or teaching is engaged in with evil intent. We hold that it does not."[22]

On 20 January 1958 the Hawaii Seven became beneficiaries of the *Yates* decision. Eight and one-half years after their original arrest, their legal ordeal finally ended.

PART FOUR

THE SPECTER FADES

Chapter 18

A New Hawaii

The anticommunist impulse in Hawaii did not die with the end of the Smith Act trial. But the immediacy of the issue disappeared as rapidly as the series of protest strikes that greeted the conviction of Jack Hall and his six fellow defendants. Jack Hall was no Alger Hiss, and the Fujimotos were not the Rosenbergs. Jack Kawano's testimony notwithstanding, few residents of Hawaii saw any real connection between the Communist Party of Hawaii and Moscow.

The real story of communism in Hawaii had been substantially revealed during the year between 11 November 1947, with Governor Stainback's Armistice Day speech, and 29 October 1948, with the dismissal of John and Aiko Reinecke. That story was subject to a variety of interpretations, but the basic facts were virtually in place. The Izuka pamphlet and its elaboration in the Reinecke hearing became the basic working document of the anticommunists. Those accused of communist associations had learned from the Reineckes' experience that the times did not allow for the luxury of a philosophical elaboration of the radical political persuasion. As I. F. Stone put it in 1951, "If I were a lawyer with a radical client in these days I wouldn't let him assert under oath that he wasn't a two-headed calf."[1]

By 1955 the irresponsible career of Joseph McCarthy had come to an abrupt halt, after his humiliation during the Army-McCarthy hearings and his formal censure by the U.S. Senate in December 1954. In April 1955 Attorney General Herbert Brownell announced that the Justice Department was giving up the practice of retaining full-time "consultants" on communism. Ended were the careers of such noted former communists as John Lautner, Paul Crouch, and Louis Budenz who, in the words of I. F. Stone, had told their "familiar story of the Communist conspiracy with the glibness of a traveling evangelist describing the details of hell."[2]

Many Americans had arrived at the point that Arthur Garfield Hays, the liberal lawyer for the ACLU, had reached when he described William Z. Foster and Earl Browder, the leaders of the CPUSA, as "confused, futile men who have been able to get nowhere in all these years. Why we treat them as important people developing a big political movement," he continued, "is beyond my comprehension."[3] In 1956 the small following the CPUSA still had was decimated in the wake of the Soviet attack on Hungary. The cold war had not died, indeed it had yet to reach its apex, but the idea of a dangerous communist movement in the United States had passed.

The Truman administration had given way to the administration of Dwight D. Eisenhower. The new president had gone to Korea and negotiated an end to the struggle there in a way that might well have led to threats of impeachment had Truman struck the same deal. Despite the rhetoric of Eisenhower's highly moralistic secretary of state, John Foster Dulles, the new president had no wish to take on the mantle of French colonialism in Indochina in the name of anticommunism. Nor did Eisenhower intend to roll back the Iron Curtain in Europe if a substantial risk of war were involved.

By 1954 the Democrats of Hawaii were tired of apologizing for the communist albatross the Republicans had so long wrapped around their necks. In his book *Journey to Washington*, Daniel Inouye described a dramatic moment in the 1954 election campaign when a Democratic rally was interrupted by a so-called Republican truth squad. The leader of the interloping Republicans told the audience that the Democratic party was in the hands of men who were "the willing tools of ILWU leader Harry Bridges and hence, at the very least, soft on communism." Inouye, the one-armed war hero who was running for the territorial House of Representatives, recalled rising from his seat, taking the microphone from the head of the "truth squad," and addressing the audience as follows:

> I cannot help wondering whether the people of Hawaii will not think it strange that the only weapon in the Republican arsenal is to label as communists men so recently returned from defending liberty on the firing lines of Italy and France. Let me speak for those of us who didn't come back—I know I speak for my colleagues on this platform, and for good Democratic candidates everywhere in these Islands—when I say that we bitterly resent having our loyalty and patriotism questioned by cynical political hacks who lack the courage to debate the real issues in this campaign. . . .
>
> I gave this arm to fight fascists. If my country wants the other one to fight communists, it can have it![4]

Strangely enough, the largest dose of anticommunist rhetoric the Democrats faced in 1954 came from within the ranks of their own party. Maverick Democrat Frank Fasi, in his bid for mayor of Honolulu, was vocally anticommunist in his 1954 primary campaign. His candidacy was an isolated throwback to the 1950 struggle between the Walkout and Standpat Democrats. Fasi's anticommunist rhetoric reached its peak during a twenty-hour "talkathon" he did on radio station KULA. Two hours of the event was carried on KULA-TV. One caller was concerned because Fasi had branded the ILWU as a communist union. The caller was both a member of the ILWU and a World War II veteran. He asked Fasi, "Would you classify me as a communist?" Fasi responded:

> No, I wouldn't call you a communist because you happen to be a member of the ILWU. But your leaders have been classified as such by a jury of twelve in our Federal court. . . . Someday we may fight Communist Russia, and when that day comes I want you ILWU rank and file union members who are loyal Americans to consider the fact that your leaders will probably be interned immediately. And I am very much concerned that once your leaders are put away in prison for the duration of the war, what is going to happen to you and your union movement.[5]

Another question had to do with pressure the Wilson administration was putting on city employees to give time and money to the Wilson campaign. Fasi responded:

> These professionals who believe and say in all sincerity—and I quote—"We don't care where the votes come from—communists, fascists, kanakas, or Japanese." They say that, and the *Honolulu Record*, the Communist *Daily Worker* of Hawaii, supports them in print. While communist propagandist Robert McElrath supports them on the radio. They are the type that will make deals with the devil, himself, just to stay in office.[6]

Even Fasi claimed to have minimum standards for his anticommunism. When asked his opinion of the recently diminished Joseph McCarthy, Fasi was quick to say

> I think that McCarthy—even though he's an ex-marine and belongs to the same religious faith as I do—is a disgrace to the United States Senate. Some people say that at least he has had the guts and courage to expose [the communists]. But I resent a man that exposes communism with the tactics that he has used, the complete disregard for the rights—the human rights and the civil rights—of American citizens with the excuse that he is fighting an evil. . . . I am opposed to that type of man conducting hearings the way he conducted them, just for himself, and not so much to ferret out the Communists in our government. . . . I am against McCarthyism and everything he stands for.[7]

Fasi would have to wait another fourteen years before he was finally successful in his bid to become mayor of Honolulu.

Another who had to wait after the 1954 elections, although not so long as Frank Fasi, was John A. Burns. Joe Farrington, the popular Republican delegate to Congress, died before the 1954 elections. On 31 July 1954, in a special election, Elizabeth Farrington was overwhelmingly elected to finish out the last three months of her husband's term. So impressive was her two-to-one victory over Judge Delbert Metzger that the Republican party asked her to stand for reelection in the fall. In spite of the Democratic landslide of 1954, Mrs. Farrington was re-elected as delegate to Congress. The margin over Democratic party chairman John A. Burns was less than one thousand votes out of 140,000 votes cast. Burns would be elected in 1956.

In the political revolution of 1954, the Democrats found themselves with two-thirds majorities in the territorial House and Senate. Hawaii's "normal" Republican majority had become a "normal" Democratic majority. The Republicans continued to give lip service to anticommunism. A review of Republican party platforms in Hawaii reveals that the party continued to oppose communism and support the territorial Subversive Activities Commission until 1962, when this biennial pledge was dropped.

In 1956 U.S. Senate opponents of Hawaiian statehood sought to revive the specter of communism in Hawaii by holding yet another set of hearings on the subject. Senator James O. Eastland, a blatantly racist Mississippi Democrat, brought his Senate Internal Security Subcommittee to Honolulu. Former Governor Ingram M. Stainback used this forum to justify the anticommunist actions taken during his administration. The territorial Subversive Activities Commission complained to the senators that the Democratic legislature in Hawaii had cut the commission's 1956 budget request by 50 percent. Some of the original members of the Reluctant Thirty-nine were paraded before the committee, once again invoking the Fifth Amendment. This time, however, there would be no charges of contempt of Congress. More than 3,000 of the 24,000 ILWU members walked off their jobs to protest the Eastland hearings.[8] By this time, however, Hawaii's employers were more interested in statehood and good labor relations than they were in making a few meaningless anticommunist points. The feeling was that if Jack Hall and his fellow union leaders had, indeed, been members of the Communist party in the past, they surely were no more. The ILWU was proving itself a force with which they could deal.

Regarding former Governor Ingram M. Stainback, perhaps the most accurate judgment of his anticommunist crusade came from one who had been an admirer. J. Russell Cades, a distinguished Honolulu attorney, said of Stainback in 1982: "I knew Stainback fairly well. In his day he was a highly competent, fine lawyer. I think he was unusually capable. I thought he went berserk on the question of the communist scare and all that."[9] Cades felt that much of the anticommunist activity was a smoke screen for opposition to statehood.

In 1958 John A. Burns, then Hawaii's delegate to Congress, met the charge of communist penetration in the Democratic party by quoting

FBI reports. The Communist Party of Hawaii, according to the FBI, had 160 members in 1946; by 1952, that number had dwindled to 36. The success of the Democratic party, Burns asserted, had killed any communist menace that may have existed.[10] Burns was only half right in his statement, and he knew it. It was the success of the Democratic party *and* the success of the ILWU that had eliminated the need for a radical political party in the territory of Hawaii. This view was accepted by all but a handful of those who had been members of the Communist Party of Hawaii.

John Burns, easily the most important political figure in Hawaii during the thirty years following World War II, had no illusions about the presence of communism in Hawaii. He did, however, have a perspective that served him and the state of Hawaii well. Burns recalled the era of communist ascendancy in 1975:

> Every guy in the organization, the ILWU, was at one time or another a member of the Communist Party of America. This is where they got their organizational information and how to organize, and how to bring groups together and how to create cells and how to make movements that are undetected by the bosses and everything else. . . . I knew what they were about. I said this is the only way they are going to organize.[11]

The nature of the Communist Party of Hawaii had changed by the mid-1950s. There is evidence that the more ideological members of the Party felt betrayed by their more pragmatic brethren from the ILWU. The pragmatists, like Jack Hall, had dropped out of the Party when it became an impediment to the achievement of their goals as union leaders. The ILWU had become a part of the establishment. Its primary interest was in consolidating and protecting its considerable gains. As Jack Hall said in 1968: "The radicals are no longer in the unions. They are on the campuses."[12]

In 1983 Noel Kent wrote of Jack Hall in terms that many would not recognize. "No one," Kent wrote in *Hawaii: Islands Under the Influence,* "personifies the tragedy of the ILWU more clearly than Jack Hall, whose great leadership abilities were channeled into the narrow confines of conservative (and increasingly autocratic) trade unionism."[13] There *is* an element of tragedy to the end of Jack Hall's life. The challenge had obviously gone out of his work. His health had deteriorated dramatically as a result of his stubborn unwillingness to take proper care of himself and the continuation of his destructive drinking habits. As Sanford Zalburg pointed out, "In the end it all came apart: he had diabetes, prostate trouble, high blood pressure, arteriosclerosis, gout, [and] Parkinson's disease."[14] By the end, the 220 pounds he carried on his six-foot-two-inch frame had dwindled to 160 pounds. But this was not the tragedy of which Kent was speaking. Kent, unwilling to accept the success of the ILWU as something laudable, saw it this way: "For the people of Hawaii, the disintegration of the ILWU as a force committed to the powerful socialist ideas of economic justice, mass democracy, and workers' power was a tragedy of the first order."[15] Kent's critique that Jack Hall "died a defeated man" fails to appreciate the intensely pragmatic nature of the man. As Hall once told Art Rutledge, "I don't want to write history, I want to make it." And make it he did.

The consensus view of Jack Hall, when he died in 1971, was that he had become something of a labor statesman. Gene Hunter, associate editor of Hall's old nemesis the *Honolulu Advertiser*, wrote on Hall's death:

> Although sometimes accused of being a Communist and once arrested for allegedly conspiring to teach and advocate the overthrow of the United States government, a violation of the Smith Act, Mr. Hall, long before his death was recognized as a respected community leader, working on a variety of civic programs with some of the same businessmen he at one time counted among his bitterest enemies. . . .
>
> Throughout his life he was to fight for racial equality, for higher wages and better working conditions for laboring men and women and for the improvement of social conditions which he found abhorrent—sometimes at peril to his life and reputation.[16]

The business community had, indeed, come to terms with Jack Hall —and it was on his terms, not theirs. Frederick Simpich, Jr., was the epitome of a Big Five businessman. A vice-president and director of Castle & Cooke, director of Dole Pineapple and Matson Navigation, and president of Oceanic Properties, Simpich wrote of Hall in 1971:

> While ruthless in keeping members from drifting out of the union or in retaliation against any disaffecting politician at the polls, Hall and his staff were scrupulously honest in personal money matters. . . . There was never the suggestion of scandal about Hall's administration of the union. If Merchant Street has any debt to him, it is that the ILWU presence prevented gangster-type unions from entering the islands.
>
> In maturing, Hall came to question a youthful belief in the practicality of socialism, served with Lowell Dillingham as co-chairman of the United Fund Drive and was even elected vice-president of the Hawaii Visitors' Bureau.[17]

Hall's participation in the Hawaii Visitors' Bureau was not without its pragmatic purpose. As Hall guided the ILWU through the inevitability of agricultural and waterfront automation, he targeted tourism as the union's next frontier for jobs. Had he simply fought automation, he might have gone down as a heroic figure, but he surely would have gone down. He might even have taken the ILWU with him. Now *that* would have been a tragic ending for this man who had helped shape modern Hawaii.

With the coming of the Eisenhower administration, the territory of Hawaii had its first Republican governor in twenty years. The new president tapped the noncontroversial Samuel Wilder King. Gavan Daws described King as "a Republican with a dash of New England blood and a dash of Hawaiian blood to balance it."[18] Although King was not actively anticommunist, he did appear at the Smith Act trial, reluctantly, to say that he did not consider Jack Hall to be a "very good citizen," in that "he does not seem to believe in the American system of democracy." During Eisenhower's second term, King was replaced by William F. Quinn, a popular attorney who had come to Hawaii after graduating from law school shortly after the end of World War II. In 1984 Quinn recalled his first meeting with President Eisenhower. "The first thing he says to me was, 'Well, doesn't Harry Bridges, the Communist, control those islands?' And I had to reassure him that he didn't."[19] When he was running for governor in 1959, after statehood had been achieved, Quinn recalled the following conversation with Vice-President Richard M. Nixon:

> NIXON: I think you're going to have to take off the gloves and come out fighting out there. You've got Jack Burns, who's so tied into the ILWU—which is Harry Bridges—and is a Communist. . . . You've got to lay all that out. You've got to get out there and let people know this, and you've got to really hit them hard.
>
> QUINN: Mr. Vice-President, one, it's not true and two, it's just not my style.[20]

Had Quinn followed Nixon's advice, he might well have lost the race in which he became the state of Hawaii's first elected governor.

In a 1975 interview A. A. Smyser, then editor of the *Honolulu Star-Bulletin*, expressed the feeling that there had been an overreaction to the communist threat in the late 1940s and early 1950s. Smyser emphasized that this reaction must be seen in the context of the times. "This was never more true," Smyser said, "than during the 1949 longshore strike, when so many institutions, all in a state of flux, were so severely tested."[21]

In another 1975 interview, Smyser elaborated on the corporate view of the communist threat by his newspaper:

> [The *Star-Bulletin*] tended to agree with [Burns] that the communist issue was seized upon by different groups in the community for their own interests. . . . Any opposition to Statehood on the grounds that labor leaders might get into power, or the Japanese people might get into power was an un-democratic, and un-American reason that you couldn't really espouse.

And so the people who felt that—and there were people who felt that—retreated to communism as the cover for their opposition. Burns was aware of this, the *Star-Bulletin* was aware of it, and in this we could make common cause. Although I would say the *Star-Bulletin*—Riley Allen and Joe Farrington (but Riley in particular)—nonetheless considered communism a matter of serious concern in the community at that time.[22]

A similar feeling was expressed by Howard K. Hoddick in 1975. Hoddick, as acting U.S. attorney at the time of the Smith Act trial, had carried most of the burden in the preparation of the government's case against the Hawaii Seven. Commenting from the perspective of almost a quarter of a century's distance, Hoddick said of the trial: "Looking back, we probably wasted a lot of time. The trail was too thin, if there was any trail at all. But we believed it at the time."[23]

There was at least one person who had no regrets over his views of the communist menace in Hawaii, when looking back over the years: Dr. Lyle G. Phillips, the former president of IMUA. Dr. Phillips said in 1975 that he believed the communist threat was every bit as large as IMUA had painted it during the peak years of the Hawaii Residents' Association's influence. He maintained that the communists had actually won out in the struggle without the public ever realizing it. Dr. Phillips was particularly critical of the Big Five, the principal means of support for IMUA. "They quit a few years ago, and IMUA is falling apart now."[24]

Few bemoaned the passage of IMUA. Former Governor Bill Quinn recalled: "Dr. Lyle Phillips was making speeches all around the country saying that I was a communist."[25] Quinn was occasionally accused of being a "closet Democrat," but Phillips was the only person who appears to have gone on record to accuse him of having been a communist. Quinn saw it all as a part of the effort to stop statehood.

Another to repudiate Phillips was his onetime close associate Tony Todaro. In 1955 Paul Crouch, one of the government's professional ex-communists in the Smith Act trial, wrote a letter attacking statehood. Todaro responded:

[Crouch's letter] compels me to dust off my soap box abandoned two years ago after severing relations with IMUA. . . . I cannot go along with Crouch that the Communist menace in Hawaii is grave enough to warrant a denial of statehood. . . . I strongly disagree with my good friend, Dr. Lyle G. Phillips, of IMUA, that nowhere in the Mainland has the Communist Party progressed towards its evil aims as has the Communist Party in Hawaii. . . . I challenge IMUA, Paul Crouch and all prejudiced congressmen to submit to the public a list of names that could be elected to sit in congress as Moscow agents and another list of political issues these "Moscow agents" would try to force upon the national congress that would benefit Russia. I challenge these people, also, to pinpoint their charges that the legislature of Hawaii is dominated or influenced by Communists or

> Communist philosophy. Give us names and specific action and not a general charge that McElrath was seen talking to certain lawmakers at Iolani Palace.[26]

Todaro had come a long way from the days when he, himself, had written of the evil spells of Robert "McElmouse."

One of the more interesting retrospective views of the issue of communism in Hawaii came from Yasuki Arakaki. Arakaki, close personal and political friend of John A. Burns, said in a 1977 interview:

> Nobody can prove that I am a Communist. I have read and I had at that time in my possession much of the literature written by Karl Marx and other people who advocated socialism. And I offered an opinion—even until today—that someday the world cannot afford capitalism. The people in this world will realize that they have to share their wealth and capitalism doesn't share wealth. . . . And we are having too many people . . . exploiting the natural resources. . . . I still believe today the country that is going to save the world is the People's Republic of China. . . . Whatever "ism" you might call it, I think they have a solution.

Interviewer Dan Boylan pursued the question, asking whether Arakaki had ever expressed such views to John Burns. Arakaki responded: "On many occasions, yes. Jack knew what I believed. He always counseled me and said, 'Your belief is something which a lot of people won't understand.' In other words, keep quiet."[27]

To have kept quiet is probably what Jack Kawano, the truly tragic figure in this struggle, wished he had done. By 1975 he could look back philosophically. When asked whether he thought he had been used by those who urged him to go public with the story of his communist past, Kawano said no, "they just had to ride another horse when they found out that I was not useful to them." Asked whether he was bitter or angry, he replied:

> When I look back at it I'm not angry because I feel that that's the normal way a man should go, because when two men is going into a fight, or going into war, there's no reason why two men should die because one is dead. I think the other, if he's not dead, should live to fight another day. And I think that's what Burns and Kido and those people did. So I have no feelings against them.[28]

Kawano could easily have felt betrayed by his Democratic party friends. This son of Hawaii was forced into virtual exile after his liquor business failed. When Kawano was unable to get a decent job in Hawaii, Rex McKittrick of the U.S. attorney's office prevailed upon Lockheed Aircraft to hire him in Burbank, California. Even when Kawano was in California he was not beyond being used by men who called themselves his friends. In 1962, the year John Burns won his first governor's race, Kawano was brought to Hawaii by Kenji Kimball of the Halekulani Hotel. It is not entirely clear whether Kawano knew what was expected of him when he accepted the money for his airline ticket and expenses from Kimball. If he did not know before, he found out when he arrived. "They wanted me to make a statement denouncing Jack Burns," Kawano said in 1975, " . . . say that Burns was a pro-Communist."[29]

Chuck Mau, Kawano's trusted old friend and advisor, recalled in 1975 that he had gone to Kawano's hotel room, heard what Kimball and his Republican friends wanted Kawano to do, and had advised him "that it would not be a fair thing to do because it would not be true." "The worst that could be said [of Burns]," Mau reports telling Kawano, "because of his close relationship with certain leaders of the ILWU, would be that he was an opportunist and wanted to play ball with them just to get their support and their votes."[30]

Confronted with the reality of turning on his old friend Jack Burns, Kawano would not do so. Whether it was Chuck Mau, his own conscience, or a combination of the two, he balked. "I went out there but I didn't do it," Kawano said. "And in fact, Jack [Burns] used my statements about him, proper statements about him, in his campaign to help prove he wasn't a Communist."[31]

When attempting to assign motivation for people's actions related to the issue of communism in the United States during the late 1940s and early 1950s, one should remember that fear is one of the greatest motivators we know. Fear does not have to be reasonable in order to be deeply felt. A fear of communism during this period is not to be dismissed, considering the geopolitical circumstances in which we found ourselves at the end of World War II. But fear was not the exclusive companion of one side during these troubled years. David Thompson, the ILWU's longtime educational director, commented in 1975 about some of the fears of organized labor, "especially the Japanese who had been through it before." Thompson spoke of "the fear of losing a job, of being overcommitted to the union, and of the possible failure of unionism."[32]

Fear is a breeder of conspiratorial thinking. In the period following World War II, there were many possible sources of fear. Besides the international and national concerns that made their way into the territory's consciousness, there were more immediate sources of concern: the Japanese Americans' experience both at home and abroad during World War II, the changing relations between labor and management that had been dimly perceived before World War II and were so explosively apparent by the end of the war, and the sense of a new day dawning in Hawaii's politics. Change was in the air, and change creates fear. In the final analysis, both the "bosses' conspiracy" and the "communist conspiracy" were exaggerated.

It took time for the new world that rose out of the ashes of World War II to begin to come to terms with itself. That process continues to this day. In Hawaii, the new relationships that produced the revolution of 1954 have become established and generally accepted. The lion has learned to live with the lamb. In these days, it is hard to tell which is which.

Notes

Abbreviations

HA	*Honolulu Advertiser*
HH	U.S. Congress, House, Committee on Un-American Activities, *Hearings Regarding Communist Activities in the Territory of Hawaii* (HUAC hearings)
HR	*Honolulu Record*
HSB	*Honolulu Star-Bulletin*
HTH	*Hilo Tribune-Herald*
JBOHP	John A. Burns Oral History Project
RH	*Department of Public Instruction v. Dr. John E. Reinecke and Aiko T. Reinecke* (Reinecke hearings)

Chapter 1: The Mainland

1. Ronald Steel, *Walter Lippmann and the American Century*, p. 101.
2. David H. Bennett, *The Party of Fear*, p. 187.
3. Ibid., p. 186.
4. Ibid., p. 193. This fear of aliens was also consistent with the rise of the Ku Klux Klan in the 1920s to become an organization of more than four million members. The Klan of the 1920s was far more concerned about Catholics and Jews, the preponderance of whom were recent arrivals to the United States, than about blacks.
5. Ibid., pp. 194–195.
6. Walter Goodman, *The Committee*, pp. 6–7.
7. *New Republic*, 24 Dec. 1930, p. 58.
8. Roger Morris, *Richard Milhous Nixon*, p. 377.
9. Ibid.
10. Charles P. Larrowe, *Harry Bridges*, p. 246.
11. Ibid., p. 248.
12. Ibid., p. 340.
13. Bennett, *Party of Fear*, p. 286.
14. Richard J. Walton, *Henry Wallace, Harry Truman, and the Cold War*, p. 277.
15. Larrowe, *Harry Bridges*, p. 324.
16. Edward D. Beechert, *Working in Hawaii*, p. 305.
17. Fred J. Cook, *The Nightmare Decade*, p. 64.
18. For an excellent discussion of the ACLU and the communist issue, see "The Politics of Civil Liberties" by Mary S. McAuliffe in *The Specter*, ed. Robert Griffith and Athen Theoharis, pp. 154–170.
19. Cook, *Nightmare Decade*, p. 64.

20. *Congressional Record, House of Representatives*, 29 July 1939, p. 10,452.
21. Ibid., p. 10,452.
22. *Congressional Record, Senate*, 10 June 1940, p. 2,818.
23. Goodman, *The Committee*, p. 99n.
24. *Dennis v. United States*, 341 U.S. 494 (1951).
25. David A. Shannon, *The Decline of American Communism*, pp. 195–203.
26. Joseph R. Starobin, *American Communism in Crisis, 1943–1957*, pp. 183–184. For the most comprehensive, if sympathetic, account of the Wallace campaign in 1948, see Curtis D. MacDougall, *Gideon's Army*.
27. Stephen E. Ambrose, *Nixon: The Education of a Politician, 1913–1962*, p. 129.
28. Morris, *Richard Milhous Nixon*, p. 332.
29. Fawn M. Brodie, *Richard Nixon: The Shaping of His Character*, p. 171.
30. Goodman, *The Committee*, p. 271.
31. Robert J. Donovan, *Tumultuous Years*, p. 133.
32. For the most comprehensive study of the Hiss case, see Allen Weinstein, *Perjury*.
33. For a highly readable account of these events, see Louis Nizer, *The Implosion Conspiracy*.
34. *Honolulu Star-Bulletin (HSB)*, 22 Sept. 1950, p. 1.
35. *HSB*, 23 Sept. 1950, p. 1.
36. *Honolulu Advertiser (HA)*, 30 Aug. 1950, p. 1.
37. For an excellent short legislative history of the McCarran Act, see the chapter titled "The Internal Security Act of 1950" by William R. Tanner and Robert Griffith, in *The Specter*, ed. Griffith and Theoharis, pp. 174–189.
38. *HSB*, 13 Oct. 1950, p. 4.
39. *HSB*, 1 Jan. 1951, p. 1.
40. Brodie, *Richard Nixon*, p. 241.
41. Richard H. Rovere, *Senator Joe McCarthy*, p. 102.
42. Bennett, *Party of Fear*, p. 293.
43. Rovere, *Senator Joe McCarthy*, pp. 132–134.
44. Morris, *Richard Milhous Nixon*, p. 749.
45. Donovan, *Tumultuous Years*, p. 170.
46. Cook, *Nightmare Decade*, pp. 297–298.
47. Rovere, *Senator Joe McCarthy*, p. 65.
48. Owen Lattimore, *Ordeal by Slander*, pp. 7–8.
49. Cook, *Nightmare Decade*, p. 236.
50. Ibid., p. 237.
51. Robert Griffith, *The Politics of Fear*, p. 83.
52. Cook, *Nightmare Decade*, pp. 261–262. The senators who joined Mrs. Smith were Charles W. Tobey of New Hampshire, George D. Aiken of Vermont, Wayne L. Morse of Oregon (then a Republican), Irving M. Ives of New York, Edward J. Thye of Minnesota, and Robert C. Hendrickson of New Jersey.
53. Bennett, *Party of Fear*, p. 310.

Chapter 2: The Territory of Hawaii

1. Quoted in Edward D. Beechert, *Working in Hawaii*, pp. 222–223.
2. Lawrence Fuchs, *Hawaii Pono*, p. 363.
3. Beechert, *Working in Hawaii*, p. 213. The charges against Wright were

picked up by Edward Johannessen in his 1956 work *The Hawaiian Labor Movement* (see p. 146). Johannessen also refers to an organization called the Hawaiian Proletarian Soviet that he said "was organized and at one time claimed a membership of 2,500 although this figure is undoubtedly exaggerated." I have not been able to find any other references to the Hawaiian Proletarian Soviet. If it did exist, it certainly did not have 2,500 members.

4. Beechert, *Working in Hawaii*, p. 132.

5. Ibid., p. 244.

6. Ibid., p. 241.

7. Ibid., p. 253.

8. Sanford Zalburg, *A Spark Is Struck*, p. 4.

9. Ibid., pp. 5–6.

10. Ibid., p. xiv.

11. Jack Kimoto, interview with author, 22 Nov. 1976.

12. Bill Bailey, interview with author, 13 March 1992. Bailey said that some of the German sailors pretended to be beating him harder than they actually were and whispered words of encouragement to him.

13. Louis Goldblatt, *Working Class Leader in the ILWU, 1935–1977*, p. 384.

14. William Schneiderman, Oleta O'Conner Yates, and twelve others were convicted of having violated the Smith Act in 1952. See Shannon, *Decline of American Communism*, pp. 195–203.

15. Zalburg, *A Spark Is Struck*, p. 19.

16. Bill Bailey, interview with author, 13 July 1992.

17. Beechert, *Working in Hawaii*, p. 227.

18. Fuchs, *Hawaii Pono*, p. 233. According to Fuchs: "To suppress strikes, the territorial legislature enacted laws against 'criminal syndicalism, anarchistic publications, and picketing' between the years 1919 and 1923. Under the first law, anyone who advocated violence or sabotage as a means for dealing with an industrial dispute could be imprisoned for ten years." Ibid.

19. Zalburg, *A Spark Is Struck*, p. 25.

20. Bill Bailey, interview with author, 13 July 1992. Bailey claimed that Jack Hall had jumped ship in Marseilles, presumably in 1937, to join the Abraham Lincoln Battalion. He was scheduled to ship out on the *Barcelona* but did not show up. If it did happen, it was Hall's good fortune that he missed the sailing, for the *Barcelona* was torpedoed on the way to Spain, with heavy loss of life.

21. Beechert, *Working in Hawaii*, p. 258.

22. Ibid., p. 257.

23. Zalburg, *A Spark Is Struck*, p. 33.

24. Ibid., p. 35.

25. Ibid., p. 39.

26. John E. Reinecke, *Report on the Inter-Island Strike*, undated, probably written in late 1938 or early 1939, pp. 47–48.

27. Ibid., p. 44.

28. Zalburg, *A Spark Is Struck*, p. 40.

29. Fuchs, *Hawaii Pono*, pp. 363–364.

30. A copy of the history syllabus used by Hawaii's participants in the California Labor School can be found at the Center for Labor Education and Research, University of Hawaii, College of Continuing Education and Community Service.

31. Zalburg, *A Spark Is Struck*, p. 47.
32. Ibid., p. 42.
33. Beechert, *Working in Hawaii*, p. 278.
34. Zalburg, *A Spark Is Struck*, p. 49.
35. Ibid., p. 51.
36. Ibid., p. 55.
37. Beechert, *Working in Hawaii*, pp. 283–284.
38. Zalburg, *A Spark Is Struck*, p. 61.
39. Fuchs, *Hawaii Pono*, p. 303.
40. Ibid., p. 306.
41. Zalburg, *A Spark Is Struck*, p. 68.
42. Ibid., p. 82.
43. Ibid., p. 99.
44. Goldblatt, *Working Class Leader*, p. 318.
45. Zalburg, *A Spark Is Struck*, p. xiv.
46. Fuchs, *Hawaii Pono*, p. 357.
47. Goldblatt, *Working Class Leader*, p. 320.
48. Zalburg, *A Spark Is Struck*, p. 126.
49. Ibid., p. 127.
50. Ibid., p. 559ff.
51. Ibid., p. 154.
52. Ibid., p. 154.
53. Ibid., p. 155.
54. Ibid., p. 159.
55. Beechert, *Working in Hawaii*, p. 306.
56. *HA*, 19 Sept. 1946, p. 1.
57. *HSB*, 3 Oct. 1946, p. 1.
58. *Time*, 28 October 1946, p. 11.
59. *HA*, 7 Nov. 1946, p. 2.
60. *HSB*, 8 Oct. 1946, p. 2.
61. *HA*, 4 Nov. 1946, p. 1.
62. Jack Kimoto, letter to author, 15 April 1977.
63. *HSB*, 20 Nov. 1946, p. 2.
64. *HA*, 8 Nov. 1946, p. 1.

Chapter 3: The Stainback Battalion

1. *HA*, 15 Nov. 1947, p. 22.
2. *HA*, 12 Nov. 1947, p. 12.
3. *HSB*, 17 Nov. 1947, p. 1.
4. Ibid.
5. *HA*, 12 Nov. 1947, p. 12.
6. Ibid.
7. *HA*, 29 Nov. 1947, p. 4.
8. Harriet Bouslog, interview with author, 14 June 1973. Bouslog had done legal research for the Big Five law firm of Stanley, Vitousek, Pratt, and Winn in Hawaii while studying for her bar examination in 1941. She passed the bar in December, just in time for the closing of the civil courts following the bombing of Pearl Harbor.
9. *HA*, 27 Nov. 1947, p. 5.

10. Ibid.
11. *HA*, 12 Nov. 1947, p. 12.
12. *HA*, 29 Nov. 1947, p. 4.
13. *HA*, 30 Nov. 1947, p. 1.
14. *Hilo Tribune-Herald (HTH)*, 1 Dec. 1947, p. 2.
15. *HSB*, 26 Nov. 1947, p. 10.
16. *HA*, 14 Nov. 1947, p. 22.
17. *HA*, 13 Nov. 1947, p. 22.
18. This organization will appear in this work abbreviated in various forms. Often referred to as the CIO-PAC, it was more commonly known simply as the PAC. Since the ILWU was the dominant CIO union in Hawaii, the abbreviation ILWU-PAC was also used. However designated, the PAC was founded by CIO leaders, particularly Sidney Hillman, after the Democratic losses in the 1942 congressional elections. The PAC had a significant impact on national politics in the elections of 1944 and 1946, but by 1948 the interest of the left had shifted to Henry Wallace's Progressive party, and the CIO was deeply locked in its struggle to purge the union of the taint of communism.
19. *HSB*, 17 Nov. 1947, p. 6.
20. Victor Riesel, letter to Ingram Stainback, 25 March 1948.
21. Arthur Coolidge, letter to Ingram Stainback, 17 Dec. 1947.
22. Ingram Stainback, letter to Arthur Coolidge, 11 Feb. 1948.
23. Arthur Coolidge, speech made in Quincy, Massachusetts, on 24 Feb. 1948.
24. Ingram Stainback, letter to Victor Riesel, 17 May 1948.
25. *HA*, 28 November 1947, p. 6.
26. Jack B. Tenney, letter to Ingram Stainback, 26 Jan. 1949.

Chapter 4: The Truth

1. Ichiro Izuka, *The Truth about Communism in Hawaii*, p. 3.
2. Ibid., p. 8.
3. Ibid., p. 7.
4. Ibid., p. 8.
5. Ibid.
6. Ibid., pp. 9–10.
7. Ibid., p. 10.
8. Ibid., p. 8.
9. Ibid., p. 10.
10. Ibid., p. 22.
11. Ibid.
12. Ibid.
13. Ibid., p. 28.
14. Ibid., pp. 30–31.

Chapter 5: Trouble in the Ranks

1. James H. Shoemaker, *The Economy of Hawaii*, p. 188.
2. ILWU Local 142, Minutes of Executive Board, Hawaii Division, United Sugar Workers, 14 Dec. 1947, p. 1.
3. Ibid., p. 2.
4. Ibid., pp. 4–5.

5. Ibid., p. 9.
6. David Thompson, interview with author, 13 March 1975.
7. *HTH*, 15 Dec. 1947, p. 1.
8. Ibid.
9. *The Garden Island*, 16 Dec. 1947, p. 1.
10. Ibid.
11. *HTH*, 16 Dec. 1947, p. 1.
12. *The Garden Island*, 23 Dec. 1947, p. 1.
13. *HA*, 17 Dec. 1947, p. 22.
14. *HSB*, 19 Dec. 1947, p. 1.
15. *HSB*, 22 Dec. 1947, p. 14.
16. *HA*, 3 Jan. 1948, pp. 1–2.
17. *Maui News*, 7 Jan. 1948, p. 1.
18. *HTH*, 4 Jan. 1948, p. 1.
19. Thomas Lawrence O'Brien, *The Plot to Sovietize Hawaii*, p. 48.
20. Ichiro Izuka, interview with author, 21 June 1973.
21. Steve Murin, interview with author, 7 June 1973.
22. Ichiro Izuka, interview with author, 7 June 1973.
23. ILWU, *The Mysterious Stranger*, p. 4.
24. Ibid., p. 7.
25. Ibid., p. 20.
26. *HA*, 4 Jan. 1948, p. 11.
27. U.S. Congress, *Proceedings of the Roberts Commission, Pearl Harbor Attack*, item 32.
28. *HA*, 3 December 1947, p. 6.
29. ILWU, *The Big Lie*, pp. 4–5.
30. Zalburg, *A Spark Is Struck*, p. 217.
31. *HA*, 21 Feb. 1948, p. 1.
32. *HA*, 23 July 1948, p. 1.
33. John E. Reinecke, *Labor Unions of Hawaii: A Chronological Checklist*, p. 26.

Chapter 6: The Waiting

1. *HSB*, 26 Nov. 1947, p. 10.
2. *HA*, 16 Dec. 1947, p. 1.
3. Robert McElrath, interview with author, 21 March 1975.
4. *Maui News*, 13 Dec. 1947, p. 10.
5. Abraham Akaka, interview with author, 31 Aug. 1974.
6. *Maui News*, 17 Dec. 1947, p. 1.
7. *Maui News*, 20 Dec. 1947, p. 10.
8. *HSB*, 10 Jan. 1948, p. 1.
9. Marian Lai, letter to Ingram Stainback, undated, presumed to have been written in 1948.
10. *HA*, 11 Aug. 1946, p. 32.
11. See the chronology in Richard Pipes, *The Russian Revolution*, pp. 851–855.
12. W. Harold Loper, "Zeal for Democracy."
13. *HA*, 24 June 1948, p. 22.
14. *HSB*, 2 Aug. 1948, p. 8.

Chapter 7: The Ideals of Democracy

1. Herbert L. Packer, *Ex-Communist Witnesses*, p. 6.
2. *HA*, 4 Aug. 1948, p. 1.
3. Ibid., p. 6.
4. Aiko Reinecke, interview with author, 22 Nov. 1976.
5. *Department of Public Instruction v. Dr. John E. Reinecke and Aiko T. Reinecke* (cited hereafter as RH [Reinecke hearing]), 4 Aug. 1948, p. 30.
6. Ibid., p. 69.
7. RH, 5 Aug. 1948, p. 12.
8. *HA*, 7 Aug. 1948, p. 1.
9. RH, 5 Aug. 1948, p. 57.
10. Ibid., p. 61.
11. Ibid., p. 77.
12. Louis Budenz, *This Is My Story*.
13. Packer, *Ex-Communist Witnesses*, p. 124.
14. RH, 9 Aug. 1948, pp. 22–26.
15. Ibid., p. 97.
16. Ibid., p. 98.
17. RH, 10 Aug. 1948, p. 53.
18. Ibid., pp. 79–80.
19. RH, 11 Aug. 1948, p. 22.
20. *HSB*, 16 Aug. 1948, p. 2.
21. *HA*, 18 Aug. 1948, p. 1.
22. RH, 13 Aug. 1948, p. 32.
23. RH, 20 Aug. 1948, p. 12.
24. Ichiro Izuka, interview with author, 7 June 1973.
25. RH, 23 Aug. 1948, pp. 55–57.
26. RH, 25 Aug. 1948, p. 60.
27. Ibid., pp. 78–79.
28. Ibid., pp. 87–88.
29. Ibid., pp. 99–100.
30. RH, 27 Aug. 1948, p. 8. Quoted from the *Federal Register*, Tuesday, 25 March 1947, vol. 12, no. 59, p. 1938.
31. RH, 27 Aug. 1948, pp. 26, 35–36.

Chapter 8: In Their Defense

1. In the 1950 hearings of the House Committee on Un-American Activities, the so-called Reluctant Thirty-nine exercised their Fifth Amendment rights against self-incrimination when called as witnesses. Jack Kawano, one of the Reluctant Thirty-nine *did* go to Washington, D.C., to testify before HUAC in 1951. In the Smith Act trial of 1952 to 1953, none of the defendants took the stand.
2. RH, 30 Aug. 1948, p. 55.
3. RH, 31 Aug. 1948, p. 12.
4. Ibid., p. 33.
5. Ibid., p. 48.
6. Ibid., p. 6.
7. Ibid., p. 13.

8. Ibid., p. 23.
9. Ibid., pp. 44–45.
10. Ibid., p. 45.
11. *HA*, 3 Sept. 1948, p. 18.
12. RH, 31 Aug. 1948, p. 87.
13. RH, 1 Sept. 1948, p. 52.
14. Ibid., p. 53.
15. Jack Kimoto, letter to author, 15 April 1977.
16. RH, 14 Sept. 1948, p. 53.
17. Bill Bailey, interview with author, 13 March 1992.
18. Edward Berman, interview with author, 10 July 1973.
19. RH, 2 Sept. 1948, p. 84.
20. RH, 3 Sept. 1948, p. 30.
21. Ibid., p. 30.
22. RH, 25 Aug. 1948, p. 109.
23. *HSB*, 14 Sept. 1948, p. 1.
24. Ibid.
25. *HSB*, 20 Sept. 1948, p. 6.
26. *HA*, 16 Sept. 1992, p. 6.

Chapter 9: I neither Deny nor Affirm

1. RH, 9 Sept. 1948, p. 165.
2. John K. Akau, Jr., interviews with author, 9–10 Feb. 1975.
3. Jack Kimoto, letter to author, 15 April 1977.
4. RH, 9 Sept. 1948, p. 172.
5. John Reinecke, "What Must We Do?" part 2.
6. Ibid., part 3.
7. Ibid.
8. Ibid., part 4.
9. RH, 10 Sept. 1948, pp. 8–9.
10. Ibid., p. 37.
11. Ibid., p. 39.
12. Ibid., p. 14.
13. Ibid., pp. 14–15.
14. Ibid., p. 15.
15. Ibid., p. 16.
16. Ibid., p. 19.
17. For an excellent short discussion of the Massie case, see Gavan Daws, *Shoal of Time*, pp. 317–327.
18. RH, 10 Sept. 1948, p. 22.
19. Ibid., p. 27.
20. Ibid., pp. 27–28.
21. Ibid., p. 32.
22. Ibid., p. 36.
23. RH, 13 Sept. 1948, pp. 1–5.
24. This statement, published in the *Annals* of the American Law Institute, Jan. 1946, pp. 18–26, can be found in RH, 13 Sept. 1948, pp. 33–38.
25. RH, 13 Sept. 1948, p. 35.

26. Ibid., p. 43.
27. Ibid., pp. 44–45.
28. Ibid., pp. 45–46.
29. Ibid., pp. 46–47.
30. Ibid., pp. 85–87. The statement was read into the record from Bert Andrews, *Washington Witch Hunt*, pp. 121–123.
31. RH, 13 Sept. 1948, p. 89.
32. RH, 14 Sept. 1948, pp. 110–112.
33. John E. Reinecke, interview with author, 15 Sept. 1974.
34. RH, 14 Sept. 1948, pp. 115–116.
35. John E. Reinecke, interview with author, 5 June 1973.
36. RH, 15 Sept. 1948, p. 109.
37. Ibid., p. 111.
38. Ibid., p. 149.
39. Ibid., p. 152.
40. RH, 16 Sept. 1948, p. 5. Quoted from Howard Selsam, *Socialism and Ethics*, pp. 38–42.
41. RH, 16 Sept. 1948, p. 8.
42. Ibid., pp. 89–90.
43. *HA*, 22 Sept. 1948, p. 18.

Chapter 10: Teachers No More

1. *HA*, 20 Sept. 1948, p. 16.
2. *HSB*, 20 Sept. 1948, p. 6.
3. RH, 13 Oct. 1948, p. 12.
4. Ibid., pp. 21–24.
5. Ibid., pp. 27–28.
6. Ibid.
7. Interview with John Reinecke, 29 May 1973.
8. RH, 13 Oct. 1948, p. 28.
9. Ibid., p. 29.
10. Ibid., pp. 35–36.
11. Ibid., p. 39. Blatt was probably referring to the Gallup poll that was cited at the end of Chapter 6.
12. Ibid., p. 59.
13. Ibid., pp. 60–61.
14. Ibid., p. 63. From *Bridges v. Wixon*, 326 U.S. 135 (1945).
15. RH, 13 Oct. 1948, pp. 63–64.
16. Ibid., p. 76.
17. Ibid., p. 79.
18. Ibid., p. 95.
19. Ibid., pp. 98–99.
20. Ibid., p. 101.
21. Ibid., p. 117.
22. *HA*, 16 Oct. 1948, p. 1.
23. *HSB*, 21 Oct. 1948, p. 8.
24. *HA*, 24 Oct. 1948, p. 16.
25. RH, 29 Oct. 1948, p. 3.

26. Ibid., pp. 6–7.
27. Ibid., p. 8.
28. Ibid., p. 10.
29. Aiko Reinecke, interview with author, 20 June 1973.

Chapter 11: Hawaii's Politics in 1948

1. *The Garden Island*, 9 Dec. 1947, p. 8.
2. *HSB*, 10 Jan. 1948, p. 4.
3. *HA*, 11 Feb. 1948, p. 1.
4. *HA*, 26 March 1948, p. 8.
5. Ibid., p. 6.
6. Ibid.
7. Fuchs, *Hawaii Pono*, p. 312.
8. Ibid., p. 313, quoting from a letter from Governor Ingram M. Stainback to Attorney General J. Howard McGrath, dated 14 May 1948.
9. *HA*, 5 Aug. 1948, p. 8.
10. *The Garden Island*, 17 Aug. 1948, p. 8.
11. Ibid., p. 7.
12. *HA*, 19 Aug. 1948, p. 8.
13. Resolution adopted by Young Buddhists' Association, Hilo, 18 Aug. 1948, Stainback Papers, Communism, 1942–1948.
14. *HA*, 18 Jan. 1948, p. 2.
15. *HA*, 29 Aug. 1948, p. 1.
16. O'Brien, *Plot*, p. 3.
17. Ibid., p. 69.
18. Ibid., pp. 71–73.
19. *HSB*, 4 Sept. 1948, p. 3.
20. Fuchs, *Hawaii Pono*, p. 312, quoting from *HSB*, 7 Nov. 1956.
21. John A. Burns, interview for the John A. Burns Oral History Project (JBOHP), 29 Jan. 1975, p. 2.
22. *HA*, 3 Sept. 1948, p. 1.
23. *HA*, 27 Sept. 1948, p. 1.
24. *HSB*, 1 Oct. 1948, p. 11.
25. *HA*, 13 Sept. 1948, p. 2.
26. *HA*, 17 Sept. 1948, p. 2.
27. *HSB*, 25 Sept. 1948, p. 7.
28. Art Rutledge, interview with author, 29 Aug. 1974.
29. *HA*, 24 Sept. 1948, p. 2.
30. Art Rutledge, interview, 29 Aug. 1974.
31. *HA*, 2 Oct. 1948, p. 2.
32. *HSB*, 2 Oct. 1948, p. 1.
33. Ibid., p. 2.
34. *HA*, 4 Oct. 1948, p. 1.
35. *HSB*, 3 Oct. 1948, p. 1.

Chapter 12: The 1949 Longshore Strike

1. Zalburg, *A Spark Is Struck*, p. 244.
2. Ann Fagan Ginger and David Christiano, eds., *The Cold War against Labor*, p. 461.

3. Zalburg, *A Spark Is Struck*, p. 244.
4. *HA*, 4 May 1949, p. 1.
5. *Honolulu Record (HR)*, 5 May 1949, p. 1.
6. *HA*, 23 May 1949, p. 16.
7. *HSB*, 21 May 1949, p. 8.
8. Ginger and Fagan, *Cold War*, p. 469.
9. *HR*, 2 June 1949, p. 4.
10. *HA*, 4 Oct. 1948, p. 1.
11. *HA*, 7 June 1949, p. 1.
12. *HR*, 6 June 1949, p. 1.
13. Zalburg, *A Spark Is Struck*, p. 256.
14. Ibid., p. 259.
15. *HA*, 15 June 1949, p. 1. IMUA is the Hawaiian word for "forward." The term has been used by many organizations in Hawaii, both before and since the Hawaii Residents' Association borrowed it.
16. *HA*, 26 June 1949, p. 1.
17. Hugh Butler, *Statehood for Hawaii*, p. 14.
18. *HSB*, 25 June 1949, p. 8.
19. Charles P. Larrowe, *Harry Bridges*, p. 276.
20. Zalburg, *A Spark Is Struck*, p. 264.
21. Ibid., p. 265.
22. *HA*, 25 June 1949, p. 12.
23. Steve Woods, "How to Capture an Island," p. 1.

Chapter 13: HUAC Comes to Hawaii

1. Territory of Hawaii, *Journal* (House of Representatives), 1949, pp. 354–355.
2. *HR*, 13 Oct. 1949, p. 4.
3. *HA*, 8 Oct. 1949, p. 2.
4. Territory of Hawaii, *Laws of the Territory of Hawaii*, 1949, Joint Resolution 5.
5. *HSB*, 7 Oct. 1949, p. 8.
6. *HA*, 16 Oct. 1949, p. 6.
7. *HR*, 20 Oct. 1949, p. 8.
8. *HA*, 16 Oct. 1949, p. 10.
9. *HR*, 9 Feb. 1950, pp. 1, 6.
10. Ibid., p. 4.
11. *HSB*, 2 March 1950, pp. 1, 6. John Reinecke had met Bassett in Carmel in the 1920s. Bassett filled Reinecke with information about Hawaii, where he was headed on his way to China.
12. *HSB*, 7 March 1950, p. 1.
13. *HSB*, 4 April 1950, p. 3.
14. U.S. Congress, House, Committee on Un-American Activities, *Hearings Regarding Communist Activities in the Territory of Hawaii* (cited hereafter as HH [HUAC hearings]), p. 1,345.
15. HH, p. 1,359.
16. HH, p. 1,369.
17. *HR*, 13 April 1950, p. 8.
18. *HA*, 11 April 1950, p. 2.

19. *HA*, 14 April 1950, p. 1.
20. *HA*, 24 April 1950, p. 8.
21. Stainback papers, Communism 1949–51.
22. *HSB*, 11 April 1950, p. 1.
23. Richard Kageyama, interview with author, 28 Sept. 1974. At the time of this interview, Kageyama was attempting a second comeback. Seeking a Democratic nomination for a seat on the city council (the new name for the board of supervisors), Kageyama finished a distant fourth in a four-way race.
24. HH, pp. 1,426–1,427.
25. HH, p. 1,471.
26. *HA*, 21 April 1950, p. 2.
27. David Thompson, interview with author, 13 March 1975.
28. *HSB*, 13 April 1950, p. 3.
29. HH, p. 1,490.
30. *IMUA Spotlight*, April 1950, p. 1.

Chapter 14: The Crest

1. *HR*, 13 April 1950, p. 3.
2. *HA*, 30 April 1950, p. 6.
3. *HR*, 27 April 1950, p. 8.
4. *HR*, 4 May 1950, p. 8.
5. *HA*, 1 May 1950, p. 10.
6. Ibid.
7. *HA*, 9 May 1950, p. 11.
8. *HA*, 15 June 1950, p. 12.
9. *HA*, 16 June 1950, p. 9.
10. *HA*, 14 May 1950, p. 6.
11. Ibid., p. 1.
12. *HA*, 25 May 1950, p. 7.
13. *HA*, 2 June 1950, p. 13.
14. Tony Todaro, interview with author, 15 March 1975.
15. *HA*, 6 June 1950, p. 10.
16. *HA*, 13 July 1950, p. 12.
17. *HA*, 27 June 1950, p. 5.
18. *HA*, 21 July 1950, p. 8.
19. *HSB*, 12 Jan. 1951, p. 1.
20. *HSB*, 22 Sept. 1950, p. 3.
21. *HSB*, 21 Sept. 1950, p. 4.
22. *HSB*, 9 Oct. 1950, p. 12.
23. Ibid., p. 10.
24. Larrowe, *Harry Bridges*, pp. 330–331.
25. *HA*, 20 Aug. 1950, p. 11.
26. *HA*, 8 Aug. 1950, p. 4.
27. *HA*, 11 Aug. 1950, p. 3.
28. *HA*, 30 Aug. 1950, p. 8.
29. *HSB*, 5 Sept. 1950, p. 6.
30. *HSB*, 22 Sept. 1950, p. 1.
31. *HSB*, 29 Nov. 1950, p. 1.
32. *HA*, 25 Aug. 1950, p. 1.

33. *HSB*, 19 Sept. 1950, p. 1.
34. *Blau v. United States*, 340 U.S. 159.
35. *HA*, 16 Jan. 1951, p. 2. Since the case of the Reluctant Thirty-nine, known as *United States v. Yukio Abe et al.*, was not appealed, there was no federal reporting number attached to it. The federal district court in Honolulu could not produce as much as a docket number for the case, the records having long since been shipped to San Francisco. The transcript is presumably stored in the archives of the ninth circuit court.
36. *HA*, 19 Jan. 1951, p. 1.
37. *HA*, 20 Jan. 1951, p. 2.
38. *HR*, 25 Jan. 1950, pp. 1, 6.

Chapter 15: Kawano Goes to Washington

1. *Ka Leo O Hawaii*, 16 March 1951, pp. 1, 4.
2. Ibid.
3. *HR*, 17 May 1951, p. 8.
4. American Friends Service Committee, *Anatomy of Anti-Communism*, pp. 38–39.
5. *HSB*, 22 May 1951, p. 4.
6. *HR*, 31 May 1951, p. 5.
7. Alan Saunders, interview with author, 22 March 1975.
8. John Stalker, interview with author, 25 March 1975.
9. Chuck Mau, JBOHP, 21 Sept. 1975, p. 24.
10. Ernest Murai, JBOHP, 8 July 1975, pp. 27–28.
11. Mitsuyuki Kido, JBOHP, 31 July 1975, p. 4.
12. Chuck Mau, JBOHP, 27 Sept. 1975, pp. 22–23.
13. Mitsuyuki Kido, JBOHP, 31 July 1975, p. 4.
14. Daniel Inouye, JBOHP, 16 Aug. 1975, p. 17.
15. Ibid., p. 18.
16. Ibid., pp. 18–19.
17. *HA*, 11 Feb. 1951, pp. 1, 12.
18. Chuck Mau, JBOHP, 27 Sept. 1975, p. 23.
19. U.S. Congress, House, Committee on Un-American Activities, *Hearings Regarding Communist Activities in the Territory of Hawaii—Part 4, Testimony of Jack Kawano*, 6 July 1951, p. 9.
20. Ibid., p. 10.
21. Ibid., pp. 11–12.
22. Ibid., p. 20.
23. Ibid., p. 26.
24. Ibid., p. 29.
25. Ibid., p. 31.
26. Ibid., pp. 34–35.
27. Ibid., p. 36.
28. Ibid., p. 46.
29. Beechert, *Working in Hawaii*, p. 313.
30. HH, Kawano, 1951, p. 52.
31. *ILWU Reporter*, 22 Aug. 1951, p. 3.
32. Jack Kawano, JBOHP, 21 Aug. 1975, tape 2, pp. 8–10.
33. Chuck Mau, JBOHP, 27 Sept. 1975, p. 24.

Chapter 16: The Hawaii Seven

1. *United States v. Fujimoto et al.*, Criminal No. 10,495, p. 81 (cited hereafter as Smith Act transcript).
2. *Dennis v. United States*, 354 U.S. 494 (1951).
3. Smith Act transcript. The "overt acts" are listed on pp. 83–86.
4. Smith Act transcript, p. 81.
5. Beechert, *Working in Hawaii*, p. 315.
6. Howard K. Hoddick, interview with author, 22 March 1975.
7. *HA*, 30 Aug. 1951, p. 6.
8. *HSB*, 29 Aug. 1951, p. 10.
9. Tony Todaro, interview with author, 23 March 1975.
10. The quotes from Watumull and Burnside are from *Tony N. Todaro v. Hawaiian Paradise Park Corp., David Watumull, et al.*, Civil No. 31,187 (1972).
11. *IMUA Spotlight*, 17 Dec. 1952, p. 1.
12. Ibid., 2 July 1952, p. 1.
13. Harriet Bouslog, *Fear*, p. 4.
14. Ibid., p. 12.
15. Ibid., p. 16.
16. Ibid., p. 21.
17. Urban E. Wild, *The Answer to "Fear,"* p. 3.
18. For the complete text of the indictment in the Foley Square trial, see *Dennis v. United States* or consult George Marion, *The Communist Trial*, pp. 189–191.
19. Wild, *Answer*, p. 4.
20. Ibid., p. 5.
21. Hawaii Residents' Association, *IMUA Spotlight*, special edition, "The American Way of Life," 12 December 1951, p. 6.
22. Ibid., p. 15.
23. Ibid., p. 20.
24. ILWU, *Americanism, as Defined by Great Americans*, p. 1.
25. Transcript of conversation between David Thompson and FBI agents Richard Burress and James Condon (cited hereafter as Thompson tapes), 18 Dec. 1951, p. 4.
26. Thompson tapes, 9 Jan. 1952, p. 2.
27. *HSB*, 9 Jan. 1952, p. 14.
28. Ibid., pp. 2–3.
29. *HR*, 31 Jan. 1952, p. 1.
30. Smith Act transcript, pp. 10,028–10,029.
31. Ibid., p. 10,059.
32. Thompson tapes, 18 Dec. 1951, p. 16.
33. Ibid., 9 Jan. 1952, p. 9.
34. *HR*, 9 Oct. 1952, p. 3.

Chapter 17: The Trial

1. Smith Act transcript, p. 967.
2. Ibid., p. 5,848.

3. Ibid., p. 5,903.
4. Ibid., p. 6,133.
5. Richard English, "We Almost Lost Hawaii to the Reds," p. 17.
6. Ibid., p. 54.
7. Ibid.
8. Smith Act transcript, p. 6,733.
9. Ibid., pp. 7,321–7,322.
10. Jack Kimoto, letter to author, 15 April 1977.
11. Smith Act transcript, pp. 7,214–7,220.
12. Ibid., p. 7,268.
13. Ibid., pp. 7,197–7,201.
14. David Thompson, interview with author, 13 March 1975; Robert McElrath, interview with author, 25 March 1975.
15. Smith Act transcript, p. 48.
16. ILWU, *Running Story,* 5 Feb. 1953, P.M., p. 1. *Running Story* was a twice-a-day report on the Smith Act trial put out by the ILWU. Robert McElrath, in 1975, called it "pure propaganda." The ILWU library in Honolulu has a more objective summary of the trial that was maintained by Theodora Kreps for the union.
17. Smith Act transcript, pp. 3,250–3,251.
18. Ibid., p. 3,327.
19. Packer, *Ex-Communist Witnesses,* pp. 224–225.
20. Howard Hoddick, interview with author, 22 March 1975.
21. John A. Burns, JBOHP, 29 Jan. 1975, p. 12.
22. *Yates v. United States,* 354 U.S. 298 (1957).

Chapter 18: A New Hawaii

1. I. F. Stone, *The Truman Era,* p. 98.
2. Ibid., p. 191.
3. Brodie, *Richard Nixon,* p. 192.
4. Daniel Inouye, *Journey to Washington,* pp. 248–249.
5. Frank Fasi, transcript of telethon, radio/television station KULA, Oct. 1954, p. 14.
6. Ibid., p. 20.
7. Ibid., p. 32.
8. Fuchs, *Hawaii Pono,* p. 370.
9. J. Russell Cades, JBOHP, 29 Nov. 1982, p. 45.
10. Fuchs, *Hawaii Pono,* p. 335.
11. John A. Burns, JBOHP, 29 Jan. 1975, p. 21.
12. *HA,* 4 Jan. 1971, p. A-14.
13. Noel J. Kent, *Hawaii: Islands Under the Influence,* p. 154.
14. Zalburg, *A Spark Is Struck,* p. xiv.
15. Kent, *Hawaii,* p. 154.
16. *Honolulu Star-Bulletin and Advertiser,* Sunday edition, 3 Jan. 1971, p. 1.
17. Frederick Simpich, Jr., *Anatomy of Hawaii,* pp. 185–186.
18. Daws, *Shoal of Time,* p. 380.
19. William F. Quinn, JBOHP, 18 Jan. 1984, p. 24.
20. Ibid., p. 38.

21. A. A. Smyser, interview with author, 21 March 1975.
22. A. A. Smyser, JBOHP, 25 June 1975, pp. 9–10.
23. Howard K. Hoddick, interview with author, 22 March 1975.
24. Dr. Lyle G. Phillips, interview with author, 17 March 1975.
25. William Quinn, JBOHP, 18 Jan. 1984, p. 39.
26. *HA*, 23 May 1955, p. 4.
27. Yasutaki Arakaki, JBOHP, 25 July 1977, pp. 7–8.
28. Jack Kawano, JBOHP, 21 Aug. 1975, tape 2, p. 15.
29. Ibid., pp. 26–27.
30. Chuck Mau, JBOHP, 27 Sept. 1975, p. 28.
31. Jack Kawano, quoted by Dan Boylan during an interview with Chuck Mau, 27 Sept. 1975, p. 28.
32. David Thompson, interview with author, 13 March 1975.

Bibliography

Akaka, Abraham. Interview with author, 31 August 1974.

Akau, John K. Interviews with author, 9–10 February 1975.

Ambrose, Stephen E. *Nixon: The Education of a Politician, 1913–1962*. New York: Simon and Schuster, 1987.

American Friends Service Committee. *Anatomy of Anti-Communism*. New York: Hill and Wang, 1969.

American Law Institute. *Annals*. January 1946.

Andrews, Bert. *Washington Witch Hunt*. New York: Random House, 1948.

Arakaki, Yasutaki. John A. Burns Oral History Project. Interview on 25 July 1977.

Ariyoshi, Koji. Interview with author, 19 July 1973.

Bailey, Bill. Interview with author, 13 March 1992.

Beck, Carl. *Contempt of Congress: A Study of the Prosecutions Initiated by the Committee on Un-American Activities, 1945–1957*. New Orleans: Hauser Press, 1957.

Beechert, Edward D. *Working in Hawaii: A Labor History*. Honolulu: University of Hawaii Press, 1985.

Bennett, David H. *The Party of Fear: From Nativist Movements to the New Right in American History*. Chapel Hill: University of North Carolina Press, 1988.

Berman, Edward. Interview with author, 10 July 1973.

Blau v. United States. 340 U.S. 159 (1950).

Bouslog, Harriet. *Fear*. Honolulu: International Longshoremen's Union, 16 October 1951.

———. Interview with author, 14 June 1973.

Bridges v. Wixon. 326 U.S. 135 (1945).

Brodie, Fawn M. *Richard Nixon: The Shaping of His Character*. New York: W. W. Norton and Co., 1981.

Budenz, Louis. *This Is My Story*. New York: McGraw-Hill, 1947.

Burns, John A. John A. Burns Oral History Project. Interviews on 16 January 1975 and 29 January 1975.

Butler, Hugh. *Statehood for Hawaii: Communist Penetration of the Hawaiian Islands*. Committee on Interior and Insular Affairs, 80th Congress, 2d Session. Washington, D.C.: U.S. Government Printing Office, 1949.

Cades, J. Russell. John A. Burns Oral History Project. Interview on 29 November 1982.

Chambers, Whittaker. *Witness*. New York: Random House, 1952.

Coffman, Tom. *Catch a Wave: A Case Study of Hawaii's New Politics*. Honolulu: University Press of Hawaii, 1973.

Cook, Fred J. *The Nightmare Decade: The Life and Times of Senator Joe McCarthy*. New York: Random House, 1971.

Coolidge, Arthur W. Letter to Ingram Stainback, 17 December 1947. Stainback Papers, Communism 1942–48.

———. Speech made in Quincy, Massachusetts, 24 February 1948. Stainback Papers, Communism 1942–48.

Daws, Gavan. *Shoal of Time: A History of the Hawaiian Islands*. Toronto: Macmillan Company, 1968.

Dennis v. United States. 341 U.S. 494 (1951).

Department of Public Instruction v. Dr. John E. Reinecke and Aiko T. Reinecke. Territory of Hawaii: Attorney General's File C-6194, 1948.

Donovan, Robert J. *Tumultuous Years: The Presidency of Harry S. Truman, 1949–1953*. New York: W. W. Norton and Co., 1982.

English, Richard. "We Almost Lost Hawaii to the Reds." *Saturday Evening Post*, 2 February 1952.

Fasi, Frank. Transcript of telethon, radio/television station KULA, October 1954. Hawaiian Collection, Hamilton Library, University of Hawaii at Manoa.

Federal Register. Vol. 12, No. 59, 25 March 1947.

Fuchs, Lawrence H. *Hawaii Pono: A Social History*. New York: Harcourt, Brace & World, 1961.

Fujimoto et al. v. United States. 251 F 2d 342 (1958).

Gill, Tom. John A. Burns Oral History Project. Interview on 7 November 1975.

Ginger, Ann Fagan, and Christiano, David, eds. *The Cold War against Labor: An Anthology*. Berkeley: Meiklejohn Civil Liberties Institute, 1987.

Goldblatt, Louis. *Working Class Leader in the ILWU, 1935–1977:* Interview conducted by Estolv Ethan Ward, 1978–1979. 2 vols. Berkeley: Regents of the University of California, 1980.

Goodman, Walter. *The Committee: The Extraordinary Career of the House Committee on Un-American Activities*. New York: Farrar, Strauss, and Giroux, 1968.

Griffith, Robert. *The Politics of Fear: Joseph R. McCarthy and the Senate*. Lexington: University of Kentucky Press, 1970.

Griffith, Robert, and Theoharis, Athen, eds. *The Specter: Original Essays on the Cold War and the Origins of McCarthyism*. New York: New Viewpoints, 1974.

Hawaii Residents' Association (IMUA). "The American Way of Life." *IMUA Spotlight* special edition (Honolulu), 12 December 1951.

Hilo Tribune-Herald. 1946–1953.

Hiss, Alger. *In the Court of Public Opinion*. New York: Knopf, 1957.

Hoddick, Howard. Interview with author, 22 March 1975.

Holmes, Thomas Michael. "The Reinecke Case: A Study in Administrative Injustice." *Hawaii Bar Journal* (Honolulu), vol. 12, no. 3 (Fall 1976).

Honolulu Advertiser. 1946–1971.

Honolulu Record. 1948–1958.

Honolulu Star-Bulletin. 1946–1971.

International Longshoremen's and Warehousemen's Union. *Americanism, as Defined by Great Americans*. Honolulu, 1952.

———. *The Big Lie.* Honolulu, 1948.

———. *The Mysterious Stranger.* Honolulu, 1947.

———. *Running Story.* Honolulu, 1952–1953.

International Longshoremen's and Warehousemen's Union Local 142. Minutes of Executive Board, Hawaii Division, United Sugar Workers, 14 December 1947. ILWU Archives.

IMUA Spotlight (Honolulu). 1950–1952.

Inouye, Daniel. John A. Burns Oral History Project. Interview on 16 August 1975.

Inouye, Daniel (with Lawrence Elliott). *Journey to Washington.* Englewood Cliffs, N.J.: Prentice-Hall, 1967.

In re Harriet Bouslog Sawyer. 2 L 2d 1473 (1959).

Izuka, Ichiro. Interviews with author, 7 June 1973 and 21 June 1973.

———. *The Truth about Communism in Hawaii.* Honolulu, 1947. Pamphlet privately published.

Johannessen, Edward. *The Hawaiian Labor Movement: A Brief History.* Boston: Bruce Humphries, Inc., 1956.

John A. Burns. Oral History Project. Tapes and transcripts of interviews with over ninety individuals who were associated with Governor Burns in one way or another. Interviews were done by Stuart Gerry Brown, Dan Boylan, and Paul Hooper between 1975 and 1983. The materials are housed at the University of Hawaii, Hamilton Library, Hawaiian and Pacific Collection.

Kageyama, Richard. Interview with author. 28 September 1974.

Ka Leo O Hawaii. Honolulu. 16 March 1951.

Kawano, Jack. John A. Burns Oral History Project. Interview on 21 August 1975.

Kent, Noel J. *Hawaii: Islands Under the Influence.* New York: Monthly Review Press, 1983.

Kido, Mitsuyuki. John A. Burns Oral History Project. Interview on 31 July 1975.

Kimoto, Jack. Interview with author, 22 November 1976.

———. Letter to author, 15 April 1977.

Lai, Marian. Letter to Ingram Stainback. Stainback Papers, Communism 1942–48. Letter undated, presumed to have been written in 1948.

Larrowe, Charles P. *Harry Bridges: The Rise and Fall of Radical Labor in the United States.* New York: Lawrence Hill and Company, 1972.

Lattimore, Owen. *Ordeal by Slander.* Boston: Little, Brown and Company, 1950.

Loper, W. Harold. "Zeal for Democracy." Department of Public Instruction, Honolulu, Principals' Circular No. 943, 16 March 1948. Stainback Papers, Communism 1942–1948.

MacDougall, Curtis D. *Gideon's Army.* 3 vols. New York: Marzani & Munsell, 1965.

Marion, George. *The Communist Trial: An American Crossroads.* New York: Fairplay Publishers, 1950.

Mau, Chuck. John A. Burns Oral History Project. Interviews on 21 September 1975 and 27 September 1975.

Maui News. 1946–1953.

McAuliffe, Mary S. "The Politics of Civil Liberties." In *The Specter: Original Essays on the Cold War and the Origins of McCarthyism,* edited by Robert Griffith and Athen Theoharis. New York: New Viewpoints, 1974.

McElrath, Robert. Interviews with author, 21 March 1975 and 25 March 1975.

McNamara, Robert M. "Hawaii's Smith Act Case." Master's thesis, University of Hawaii, 1960.

McWilliams, Carey. *Witch Hunt: The Revival of Heresy.* Boston: Little, Brown and Company, 1950.

Morris, Roger. *Richard Milhous Nixon: The Rise of an American Politician.* New York: Henry Holt and Company, 1990.

Murai, Ernest. John A. Burns Oral History Project. Interview on 8 July 1975.

Murin, Steve. Interview with author, 7 June 1973.

New Republic. 24 December 1930.

Nixon, Richard M. *Six Crises.* Garden City, N.Y.: Doubleday, 1962.

Nizer, Louis. *The Implosion Conspiracy.* Garden City, N.Y.: Doubleday, 1973.

O'Brien, Thomas Lawrence. *The Plot to Sovietize Hawaii.* Hilo, 1948. Pamphlet privately published.

Okada, Hideo. John A. Burns Oral History Project. Interview on 26 July 1978.

Packer, Herbert L. *Ex-Communist Witnesses: Four Studies in Fact Finding.* Stanford, Calif.: Stanford University Press, 1962.

Phillips, Dr. Lyle G. Interview with author, 17 March 1975.

Pipes, Richard. *The Russian Revolution.* New York: Alfred A. Knopf, 1990.

Quinn, William F. John A. Burns Oral History Project. Interview on 18 January 1984.

Reinecke, Aiko. Interviews with author, 20 June 1973, 23 June 1973, and 22 November 1976.

Reinecke, John E. Interviews with author, 29 May 1973, 5 June 1973, 20 June 1973 and 15 September 1974.

———. *Labor Unions of Hawaii: A Chronological Checklist.* Honolulu: University of Hawaii Industrial Relations Center, 1966.

———Letter to author, 1 July 1978.

———. *Report on the Inter-Island Strike.* Honolulu: Hawaii Educational Association. Report undated, presumed to have been written in late 1938 or early 1939.

———. "What Must We Do?" Unpublished manuscript, written in late 1934 or early 1935. Stainback Papers, Communism 1942–48.

Riesel, Victor. Letter to Ingram Stainback, 25 March 1948. Stainback Papers, Communism 1942–48.

Rohrbough, Ed. John A. Burns Oral History Project. Interview on 8 August 1977.

Rovere, Richard H. *Senator Joe McCarthy.* New York: Harcourt, Brace and Company, 1959.

Rutledge, Art. Interview with author, 29 August 1974.

Saunders, Alan. Interview with author, 22 March 1975.

Selsam, Howard. *Socialism and Ethics.* New York: International Publishers, 1943.

Shannon, David A. *The Decline of American Communism: A History of the Communist Party of the United States since 1945.* New York: Harcourt, Brace and Company, 1959.

Shoemaker, James H. *The Economy of Hawaii.* Washington, D.C.: U.S. Department of Labor, Bureau of Labor Statistics, U.S. Government Printing Office, 1948.

Simpich, Frederick, Jr. *Anatomy of Hawaii.* Honolulu: Coward, McCann and Geoghegan, 1971.

Smyser, A. A. Interview with author, 21 March 1975.

———. John A. Burns Oral History Project. Interview on 25 June 1975.

Stainback, Ingram M. Letter to Arthur Coolidge, 24 February 1948. Stainback Papers, Communism 1942–48.

———. Letter to Victor Riesel, 17 May 1948. Stainback Papers, Communism 1942–48.

———. Papers of Ingram M. Stainback. Communism 1942–48, 1949–51. Archives of Hawaii.

Stalker, John. Interview with author, 22 March 1975.

Starobin, Joseph R. *American Communism in Crisis, 1943–1957.* Cambridge: Harvard University Press, 1972.

Steel, Ronald. *Walter Lippmann and the American Century.* Boston: Little, Brown and Company, 1980.

Stone, I. F. *The Truman Era.* New York: Monthly Review Press, 1953.

Tanner, William R., and Robert Griffith. "The Internal Security Act of 1950." In *The Specter,* edited by Robert Griffith and Athen Theoharis. New York: New Viewpoints, 1974.

Tenney, Jack B. Letter to Ingram M. Stainback, 26 January 1949. Stainback Papers, Communism 1949–51.

Territory of Hawaii. *Journal.* House of Representatives of the Twenty-fifth Legislature, Special Session, 1949.

———. *Laws of the Territory of Hawaii.* Twenty-fifth Legislature, Special Session, Joint Resolution 5, 1949.

The Garden Island (Kauai). 1946–1953.

Thompson, David. Interview with author, 13 March 1975.

———. Transcript of taped conversations with FBI agents, Richard Burress and James Condon, 18 December 1951 and 9 January 1952. ILWU Archives.

Time Magazine, 28 October 1946.

Todaro, Tony. Interviews with author, 15 March 1975 and 23 March 1975.

Tony N. Todaro v. Hawaiian Paradise Park Corp., David Watumull, et al. Civil No. 31,187 (1972).

Tokunaga, Mike. John A. Burns Oral History Project. Interview on 1 June 1977.

Tuttle, Daniel W., comp. *The Hawaii Democratic and Republican Party Platforms, 1952–1962.* Honolulu: Department of Government, University of Hawaii, 1962.

United States v. Fujimoto et al. Criminal No. 10,495 (1952–1953).

U.S. Congress. *Proceedings of the Roberts Commission, Pearl Harbor Attack.* 79th Congress, 1st Session, Volume 25, Washington, D.C.: U.S. Government Printing Office, 1946.

U.S. Congress, House, Committee on Un-American Activities. *Hearings Regarding Communist Activities in the Territory of Hawaii.* 81st Congress, 2d Session. Washington, D.C.: U.S. Government Printing Office, 1950.

———. *Hearings Regarding Communist Activities in the Territory of Hawaii—Part 4, Testimony of Jack Kawano.* 82d Congress, 1st Session. Washington, D.C.: U.S. Government Printing Office, 1951.

Walton, Richard J. *Henry Wallace, Harry Truman, and the Cold War.* New York: The Viking Press, 1976.

Weinstein, Allen. *Perjury.* New York: Alfred A. Knopf, 1978.

Wild, Urban E. *The Answer to "Fear."* Honolulu: Hawaii Residents' Association, 1951.

Woods, Steve. "How to Capture an Island: 5th Column Attacks Hawaii." *Plain Talk,* vol. 3, no. 8 (1949): 1–8.

Yagi, Thomas. John A. Burns Oral History Project. Interview on 9 August 1977.

Yates v. United States. 354 U.S. 298 (1957).

Yoshinaga, Nadao. John A. Burns Oral History Project. Interview on 14 July 1977.

Young Buddhists' Association. Resolution adopted on 18 August 1948, Hilo. Stainback Papers, Communism 1942–48.

Zalburg, Sanford. *A Spark Is Struck: Jack Hall and the ILWU in Hawaii.* Honolulu: University Press of Hawaii, 1979.

Index

References to illustrations are in **boldface**

About the Author

T. Michael Holmes has taught at the University of Hawaii, Hawaii Loa College, and Franklin College in Lugano, Switzerland. He is currently collaborating with Dan Boylan on a biography of John A. Burns.